US POWERBOATING

THE POWERBOAT CERTIFICATION SERIES

Start Powerboating Right!

The National Standard for Quality On-The-Water Instruction

Copyright © 2020
Fourth Edition
ISBN 978-1-938915-40-6

The United States Sailing Association

Printed in the United States of America.

Published by the United States Sailing Association
1 Roger Williams University Way, Bristol, RI 02809

www.ussailing.org
www.uspowerboating.com

Introduction

There is a sense of freedom and adventure when you're on the water to explore, spend quality time with family and friends, to go fishing, tubing, waterskiing and wakeboarding, to connect with nature, and get away to your own private paradise. This is part of what makes boating fun.

The other part is a feeling of pride when you can handle your boat in challenging situations with no fuss or drama and you look self-assured in front of family and friends. When you have the confidence and skills as the skipper, your calm leadership sets the tone for everyone to relax and have fun.

For nearly four decades US Sailing and US Powerboating have conducted on-the-water courses while establishing standards for on-the-water instruction, and continue to certify instructors nationwide to teach on the water. US Sailing and US Powerboating are known as the on-the-water experts for sail and power. In the entry-level courses, Safe Powerboat Handling and Basic Powerboat Cruising, a person with no previous experience can progress rapidly from introductory familiarization and docking

Photo Courtesy of U.S. Coast Guard

drills to gaining the confidence to perform high speed turns and stops. These are great courses for those who want to improve their boat-handling skills. From these introductory courses, a student can go on to take courses in coastal cruising, night operation, electronic navigation and others.

There is a national network of waterfront boating centers, schools, marinas and clubs offering hands-on, on-the-water courses for sport and cruising powerboats that use US Powerboating's standards and certified instructors. Try one of these courses and experience the confidence that hands-on training brings to the fun and adventure of powerboating.

For more information on these courses and participating waterfront facilities and instructors, go to www.uspowerboating.com.

Photo Courtesy of Boston Whaler

TABLE OF CONTENTS

Chapter 1

THE POWERBOAT

KEY CONCEPTS

▶ Types of boats   ▶ How a prop & jet work

▶ Parts of a boat   ▶ Engine controls

If it had been possible to come up with the perfect powerboat design, all powerboats would look nearly alike. However, there is an infinite variety of types and sizes aimed at fulfilling different boating activities.

DISPLACEMENT BOATS

Generally, boats with displacement hulls move through the water at slow to moderate speeds rather than riding on top of the water. This motion creates waves at the *bow*, along the sides and at the *stern*. As speed increases, the waves become larger and the distance between them lengthens until the hull becomes trapped between a wave at its bow and another one at its stern. When this happens, the displacement hull has reached what is called *hull speed*. This is the maximum speed for this hull. One of the most familiar examples of a displacement hull at hull speed is a tugboat moving at maximum speed with its hull sunk low in the water with a large bow and stern wave. Characteristics of displacement hulls include:

This cruising powerboat is approaching its maximum speed with waves at its bow and stern, but the size of the waves are moderate, indicating a more efficient hull shape.

Photo Courtesy of Wilde Yacht Sales, LLC

- Good maneuverability

- Good ability to hold a straight course (*directional stability*)

- Good load-carrying capacity

- Good rough-water handling

- Performance not greatly affected by load

- Speed limited by length

- May roll excessively when seas are coming sideways to the hull

With its large bow and stern waves, this tugboat is at maximum speed.

PLANING BOATS

A planing hull behaves like a displacement hull at low speeds, forming waves at its bow and along the length of the hull. Upon reaching a certain speed it goes through a transition stage (*semi-displacement*) where it climbs the face of its bow wave. At this point the boat may become unstable, fuel consumption is high, and the operator may not be able to see over the raised bow. As the boat continues to accelerate it climbs on top of the bow wave and its bow levels off and the boat starts to plane along the top of the water with less wave making and using less fuel. But as the boat increases its speed past this point, wind and water friction on the hull also increases, causing a significant increase in fuel consumption. For most planing hulls the optimum fuel consumption with respect to distance traveled is achieved just as the boat has come comfortably on a plane. When a planing boat encounters waves, its ride can often become uncomfortable and at times even dangerously unstable. It may have to be slowed back to the displacement mode where it doesn't operate as well as its displacement cousin. There are several different shapes that can be used on a planing hull: flat, V and cathedral.

A planing hull is designed to ride on top of the water once it has reached sufficient speed.

FLAT-BOTTOM HULLS

Many planing hulls are variations of the flat-bottom hull. Flat-bottom characteristics include:

- Good load carrying

- Inexpensive to construct

- Below average in holding a course at low speeds—tend to slide or drift

- Rough riding in waves

Flat-bottom powerboats plane easily, but produce a bumpy ride in rough water.

V-BOTTOM HULLS

The V-shaped hull, although a flat-bottom hull, has a pronounced V shape to its bow where it cuts the water. Characteristics of this shape include:

- Good ability to hold a steered direction at speed

- Deeper Vs perform better in rough water

- Deep Vs tend to roll at rest

V-bottom powerboats have an angled bottom which improves ride and control in waves.

CATHEDRAL HULLS

Cathedral hulls have two or three V shapes forward which turn into basically a flat hull aft. This gives greatly improved stability but with some of the unpleasant rough water ride as the pure flat bottom. Cathedral characteristics include:

- Good tracking at low speeds

- Good resistance to rolling even at rest

- Good load-carrying capacity

- Tend toward lower *freeboard*

- Uncomfortable at speed in rough water

Cathedral hulls combine excellent stability and load-carrying ability but produce a bumpy ride in waves.

SOFT INFLATABLE HULLS

These inflatables tend to be flat bottomed with the same rough and wet ride experienced in the pure flat-bottomed boat, perhaps even a little wetter. Their ability to hold a straight course is notoriously poor, particularly with any wind. The plastic impregnated fabric is susceptible to the sun's ultraviolet rays and can be sliced by sharp objects and chafed when dragging the hull up a rough beach or rubbing against a dock. In spite of these shortcomings, they continue to be very popular due to their light weight, excellent buoyancy and stability at rest. Characteristics include:

Soft inflatables are popular for their light weight and convenient storage, but can be difficult to steer and are vulnerable to puncture.

- Light weight and portable

- High stability

- Very high buoyancy

- High load-carrying capacity

- Soft contact with other boats but vulnerable to damage

- Easily affected by wind

- Low ability to hold a straight course (sideslips or drifts)

- Rough, wet ride at speed

- Relatively short life

RIGID INFLATABLE HULLS

These boats combine many of the advantages of the V hull with the soft inflatable. They have a rigid V bottom (usually fiberglass) combined with the side buoyancy chambers of an inflatable. They have good performance in rough conditions, good directional stability along with the buoyancy and initial stability of the inflatable.

A Rigid Inflatable Boat (RIB) combines the advantages of an inflatable with the control and seakindliness of a rigid V-bottom hull.

They are heavier than the soft-hull inflatable and do not fold and store as conveniently. Characteristics include:

- Combined advantages of V hull with inflatable

- Good ability to hold a straight course

- High buoyancy

- Exceptional performance in rough water

- High load-carrying capacity

- Soft contact with other boats

- Not as vulnerable to damage on bottom of hull as soft inflatable

MULTIHULLS

A catamaran with its two hulls connected by a platform has excellent stability. If each hull has an engine and propeller, a catamaran will turn easily. If it has only one engine and propeller between the hulls, it will be difficult to maneuver. Characteristics include:

- Good ability to hold a course at speed

- Good resistance to rolling

- Minimum *wake*

- Relatively shallow draft

- Cut through water rather than plane

- Small turning radius with two propellers

- Large turning radius with only one propeller

- Limited boat handling in bad weather

A catamaran's narrow hulls and wide beam provide excellent stability and a smooth ride.

PERSONAL WATERCRAFT (PWC)

Personal watercraft are frequently known by their common trade names, such as Jet Ski, Sea-Doo and WaveRunner. They use a water jet drive powered by a two-stroke or four-stroke gasoline inboard engine and are operated by a driver sitting on a saddle, standing or kneeling. Characteristics include:

- Good agility and speed

- Good maneuverability except when rapidly reducing speed

- Driver may easily reboard after falling off

- No propeller or rudder to injure a person in the water

A handle bar is used to turn the nozzle of a water jet for steering a PWC.

PARTS OF A BOAT

The directions toward the ends of a boat are called *forward* (toward the front end) and *aft* (toward the back). The forward end is the bow and the back end is the stern. When looking forward, the *port* side of a boat is the left side and the *starboard* side is the right side. In Chapter 13, you will learn in the *Navigation Rules* that the sidelights, which are turned on for nighttime operation, are red on the port side and green on the starboard side.

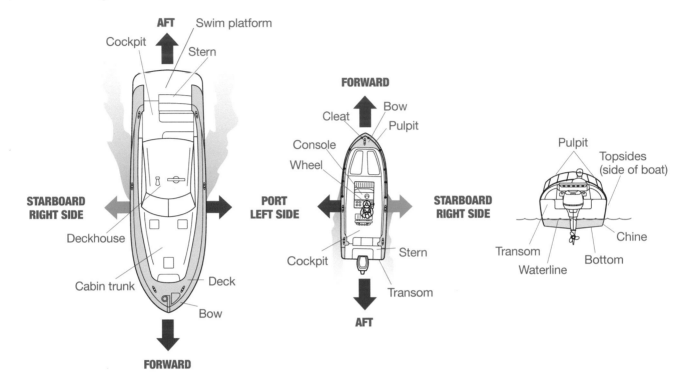

BOAT DIMENSIONS

The size of a boat is described by these dimensions:

- *Length Overall* is used to determine the minimum safety equipment required for a boat by federal and state regulations. It is measured from the forward end to the back end of a hull. It does not include any parts attached to the hull, such as outboard motors, anchor rollers or swim platforms.

- *Beam* is the maximum width of a boat.

- *Draft* is the maximum depth below the water.

- *Freeboard* is the height of the sides above the water.

- *Waterline Length* is the length of a boat measured where it floats in the water.

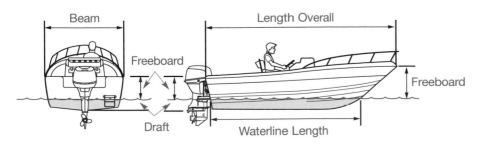

PROPULSION: PROP OR JET?

Propulsion systems generally consist of two major components: an engine that produces power, and a drive unit that propels the boat. There are two essential types of powerboat drive units:

• a propeller (prop)

• a water jet (jet drive)

HOW A PROPELLER WORKS

A rotating propeller produces thrust that moves the boat. When an engine is in FORWARD gear, the thrust from the rotating propeller drives the boat forward. When the gear is shifted into REVERSE, the propeller turns in the opposite direction driving the boat backward. Because propeller blades are optimized for forward thrust, their performance in reverse is drastically reduced.

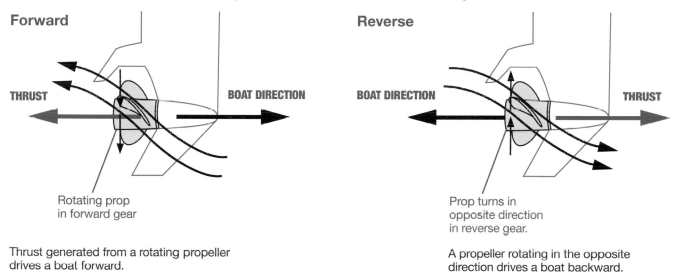

Forward

THRUST — BOAT DIRECTION

Rotating prop in forward gear

Thrust generated from a rotating propeller drives a boat forward.

Reverse

BOAT DIRECTION — THRUST

Prop turns in opposite direction in reverse gear.

A propeller rotating in the opposite direction drives a boat backward.

When viewed from behind, if a propeller drives a boat forward by rotating in a clockwise direction, it is defined as a right-hand propeller. If it is rotated in a counterclockwise direction in FORWARD gear, it would be left-handed. Whether a propeller is right- or left-handed will become important when *prop walk* is discussed in Chapter 5.

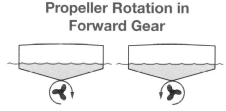

Propeller Rotation in Forward Gear

Right-Hand Propeller Left-Hand Propeller

Propeller size is defined by its *diameter* and *pitch*, and these factors have an important effect on the performance of a boat. Pitch is the distance that a propeller would move forward in a solid material in one full rotation. For example, a propeller with a 17-inch pitch would advance 17 inches. Since water is a fluid, the propeller would actually travel a distance less than 17 inches. Larger diameter propellers with less pitch that rotate at lower revolutions per minute (rpms) are used for slow-speed

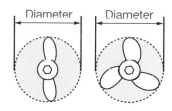

Propeller Diameter

Diameter   Diameter

boats or towing vessels, while smaller propellers with higher pitch operating at higher rpms are used for high-speed boats. A wrong propeller size may result in an engine overheating and/or a boat not reaching its designed speed.

Water flowing over the surfaces of a propeller blade produces a higher pressure on one side than the other. This pressure difference generates *lift* which results in thrust as well as a sideways force (torque). If pressure on the low-pressure side of the blades gets too low, bubbles of vaporized water (low temperature steam) will form on the blades. This bubbling action disrupts the water flow, causing the blades to lose lift and thrust and the engine to speed up. This phenomenon is called *cavitation*. When it occurs, reduce throttle and allow the propeller to regrip the water. Cavitation can happen if too much throttle is applied too quickly, or if the propeller is damaged or not the right size, or plastic debris or kelp is wrapped around the propeller.

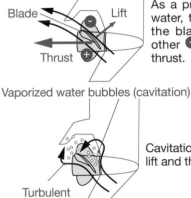

Blade — Lift

Thrust

As a propeller rotates through the water, the pressure on one side of the blades is higher ⊕ than the other ⊖, which generates lift and thrust.

Vaporized water bubbles (cavitation)

Cavitation causes the blades to lose lift and thrust.

Turbulent water flow

HOW A WATER JET WORKS

A water jet has no propeller. Instead, water enters through an intake underneath the boat and is fed into a pump, which then accelerates it through a nozzle that produces thrust to move the boat.

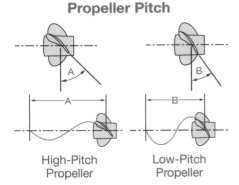

High-Pitch Propeller

Low-Pitch Propeller

A low-pitch propeller (B) moves forward a smaller distance than a high-pitch propeller (A). The higher the pitch number, the greater the pitch (distance traveled per revolution).

Contra-rotating propellers have two propellers, one in front of the other that rotate in opposite directions. This arrangement eliminates the wasteful twisting water flow from a single propeller as well as the prop walk (torque) effect. Advantages are increases in propeller efficiency, boat-handling control and fuel savings.

Forward

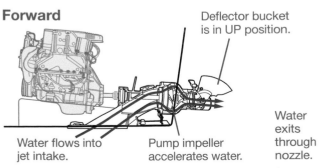

Deflector bucket is in UP position.

Water flows into jet intake.

Pump impeller accelerates water.

Water exits through nozzle.

The jet of water exiting from the nozzle generates thrust to drive the boat forward. The nozzle can be pivoted sideways to turn the boat left or right.

Reverse

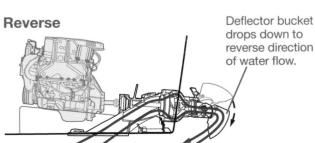

Deflector bucket drops down to reverse direction of water flow.

The deflector bucket reverses the jet of water to drive the boat backward.

TRIM & TILT CONTROL

On stern drives and many outboard motors (typically above 25 hp) and jet drives, the angle of the drive unit to the boat can be changed (trimmed) while the boat is underway to achieve better performance. This is usually done by hydraulic rams, which are activated by a toggle button normally located on the throttle control lever. These hydraulic rams can also be used to tilt the drive out of the water when leaving the boat in the water or hauling out. When operating in the trim range, the drive unit will move slowly, but once beyond the maximum UP trim position, the hydraulic speed will suddenly increase until the drive reaches its maximum tilt position. For more information on trim and how it affects a powerboat, see Chapter 5.

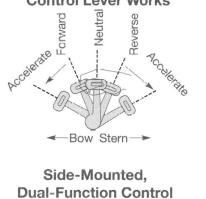

How a Dual-Function Control Lever Works

Outboard motor trimmed in down position.

Outboard motor trimmed up for optimum performance for a specific speed.

Side-Mounted, Dual-Function Control

Trim/tilt button

Neutral release lever—push into handle to move lever out of neutral.

Throttle only button—push in when lever is in neutral position to increase throttle while in neutral.

ENGINE CONTROLS

DUAL-FUNCTION CONTROL

This is the most common type and has a single lever that combines throttle (speed) and gearshift (FORWARD, NEUTRAL and REVERSE). It usually has a device that can disengage the gearshift to allow you to increase the throttle when starting or warming up the engine. Another feature of most controls prevents the engine from being started unless the gearshift is in NEUTRAL. If nothing happens when the ignition key is turned on, check to make sure the lever is in the NEUTRAL position. When shifting from FORWARD to REVERSE or REVERSE to FORWARD, pause briefly in NEUTRAL and count 1-2-3 to avoid damaging the gears.

SINGLE-FUNCTION CONTROL

Another type of control has separate single-function levers—one for the throttle and the other for the gearshift—and can often be identified by the red (throttle) and black (gearshift) knobs on the levers.

Top-Mounted, Dual-Function Control

Here is a top-mounted control with a single lever that controls throttle and gearshift.

Single-Function Control

Throttle lever (red)

Gearshift lever (black)

Twin Screw Control

The use of two dual-function levers with the port lever controlling the port engine's throttle and gearshift and the starboard lever controlling the starboard engine is frequently used. Another alternative may consist of two sets of two single-function levers with the levers of one set controlling only the throttles of the port and starboard engines and the second set controlling the gearshifts.

Using a Throttle Control

Changes in the throttle control should be done in a smooth gradual manner. When operating in conditions where the boat could impact waves or wakes, steady your hand on the base of the control and adjust the throttle with thumb and fingers.

This twin screw control's left lever controls the port engine and the right lever controls the starboard engine.

Joystick Control

A joystick system is an electronic engine control that can adjust engine rpms, drive angles and thrusters, allowing the powerboat to move in any direction: forward, backward, and sideway. It can be used on powerboats with:

Steady your throttle hand against the base for precise control, especially in wake or waves.

• two or more outboard motors;

• twin stern drives (see pages 24-25);

• traditional drive system with integrated bow and stern thrusters; and

• one or more pod drives (see page 27) with thrusters.

A joystick may also be integrated into the boat's navigation system to serve as a jog lever to change direction while on autopilot in open water without having to use the steering wheel.

Push the joystick in the direction you want the boat to go, or twist it to rotate the boat.

12

REVIEW QUESTIONS

1. The type of hull that moves through the water and has good rough-water handling is a _____ hull. At higher speeds, it is the _____ hull that rises on top of the water, but may be uncomfortable in _____ water.

2. The optimum fuel consumption (best miles per gallon) for a boat on a plane occurs when just _____ on a _____ .

3. Of the planing hull types, it is the _____ and _____ that have good performance in rough water.

4. When a planing hull begins climbing its bow wave, it is in the _____ stage. At this point the boat may become _____ , fuel consumption is high, and _____ may be poor over the raised bow.

5. Propeller size is defined by its _____ and _____.

Answers:
1) displacement; planing; rough
2) comfortably; plane
3) V bottom; rigid inflatable
4) transition/semi-displacement; unstable; visibility
5) diameter; pitch

Chapter 2

OUTBOARD MOTORS

KEY CONCEPTS

▶ Two- & four-strokes
▶ Outboard motor parts

▶ Starting procedure
▶ Fueling & maintenance

TWO-STROKE & FOUR-STROKE

Outboard motors can range in size from small two-horsepower (hp) units that weigh 25 pounds to massive 300-horsepower (hp) engines. They can be either two-stroke (two-cycle) or four-stroke (four-cycle). Two-stroke outboards use oil mixed into the gasoline to lubricate the engine. Each compression stroke of a piston is followed by a power stroke. As the power stroke comes to its end, a new mixture of gasoline/oil and air enters the cylinder and exhaust gases are forced out along with some of the new incoming mixture. These outboards have been regarded as serious polluters, but recent innovations, such as oil injection and the replacement of carburetors with fuel injection, have reduced pollution to a level almost comparable to the four-stroke models.

Four-stroke outboards are lubricated by oil in the crankcase, similar to an automobile engine. An intake stroke, which brings in a mixture of gasoline and air, precedes each compression stroke, which is followed by a power stroke. The exhaust stroke, which forces out the exhaust gases, completes the cycle and the next cycle starts again with the intake stroke.

As concerns about air and water pollution have increased, manufacturers have developed cleaner-running outboards. Some states have stringent pollution requirements for reservoirs and inland waters that may affect the use of your boat.

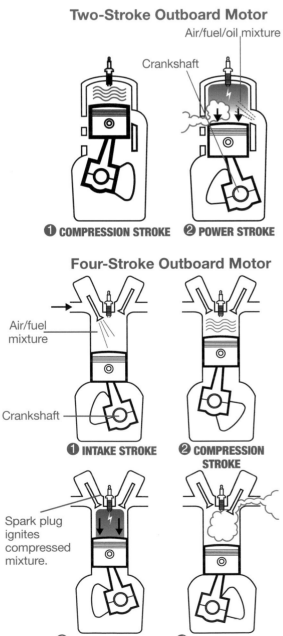

Two-Stroke Outboard Motor

Air/fuel/oil mixture

Crankshaft

❶ COMPRESSION STROKE   ❷ POWER STROKE

Four-Stroke Outboard Motor

Air/fuel mixture

Crankshaft

❶ INTAKE STROKE   ❷ COMPRESSION STROKE

Spark plug ignites compressed mixture.

❸ POWER STROKE   ❹ EXHAUST STROKE

PARTS OF AN OUTBOARD MOTOR

CHOKE

A choke reduces the air supply in the carburetor, which enriches (increases the proportion of fuel) the fuel-air mixture that enters the cylinder. This makes the mixture easier to ignite. A manual choke control is pulled out to reduce or close the air supply. Some outboards may have an automatic choke and no action is required.

This symbol indicates a choke, which reduces air to the carburetor.

PRIMER PUMPS

Primer pumps are used in many outboards. On electrically started engines, pushing in the key or just turning it to the START position activates a primer pump that injects a small amount of fuel into the cylinder. Manually activated primer pumps may be used on smaller outboards with manual pull-cord starting. At first glance these can be confused with a manual choke knob, but they are usually accompanied by a decal on the face of the engine listing instructions for use. Manual primer pump knobs must be pulled out and then pushed back in to inject the fuel. Some retract automatically while others must be pushed. If left out, the engine will not start.

Methods of choking or priming engines vary. Refer to the manufacturer's manual for starting procedures.

Two-Stroke Outboard Motor

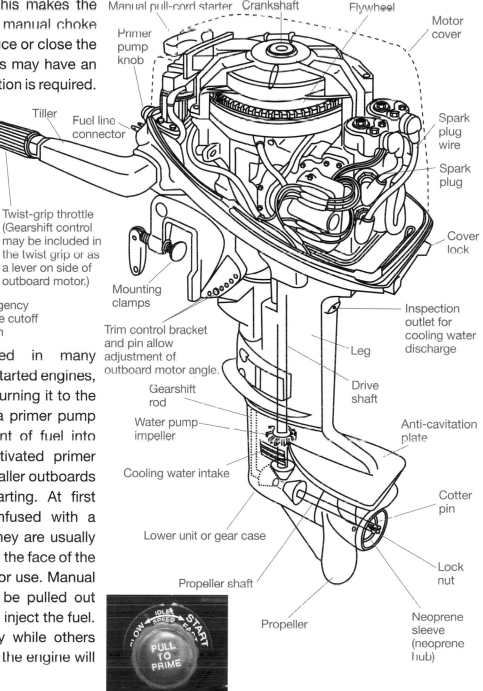

Manual pull-cord starter — Crankshaft — Flywheel — Motor cover — Primer pump knob — Spark plug wire — Spark plug — Cover lock — Tiller — Fuel line connector — Twist-grip throttle (Gearshift control may be included in the twist grip or as a lever on side of outboard motor.) — Emergency engine cutoff switch — Mounting clamps — Trim control bracket and pin allow adjustment of outboard motor angle. — Gearshift rod — Water pump impeller — Cooling water intake — Lower unit or gear case — Propeller shaft — Inspection outlet for cooling water discharge — Leg — Drive shaft — Anti-cavitation plate — Cotter pin — Lock nut — Neoprene sleeve (neoprene hub) — Propeller

This primer pump knob injects a small amount of fuel into the cylinder.

TILT-LOCK RELEASE LEVER

The tilt-lock release lever appears on small outboards without an electric hydraulic-powered trim/tilt control. The lever is in the RELEASE position when operating in FORWARD gear, which allows the outboard to kick up if it hits an underwater object. It must be placed in the LOCK position before shifting into REVERSE to prevent the outboard from tilting up.

TWIST-GRIP THROTTLE & GEARSHIFT

For outboards with a separate gearshift lever on the side of the motor, the twist-grip throttle will usually have a shift position marked on it to which the throttle should be set before shifting the lever into FORWARD, NEUTRAL or REVERSE so as to prevent serious damage to the outboard.

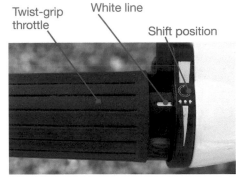

The white line on the twist-grip throttle is lined up with the shift position which will allow the gear to be shifted into forward, neutral or reverse.

Four-Stroke Outboard Motor

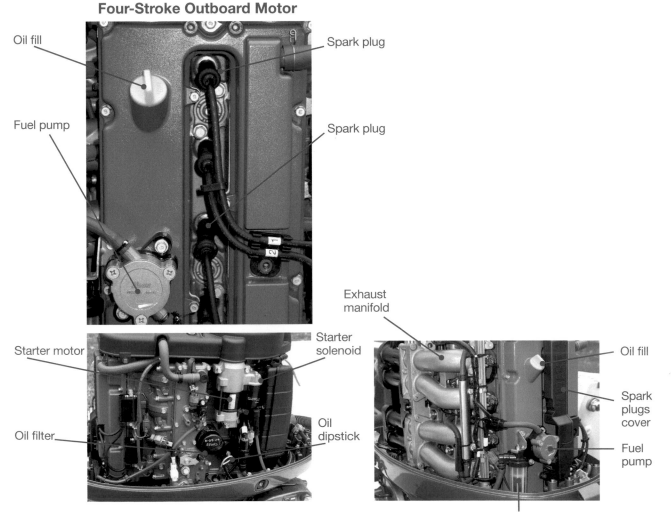

16

Shear Pins & Safety Sleeves

All outboards have a designed weak link between the propeller and the propeller shaft to protect the engine and drivetrain if the propeller hits an object. Most outboards use a neoprene sleeve (neoprene hub) that is bonded to the propeller hub. When impact occurs, the bonding is broken, which protects the outboard. If the bond fails, there is usually enough friction in the neoprene hub to allow the engine to turn the propeller very slowly, often enough to return to safety. The propeller must then be removed and repaired. Smaller outboards may use a soft metal pin called a shear pin, which will break upon impact and the propeller will no longer spin.

A shear pin breaks when a propeller hits an object, protecting the engine and the drivetrain from damage.

Outboard Inspection

- Outboard controls operate smoothly.

- Propeller blades, neoprene sleeve or shear pin are intact.

- Cooling water intake is clear.

- Oil level (applies to four-stroke or two-stroke with separate oil tank); add oil if indicated.

- Fuel tank level; add if indicated.

- Condition of fuel line (no cracks or sponginess) and connections.

- Any leaks in fuel system or gasoline odor in bilges.

- Condition of battery cables (no cracks, abrasion or frayed wire) and battery (no corrosion at terminals and proper fluid level). Cables securely fastened to battery.

- Condition of lanyard with one end securely connected to the emergency engine cutoff switch.

- Attachment of safety chain, wire or line to boat and motor (applies to outboards fastened to the transom with screw clamps).

Most modern outboards use a neoprene sleeve bonded to the propeller hub that breaks when a propeller hits an object.

Lifting an Outboard

A small outboard motor of 10 horsepower or less can usually be lifted and attached to a boat without too much effort. Although this is best done on land, secure the boat to prevent movement when transferring the outboard while on the water. Have someone pass the outboard to a person in the boat. As a precaution against accidentally losing the motor overboard during the transfer, tie a retrieval line to the motor and fasten it to the dock or boat.

Retrieval line connecting motor and boat prevents motor from sinking to bottom if you lose your grip.

OUTBOARD STARTING PROCEDURE

For best results, follow the procedures described in the manufacturer's manual.

1 Complete the inspection.

2 Turn battery switch to correct setting.

3 Lower outboard into DOWN position.

4 Pump the fuel primer bulb until it is firm (if using a portable or integral tank with an air vent, open the vent before pumping the bulb). Also pump oil bulb, if applicable.

5 Attach one end of the lanyard to the driver and make sure the other end is attached to the emergency engine cutoff switch at the key ignition or on the tiller.

6 Center outboard motor.

7 Put gearshift in NEUTRAL and throttle to START position.

8 If starting manually, activate the primer pump or pull the choke out all the way, then pull the starter cord until the engine starts. When using the cord, remove any slack in it before pulling; don't yank on it or let it snap back on the rewind. On an outboard with a choke, push the choke in all the way (unless it is very cold) once the engine fires. If, after the third pull on the starter rope the engine hasn't started, push the choke in halfway and pull the rope again. When using an electric start, push the ignition key in at the START position to activate the primer pump or choke. When the engine starts, release the key from the START position. It may be necessary to cycle the pump two or three times before engine fires. NOTE: *If starting a warm engine, do not use the primer pump or choke.*

9 Adjust throttle to steady idle.

10 Check for a stream of water flowing from the inspection outlet for cooling water discharge. IMPORTANT: *If there is no water, turn off the outboard motor immediately to prevent damage from overheating.*

11 Check gauges, if applicable. NOTE: *If engine won't start and there is a smell of gasoline, wait several minutes before attempting to start it again.*

A lanyard attaches the driver to the emergency engine cutoff switch. If the driver falls overboard or is thrown from the steering station, the engine will immediately shut off. Wireless cutoff devices are also available.

Photo Courtesy of U.S. Coast Guard

OUTBOARD COOLING SYSTEM

Most outboard motors are water cooled. The illustration tracks the flow of cooling water which enters through the cooling water intake, and is pushed up the water feed tube by a water pump and then circulated through waterways in the engine block. The water then flows back down the leg where it mixes with the exhaust gases and exits through the propeller hub. During its journey through the engine, a bit of the cooling water is diverted through the inspection outlet for cooling water discharge to let you know that the cooling system is working. Outboards smaller than five horsepower will usually have their exhaust outlet located just above the propeller instead of through the propeller hub.

FUELING

PROCEDURE FOR TWO-STROKE OUTBOARDS

Oil is mixed with the fuel to lubricate the engine and there are two ways this can be done. To determine which method applies to your outboard, check the manufacturer's manual.

1 *Adding oil to the fuel tank.* This method is most common in older engines. Oil is usually added first followed by gasoline to mix the ingredients. If the fuel tank is empty, add a gallon of gasoline before adding the oil, then add the rest of the fuel. Many outboards use a ratio of 1 pint of oil to 6 gallons of gasoline, but check the manufacturer's manual for the recommended ratio. Serious damage to the engine can result by using an improper mixture.

2 *Adding oil to the oil tank.* Many newer two-stroke outboards have oil tanks (either as part of the engine or separately) that automatically meter the oil into the gasoline according to the engine speed.

PROCEDURE FOR FOUR-STROKE OUTBOARDS

These run on gasoline with the lubricating oil added separately to the crankcase.

No matter what type of outboard is used, it is very important that you use the type of oil recommended in the manufacturer's manual.

Outboard Cooling System

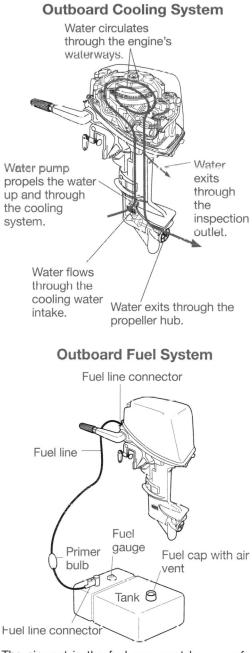

Water circulates through the engine's waterways.

Water pump propels the water up and through the cooling system.

Water exits through the inspection outlet.

Water flows through the cooling water intake.

Water exits through the propeller hub.

Outboard Fuel System

Fuel line connector

Fuel line

Fuel gauge

Primer bulb

Fuel cap with air vent

Tank

Fuel line connector

The air vent in the fuel cap must be open for fuel to flow to the outboard motor. If closed, the motor will not start or it will stop after running a short time. Vent is usually closed when a boat is not being used.

Fuel line connector

Fuel cap

New EPA-certified fuel tanks have an automatic vacuum valve instead of an air vent.

SAFETY PRECAUTIONS FOR FUELING

Always remember that gasoline vapor is heavier than air. It can settle in bilges or enclosed compartments and a spark can ignite an explosion. If the fuel tanks are portable:

- Fill them off the boat on the ground or the dock.

- Make sure the tank vents are open.

- Secure fuel fill caps and close the air vents before bringing them back on board the boat to avoid spillage.

If the fuel tank is built into the boat:

- Tie the boat to the dock to prevent it from moving and spilling gasoline during fueling.

- Close all hatches and openings before fueling.

- Shut off engine and all electrical equipment.

- Passengers should be off the boat.

- Do not overfill or force fuel through the air vents.

- Close caps on fuel fills after fueling.

- Turn on blowers (if applicable), open all hatches and openings, and allow the boat to ventilate for at least four minutes.

- Check for gasoline odor in bilges and compartments before starting.

Add gasoline fuel through the deck plate marked GAS or FUEL and carefully monitor the fuel flow.

Use these precautions for fueling any kind of tank:

- Don't smoke or use anything, such as matches, lighters or switches, that might cause a spark during fueling.

- Determine the amount of fuel needed, but do not use a metal dipstick that could cause a spark.

- Keep the hose nozzle in contact with the tank or fill pipe to prevent a buildup of static electricity which might cause a spark.

- Leave some space in the tank for thermal expansion of the fuel.

- Allow time for fuel to drain from the hose before removing the nozzle.

- Wipe up spillage immediately and deposit the rag in an appropriate container ashore.

MAINTENANCE

Outboards should be kept in good operating condition by regular inspection and maintenance and serviced periodically by a qualified mechanic. A tool kit with spare parts and manufacturers' manuals should be kept on the boat in a waterproof container.

BASIC TOOLS & SPARES

- pliers
- spark plug wrench
- screwdrivers (various types)
- knife
- sandpaper
- electrical & duct tape
- shear pins (if applicable)
- cotter pins
- starter rope (if applicable)
- spark plugs

REVIEW QUESTIONS

1. Two-stroke outboards are lubricated by oil that is _____ into the fuel while four-stroke engines are lubricated by oil in the _____.

2. When starting a cold outboard, either a primer pump is used to inject a small amount of _____ into the _____ or a choke is used to reduce the _____ supply in the _____.

3. When a propeller hits an object, the rest of the outboard is protected from damage by breaking the bonding of the_____ to the propeller hub or breaking the _____.

4. When starting an outboard, it is important to check for a stream of _____ from the inspection outlet. If there is no _____ , the outboard motor should be _____.

5. After filling a built-in fuel tank, hatches should be opened to allow the boat to ventilate because gasoline vapor is _____ than air and can settle in the bilge.

PREVENTATIVE MAINTENANCE CHECKLIST

Perform routine checks and maintenance of the engine, systems and hull as recommended by the manufacturer.

- ☐ Fuel system (inspect for leaks and condition)
- ☐ Fuel and oil filters (inspect, replace)
- ☐ Oil changes (engine and gear, inspect for leaks)
- ☐ Grease points (lubricate)
- ☐ Spark plugs (condition, clean/replace)
- ☐ Cooling system (flush to prevent buildup of salt, sandy or muddy sediment)
- ☐ Battery condition
- ☐ Battery terminals (clean and tight)
- ☐ Power trim & tilt (condition of rams, inspect for leaks)
- ☐ Propeller and attachment (condition)
- ☐ External anodes (clean, replace as needed)
- ☐ Through-hull fittings (condition)
- ☐ Trim tabs (condition of rams, inspect for leaks)
- ☐ Hull (condition, inspect for leaks)

Answers: 1) mixed; crankcase 2) fuel; cylinder; air; carburetor 3) neoprene sleeve/hub; shear pin 4) water; water; turned off 5) heavier

Chapter 3

INBOARD ENGINE SYSTEMS

KEY CONCEPTS

▶ Types of engines   ▶ Types of drives

▶ Starting procedures   ▶ Fueling & maintenance

Inboard engines use either gasoline or diesel fuel. With their relatively lighter weights and higher rpms, gasoline engines often power high-performance sportboats. Diesel engines are typically used on large or moderate-speed vessels for their reliability and low-speed torque. Diesel fuel does not have the fire hazards of gasoline.

GASOLINE ENGINE SYSTEMS

GASOLINE ENGINE INSPECTION

- Oil level; add if indicated.

- Coolant level; add if indicated.

- Fuel tank level; add if indicated.

- Condition of fuel line (no cracks or sponginess) and connections.

- Any leaks in fuel system or gasoline odor in bilges.

- Belts should be snug; look for signs of wear.

- Raw water *seacock* (valve) should be open.

- Raw water strainer; clean out debris.

- Engine control levers operating smoothly.

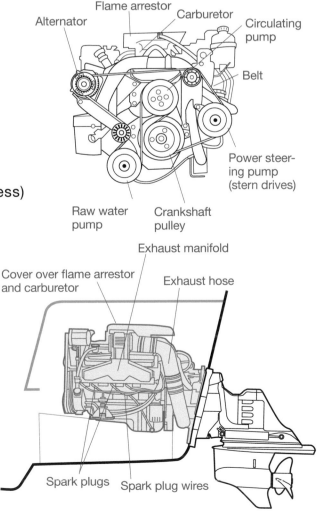

Gasoline Starting Procedure

Follow procedures in the manufacturer's manual for recommended steps.

1. Complete the inspection.

2. Turn battery switch to correct setting.

3. Engage engine blower for at least four minutes or until all traces of gasoline odor have disappeared.

4. Tilt stern drive into DOWN position and center it (if applicable).

5. Put gearshift in NEUTRAL (throttle slightly open if necessary).

6. Turn ignition key to ON to start engine.

7. Adjust throttle to steady idle.

8. Check gauges (oil pressure, water temperature, ammeter).

9. Check exhaust outlet for consistent water flow. If you don't see any water or there is an abnormal sporadic flow, immediately turn off the engine to prevent damage from overheating.

DIESEL ENGINE SYSTEMS

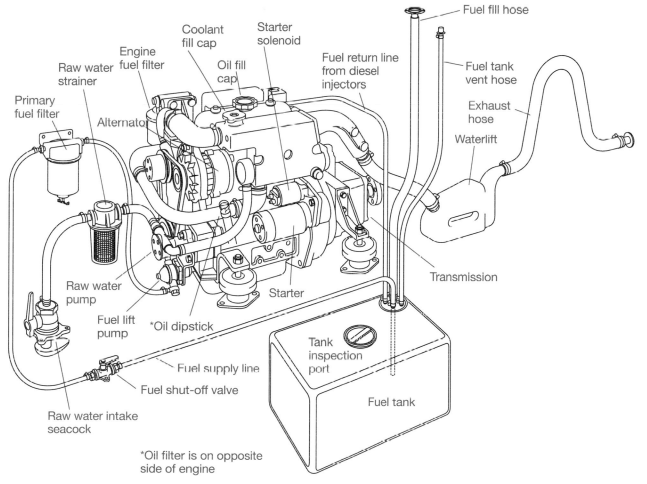

Fuel fill hose

Coolant fill cap

Starter solenoid

Engine fuel filter

Oil fill cap

Raw water strainer

Fuel return line from diesel injectors

Fuel tank vent hose

Primary fuel filter

Alternator

Exhaust hose

Waterlift

Raw water pump

Fuel lift pump

*Oil dipstick

Starter

Transmission

Fuel supply line

Tank inspection port

Fuel shut-off valve

Raw water intake seacock

Fuel tank

*Oil filter is on opposite side of engine

DIESEL ENGINE INSPECTION

- Engine oil level; add if indicated.
- Coolant; add if indicated.
- Fuel tank level; add if indicated.
- Condition of fuel line (no cracks or sponginess) and connections.
- Belts should be snug; look for signs of wear.
- Engine pan and bilge for fuel, water or oil.
- Raw water seacock (valve) is open.
- Raw water strainer; clean out debris.
- Engine control levers for smooth operation.

DIESEL STARTING PROCEDURE

Follow procedures in the manufacturer's manual for recommended steps.

1. Complete the inspection.
2. Turn battery switch to correct setting.
3. Put engine control in RUN position.
4. Put gearshift in NEUTRAL (throttle slightly open if necessary).
5. Preheat with glow plug control for 10-30 seconds, if applicable.
6. Turn on ignition (oil pressure alarm should sound) and start engine.
7. Adjust throttle to steady idle (oil pressure alarm should stop).
8. Check gauges (oil pressure, water temperature, ammeter).
9. Check exhaust outlet for consistent water flow. If you don't see any water or there is an abnormal sporadic flow, immediately turn off the engine to prevent damage from overheating.

All diesel engines are stopped by depriving the engine of fuel. This is achieved by either a mechanical pull or an electromechanical device using a button or a different key position. CAUTION: *Do not stop engine when in FORWARD or REVERSE gear.*

COOLING SYSTEMS

Nearly all inboard engines use seawater (raw water) to cool the internal coolant, unlike a car which uses air to cool the internal coolant.

TYPES OF DRIVES

STERN DRIVES

Stern drives, sometimes called inboard/outboards (I/O) or outdrives, combine features of both an inboard engine and outboard motor. The gasoline or diesel engine is mounted inside the boat and the powertrain goes through the transom to a stern drive that resembles the lower part of an outboard motor. The stern drive is turned to steer the boat and is also capable of being tilted upward when not in use.

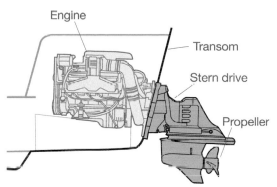

Shown is a typical stern drive driven by an inboard engine.

STERN DRIVE INSPECTION

• Hydraulic fluid for power trim control (reservoir generally mounted on inside of transom); add if indicated.

• Propeller blades and neoprene sleeve are intact.

SHAFT DRIVES WITH FIXED (NON-SWIVELING) PROPELLERS

The propeller shaft starts at the gearbox transmission and passes through a sealed stern tube in the bottom of the hull. Since the propeller cannot be turned like an outboard motor or stern drive, a rudder is required to steer the boat.

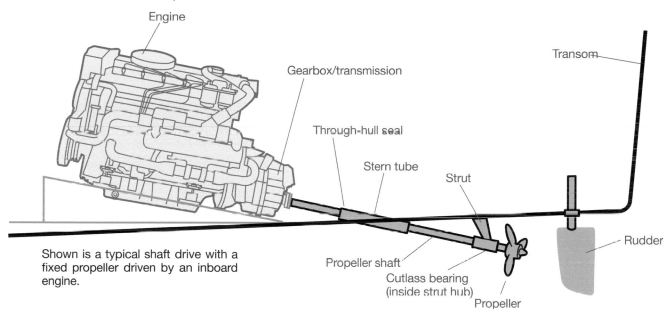

Shown is a typical shaft drive with a fixed propeller driven by an inboard engine.

PROPELLER SHAFT THROUGH-HULL SEAL

There are various arrangements for sealing the shaft as it passes through the hull. The most common is the dripless (packless) seal which uses carbon or PTFE (Teflon). Another type is a stuffing box packed with flax rings which is designed to leak a small amount of water, a few drops per minute, when the shaft is turning to help keep it lubricated. A packing nut on the stuffing box is tightened against the packing material to keep the water flow to a few drops per minute.

Stuffing Box Seal

Dripless (Packless) Seal

JET DRIVES

Jet drives use a large water pump impeller powered by either a gasoline or diesel engine to accelerate water flow through a nozzle to produce propulsive thrust. Jet drives have good steering ability at all speeds except when slowing down. Most mid- to large-size jet drives use deflectors for steering and reverse by deflecting the water flow from the nozzle to change direction. Smaller jet drives used on personal watercraft (PWC) and small sportboats may use a swiveling nozzle for steering and a reversing deflector.

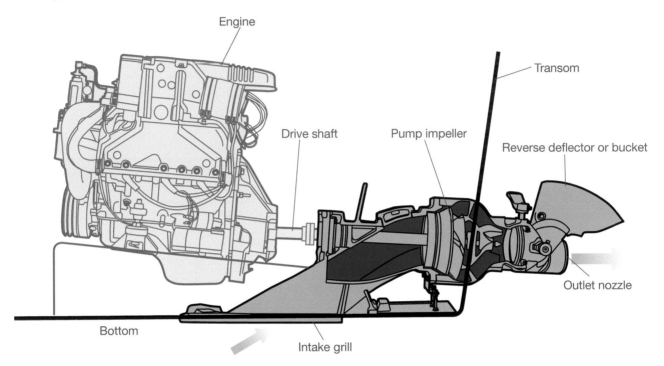

Engine

Transom

Drive shaft

Pump impeller

Reverse deflector or bucket

Outlet nozzle

Bottom

Intake grill

JET DRIVE INSPECTION

- Jet drive control should operate smoothly.

- Hydraulic oil level; add if indicated.

- Condition of jet drive's impeller; inspect through access cover (engine must be turned off and transmission in NEUTRAL).

- Jet drive should rotate freely (engine must be turned off and transmission in NEUTRAL).

POD DRIVES

Pod drives are another form of directed thrust propulsion found on powerboats in the mid 30-foot length and larger. The pods are located near the stern and mounted to the bottom of the hull. This system uses a combination of throttle controls and steering wheel for less confined areas and higher speed use, while a joystick control is used for more precise or close-quarters maneuvering.

Generally, they come in a twin pod configuration but can have triple and quad pod installations on larger powerboats. Pods are similar in design with one key difference: those that have forward facing contra-rotating propellers (Volvo IPS) and those with rear facing contra-rotating propellers (Mercury Zeus and ZF Pods). With either orientation, they provide:

• Reduced fuel consumption

• Greater maneuverability

• Smoother ride with little to no vibration or resonance

• Significant noise/sound reduction

Pods allow for powerboats to rotate on their pivot point in a boat length by twisting the joystick. They also have the ability to move the powerboat sideways, toward or away from the dock by moving the joystick 90 degrees to the centerline of the boat.

Volvo's Dynamic Positioning System (DPS) and Mercruiser's Skyhook feature can hold a powerboat in position using a GPS signal with the touch of a button. The pods also have safety features such as a skeg and drive units which can break free if they strike a submerged object, preventing water from entering the engine compartment.

POD DRIVE INSPECTION

• Check hydraulic oil level on drive unit. Some drives have more than one type of oil (e.g., Zeus has three).

• Check hoses and fittings for signs of wear and leaking.

• Check that no water is accumulating in the base.

**Forward-Facing
Contra-Rotating Pod Drive**

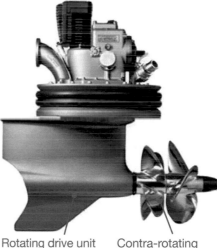

Rotating drive unit (360°)   Contra-rotating propellers

Photo courtesy of Volvo Penta

**Rear-Facing
Contra-Rotating Pod Drive**

Transmission unit

Coupling for engine drive shaft

Contra-rotating propellers   Rotating drive unit (360°)

Photo courtesy of Mercury Marine

FUELING

GASOLINE ENGINES

These engines use gasoline fuel with lubricating oil added to the engine through the oil fill opening. Remember that gasoline vapor is heavier than air and can settle in bilges or enclosed compartments. All it takes is a spark to ignite the vapor and cause an explosion. Safety precautions for fueling:

Make sure fuel is added only through the deck plate marked DIESEL or FUEL and monitor fuel flow continuously to avoid overfill.

- Close all hatches and openings before fueling.

- Passengers should be off the boat.

- Shut off engine and all electrical equipment.

- Do not smoke or use anything that might cause a spark during fueling, such as matches, lighters or switches.

- Determine amount of fuel needed and do not overfill or force gasoline through the air vents. Allow room in the tank for thermal expansion.

- Keep the hose nozzle in contact with the fill pipe to discharge the buildup of static electricity from the fuel to prevent a spark.

- Allow time for fuel to drain from the hose before removing the nozzle from the tank.

- Close caps on fuel fills after fueling.

- Turn on blowers and open all hatches and openings and allow the boat to ventilate for at least four minutes or until all traces of gasoline odor have disappeared.

- Wipe up spillage immediately and deposit the rag in an appropriate container ashore.

DIESEL ENGINES

These run on diesel fuel with lubricating oil added separately through the oil fill opening. Although diesel fuel is much less volatile than gasoline and is considered relatively risk-free when fueling, it is still good practice to follow many of the safety precautions for gasoline fueling.

SPILL POLLUTION HAZARDS

With gasoline or diesel fuel, it is your responsibility to prevent spills into the environment. Use petroleum-absorbent pads or sheets to catch or wipe up fuel that might splash from the nozzle, the fill plate or air vents. Any visible sheen left on the water could subject you to significant fines by the U.S. Coast Guard or local authorities.

MAINTENANCE

Consult the manufacturer's manual for recommended maintenance procedures. A basic tool kit with spare parts for repairs and maintenance as well as manufacturers' manuals should be kept on board the boat in a waterproof container.

BASIC TOOLS & SPARES

- pliers (include water pump pliers)
- wrenches (include stuffing box wrench if applicable)
- spark plug wrench (if applicable)
- screwdrivers (various sizes and heads)
- hammer
- knife
- sandpaper
- duct tape
- electrical tape
- spark plugs (if applicable)

REVIEW QUESTIONS

1. Inboard engines use either _____ or _____ fuel. _____ fuel does not have the fire hazards of _____.

2. Before starting a gasoline engine, the engine blower must be turned on for at least _____ minutes.

3. After starting an inboard engine, it is important to check for _____ flowing out of the exhaust outlet. If there is no _____, immediately _____ the engine.

4. A diesel engine is normally stopped by
   a. turning off electricity to the engine.
   b. engaging the brake on the shaft.
   c. depriving the engine of fuel.
   d. depriving the engine of air.

5. Jet drives have good steering ability at all speeds except when _____.

Answers: 1) gasoline; diesel; Diesel; gasoline
2) four
3) water; turn off
4) c. depriving the engine of fuel.
5) slowing down

PREVENTATIVE MAINTENANCE CHECKLIST

Perform routine checks and maintenance of the engine, systems and hull as recommended by the manufacturer.

- ☐ Fuel system (inspect for leaks and condition)
- ☐ Fuel and oil filters (inspect, replace)
- ☐ Oil changes (engine and gear, inspect for leaks)
- ☐ Grease points (if applicable, lubricate)
- ☐ Spark plugs (if applicable, condition, clean/replace)
- ☐ Cooling system: raw water strainer (inspect, replace); coolant (condition and level)
- ☐ Belts (condition, replace as needed)
- ☐ Battery condition
- ☐ Battery terminals (clean and tight)
- ☐ Power trim and tilt (if applicable, condition of rams, inspect for leaks)
- ☐ Propeller and attachment (condition, if fixed propeller drive include shaft, through-hull seal, strut and bearings)
- ☐ External anodes (clean, replace as needed)
- ☐ Through-hull fittings/ seacocks (condition)
- ☐ Trim tabs (condition of rams, inspect for leaks)
- ☐ Hull (condition, inspect for leaks)

Chapter 4

PREPARATION & OPERATOR RESPONSIBILITIES

KEY CONCEPTS

▶ Preparation & trip planning
▶ Wearing life jackets
▶ Equipment & departure checks

▶ Operator responsibilities
▶ Crew briefing
▶ Knots & line handling

Preparation and planning are without question the most important ingredients in safe, enjoyable powerboating. Many of the things that can go wrong can be avoided with a bit of foresight.

WEARING LIFE JACKETS

Wearing life jackets is comparable to wearing seat belts in a car. If you're wearing one, it could save your life if you fall overboard or your boat gets swamped with water. Boating conditions can change rapidly and it is especially important to wear a life jacket in severe weather, cold air or water conditions, unsafe conditions such as rough inlets, high boat traffic at night, and if you're alone or in remote areas. Trying to put a life jacket on while in the water can be difficult and tiring. Your life jacket should:

- be an appropriate size;

- fit properly so it doesn't ride up when you are in the water; and

- be a visible color when in the water (yellow or orange are the most visible).

If your boat is registered anywhere in the United States, life jackets must be U.S. Coast Guard approved. For more information on the types of approved life jackets, see Chapter 10.

LIFE JACKET SAFETY TIPS

- *Life jackets should fit properly and all zippers and straps should be fastened.*

- *The use of leg or crotch straps will help prevent ride up.*

DRESS FOR BOATING

Nothing takes the fun out of boating faster than being cold—or hot. Temperatures on the water tend to be more extreme and more changeable than ashore, so the right gear and clothing are an important part of enjoying your time on the water. Using the layered approach to clothing is the best way to stay comfortable in changing conditions. In cool weather, it's important to keep your head, hands and feet warm.

Because damaging ultraviolet (UV) rays can penetrate clouds and bounce off the water's surface, it's important to protect your eyes and skin. Apply sunscreen with a sun protection factor (SPF) of 15 or higher that protects against both UVA and UVB rays. This will provide protection from both direct and reflected sunlight. Waterproof and sport sunscreens are available which will not run or rub into eyes. Wear sunglasses with good protection from:

- Sideways exposure
- UV rays (at least 90%)
- Glare off the water (polarized lenses)

A two-piece foul weather gear set with a waterproof jacket and pants (preferably with suspenders) is more versatile than a one-piece jumpsuit. The jacket and pants can be worn together or separately to suit different temperatures and conditions. When selecting a size, make sure it is loose enough for layers of warm clothing underneath.

WARM WEATHER DRESSING
☐ Light-colored hat or visor with a dark color under the bill to reduce reflection
☐ UV sunglasses with a keeper cord
☐ Light-colored, lightweight clothing with an appropriate UV protection factor (UPF). For sun-sensitive skin, a high-collared shirt with sleeves helps protect neck and arms.
☐ Life jacket in good condition zipped or clipped closed
☐ Water-resistant watch
☐ Long pants protect legs from prolonged exposure to the sun.
☐ Snug-fitting shoes with nonskid soles for firm traction on wet surfaces and foot protection
☐ Soft, water-resistant duffel bag contains foul weather gear, cold weather or spare clothing, bathing suit, towel, sunscreen and a water bottle.

COLD & WET WEATHER DRESSING
☐ A fleece or knit ski cap helps minimize heat loss through the head.
☐ Hood with brim and drawstring keeps head and neck dry and warm. A baseball cap worn under the hood provides the protection of a visor and keeps the hood out of your vision when turning your head.
☐ Fleece jacket with high collar with or without nylon shell. For colder conditions, add additional layers for warmth over synthetic (polypropylene, polyester) underwear.
☐ Life jacket should be worn outside foul weather gear.
☐ Velcro or elastic cuffs at wrists and ankles help keep water out.
☐ Lined waterproof gloves keep hands dry and warm.
☐ Foul weather gear offers protection from wind and water.
☐ For colder conditions, add a layer of fleece pants.
☐ Sea boots with wool or synthetic socks keep feet warm and dry.

CHECKING WEATHER

Develop a habit of checking local conditions and forecasts before departure and be conscious of weather developments while underway. Wind direction and speed are especially important because they can affect your route, the time of your departure and return, and even whether it is safe to make the trip. The NOAA weather radio network broadcasts local and coastal marine forecasts on a continuous cycle. Most VHF radios can receive these broadcasts, usually on a channel listed as WX1 and WX2, for example. There are numerous websites, including the National Weather Service (NWS), that provide local marine weather information as well as weather chart analysis and forecasts, radar images, and warnings. If you know the web address of your local NWS office, you can save time by going there directly. Weather applications that can be downloaded onto your smartphone are also excellent resources for current conditions, forecasts, radar images, and severe weather warnings and advisories. Many television weather reports provide live radar coverage of your boating area. This is particularly valuable in determining the potential for thunderstorms. In any event, take time to get the best weather forecast available. (For more information about weather, see Chapter 12.)

CHECKING TIDE & CURRENT

When using a boat ramp or operating in tidal waters it is important to know the status of local tides to ensure there is enough water at the ramp or along your intended route. In many areas currents can have a major effect on navigation (particularly on slower boats) or using a ramp. Currents flowing perpendicular to ramps in rivers and tidal estuaries can often make launching and hauling out a challenge. In these situations it is important to know the times of slack water (minimal or no current) and maximum current flow. Remember, slack water does not always coincide with high and low tide. Sources for tidal and current information include nautical almanacs, tidal current tables, NOAA weather radio broadcasts, applications that can be downloaded onto your smartphone, newspapers and television. (For more information about tides and currents, see Chapter 12.)

A weather forecast screen from a smartphone.

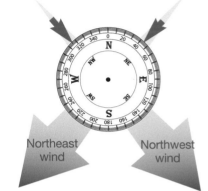

Wind direction is defined as the direction the wind is blowing from, not blowing to. A wind blowing from the northwest to the southeast is called a northwest (NW) wind. Direction may also be defined by the compass direction in degrees, such as 315 degrees. You can also determine the wind direction using visual or sensory indicators such as flags, smoke or trees on land, wind ripples on the water, or the feel of the wind on your face or neck.

TIDE DEFINITION
Tide is the vertical rise and fall of the water level due to the gravitational influence of the moon and sun.

CURRENT DEFINITION
Current is the horizontal movement of water caused by tides, wind, the flow of rivers, or ocean streams. Its direction is defined as the direction the current is flowing toward.

An example of tide information which can be downloaded onto your smartphone.

LOCAL HAZARDS

Local hazards may include shallow water, currents, rapids, weather, dams, overhead cables and traffic. It is also important to know of any special situations. These may include changes to navigation marks or information on bridge closures, diving operations and dredging. A good source for this information is the U.S. Coast Guard's *Local Notice to Mariners*, which is updated weekly and available for download from its Navigation Center. You can also sign up to receive free automatic notices by email. The U.S. Coast Guard also broadcasts marine safety information and notices to mariners twice a day on Marine VHF Channel 1022 (or old channel number 22A). Special notices are also broadcast as they occur in safety broadcasts on Channel 16 in Urgent Marine Broadcasts.

Current is flowing past this anchored buoy.

Consider local weather hazards when planning a boating trip. These may be strong onshore sea breezes that occur as the land heats up during the day, squalls, thunderstorms, lightning and fog (see Chapter 12). Use a chart to identify shallow water, bridges and other hazards.

NAVIGATION PLAN

A navigation plan should be created in advance of your departure. Although every trip on familiar waters does not require a detailed navigation plan, there should be some method to find your way home. A laminated page showing compass headings from a conspicuous, lighted, sound buoy (a navigation aid) to your destination can be invaluable in limited visibility. Unfamiliar waters demand a more detailed plan of compass headings, distances and estimated times that can be backed up with GPS positions of latitude and longitude.

NAVLOG RC TO FYC							
From	To	Crs	Dist	Speed	ETE	ETA	Remarks
RC	MK "E"	087	.5	5	0+06	0+06	
MK "E"	FG 7	048	2.3	6	0+23	0+29	
FG 7	FG 5	352	1.9	6	0+19	0+48	
FG 5	FYC	272	9.6	5.5	0+50	1+98	Slow at 9+00

This sample navigation plan depicts compass courses, distances, speeds and times for various marks along the route.

FLOAT PLAN

Someone else should know your plan—where you plan to go, your route plan, departure and arrival times, as well as a complete description of your boat, names of people on board, type of radio, boat name, and survival gear on board. Write this information down either on a sheet of paper or a prepared form. This is called a float plan.

Deliver or email the float plan to a friend or relative (not the Coast Guard) who can contact the Coast Guard if you don't return on schedule. Writing the information down is important. Not only is it difficult for someone to recall these details from memory, but the very process of writing it down forces you to think about your trip and plan more thoroughly. Upon your return, let your friend or relative know that you have arrived safely.

SAMPLE FLOAT PLAN

Complete this form before going boating and leave it with a reliable person who can notify the Coast Guard or other rescue organization, should you not return as scheduled. Do not file this plan with the Coast Guard.

1. PERSON REPORTING OVERDUE
Name _____ Phone _____

Address _____

2. DESCRIPTION OF BOAT
Registration/Documentation No. _____

Length _____ Make/Year _____ Type _____

Hull Color _____ Trim Color _____ Fuel Capacity _____

Engine _____ No. of Engines _____

Distinguishing Features _____

3. OPERATOR OF BOAT
Name _____ Age _____ Gender _____

Phone _____ Medical Conditions _____

Address _____

Operator's Experience _____

4. SURVIVAL EQUIPMENT (CHECK AS APPROPRIATE)
No. of Life Jackets _____ No. of Flares _____ Mirror _____ Smoke Signals _____

Flashlight _____ Food _____ Paddles _____ Fresh Water _____

Anchor _____ Raft or Dinghy _____ EPIRB _____

Others _____

5. MARINE RADIO
☐ Yes ☐ No   Type _____ DSC MMSI No. _____

6. TRIP EXPECTATIONS
Depart From _____ Departure Date _____ Time _____

Destination _____ Arrival Date _____ Time _____

If operator has not arrived/returned by Date _____ Time _____

call the Coast Guard or local authority at this phone number _____

7. VEHICLE DESCRIPTION
License No./State _____ Make/Year _____ Model _____ Color _____

Where is vehicle parked? _____

8. PERSON(S) ON BOARD
Name _____ Age _____ Gender _____

Phone _____ Medical Conditions _____

9. REMARKS _____

BOARDING

Your boat should be tied to the dock or slip to keep it from moving. Step aboard the boat where it's closest to the dock. If you're carrying something, place it in the boat first or have someone hand it to you after you're aboard. Use both hands to grab something solid on the boat. To get better balance when stepping onto a smaller boat, keep your body low by bending over or squatting. On small light boats, try to step as closely as possible to the centerline to minimize tipping. Once you are in the boat, your weight may affect how the boat sits in the water. Position your weight so that the boat is level from side to side and neither the bow and stern are too far down.

DEPARTURE CHECKS

A simple laminated list can be an invaluable aid to ensure that nothing has been overlooked. Some action items on your list should include:

☐ Prepare appropriate foods and liquids.

☐ Check current weather conditions and forecasts.

☐ Determine tides and currents.

☐ Identify local hazards.

☐ Review relevant charts, updates and cruising guides.

☐ Prepare a navigation plan and estimate fuel requirements.

☐ Determine viable alternatives or ports of refuge.

☐ Prepare a float plan and leave it with someone.

☐ Check that required equipment is present, up to date and in good working order.

☐ Complete the engine inspection checks (see Chapter 2 for outboard motor inspection and Chapter 3 for inspection checks of inboard gasoline and diesel engines).

☐ Remove water that has accumulated in the bilge.

☐ Add fuel for trip.

☐ Complete crew briefing.

☐ Complete the pre-start list.

OPERATOR RESPONSIBILITIES

An operator is responsible for the safety of the boat and everyone on board as well as others affected by his or her actions. To operate a boat responsibly and safely you should follow these guidelines:

- Do not exceed the Maximum Capacities label or plate. This is required for all powerboats (except inflatables) less than 20 feet in length built after October 31, 1972 and must be permanently displayed and visible to the operator. If the boat has no Maximum Capacities marking, a rough guide is to multiply the length by the beam in feet and divide by 15 to get a maximum number of people. Exceeding weight or horsepower limits could result in capsizing or swamping.

- Reduce the risk of falling overboard while underway by briefing everyone to sit in seats, not on seatbacks, side decks, the bow or transom; and if they move around to keep a secure grip on the boat.

- Avoid sudden changes in speed and direction that could cause your passengers to lose their balance or fall overboard. If you have to make a sudden change, give a timely warning.

- Always maintain a proper lookout for other vessels, hazards, swimmers and divers.

- Always operate your boat at a safe speed and observe speed limits.

- Know your boat's performance capabilities and limitations.

- Monitor fuel to make sure you have enough to return with an adequate reserve.

- Follow your navigation plan and keep track of your position.

- Be alert for any weather changes and listen periodically for weather updates on the weather channel of your VHF radio.

- Know the Navigation Rules and use them to avoid collisions (see Chapter 13). If an incident results from your neglect to comply with the Navigation Rules or take seamanlike precautions, there is nothing in the Rules that will release you from this important responsibility. You are expected to be aware of dangerous situations and a departure from the Rules may be necessary to avoid immediate danger.

- Comply with Homeland Security measures.

- Avoid impeding the passage of tug and barge traffic and large vessels that can only navigate within a channel.

A Maximum Capacities label or plate is required on powerboats less than 20 feet in length, except for inflatable boats.

For boats with outboard motors the label must display:

- Maximum number of persons and weight (persons weight is controlling)

- Maximum weight capacity including persons, engine and gear

- Maximum horsepower of the engine

For boats with inboard engines the label must display:

- Maximum number of persons and weight (persons weight is controlling)

- Maximum weight capacity including persons and gear

Note: For personal watercraft (PWC) or boats without a Maximum Capacities label, check the owner's manual or ask the manufacturer.

- Be considerate of others. Minimize the effect of your boat's wake, especially near docks or paddle craft liable to capsizing in waves. Remember, you are responsible for any damage caused by your wake.

- Be aware of the hazards of a propeller to people in the water. Position the boat to keep the propeller away from anyone in the water, or preferably turn off your engine until they are clear.

- Avoid disturbing the natural habitat of wildlife. In some areas, large animals such as manatees in Florida share the waters and you should use caution to avoid them.

TYPES OF LINES

Several different types of line (rope) are used on boats:

- Nylon is commonly used for anchor lines (rodes) and dock lines because of its strength and ability to stretch, which helps absorb shock loads.

- Polyester or Dacron line has less stretch and less ultimate strength than nylon, but is easy on the hands. It is a good all-purpose line.

- Polypropylene line is not as strong as nylon or polyester line and is very sensitive to UV rays, but it floats, which makes it popular for waterskiing towlines. It has a slippery surface and doesn't bend easily, so be careful when tying knots in polypropylene line.

CREW BRIEFING

Briefing people once they are on board the boat is an important safety measure. Boat operators too often assume their passengers have more experience than they actually have and are competent swimmers with no medical problems. Be aware of any health issues and the swimming ability of your passengers in case these become an issue if they fall overboard or the boat swamps. The briefing should include the following:

☐ Discuss the importance of keeping hands and feet inside the boat.

☐ Identify the safe (cockpit) and danger (side decks, riding on the bow) areas on a boat.

☐ Point out the location of fire extinguishers, life jackets, visual distress signals, first aid kit and bilge pumps. Show passengers how to put on a life jacket and explain why and when they should be worn.

☐ Explain garbage management and marine toilet operation.

☐ Indicate what is expected of them when leaving or returning to a dock or slip and while the boat is underway or anchoring.

☐ Describe basic emergency procedures, such as how to use the radio in an emergency, turn off the engine, what to do if a person falls overboard, or dangerous weather conditions occur.

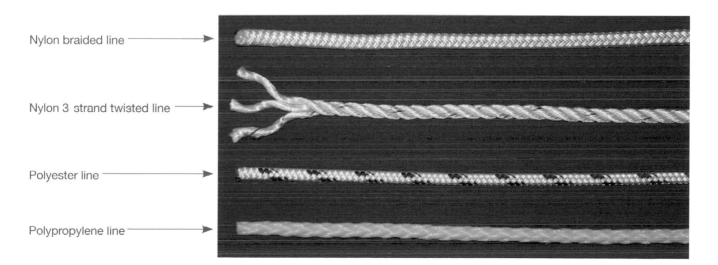

Nylon braided line

Nylon 3 strand twisted line

Polyester line

Polypropylene line

KNOTS

Safe powerboating requires basic seamanship skills such as tying up to a dock, using fenders, securing an anchor line, taking a tow, and giving another boat a tow. All of these functions involve handling a line and tying a secure knot that is also easy to untie. Several knot-tying videos are readily available online to facilitate the learning process.

CLEAT HITCH

A cleat hitch is used to tie a line to a cleat. If tied properly, the line won't jam or slip on the cleat.

   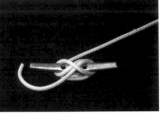

Lead the line around the far end of the cleat and wrap it around the base.

Cross the line over the top and around the end.

Then twist the line to form a loop around the other end.

The end of the line should parallel the part of the line that was originally crossed over the top of the cleat.

ROUND TURN WITH TWO HALF-HITCHES

This knot can be used to secure fender lines to rails or stanchions.

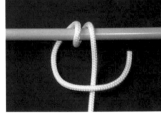 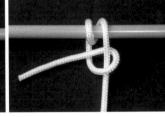 

Wrap the end of the line *twice* around the object.

Cross the end over and around the standing part, passing it inside to form a half-hitch.

Again, cross the end over and around the standing part, passing it inside to form a second half-hitch.

BOWLINE

This knot can be used to make a non-slipping loop at the end of a line to put over a piling or cleat. It becomes more secure under pressure, but remains easy to untie when pressure is released. In situations where the load on the line is not constant, it can work loose. For that reason, it is not recommended for tying an anchor line to an anchor.

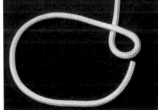 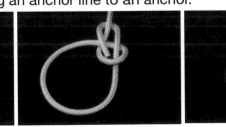 

Make a small loop near the end of the line. Make sure the end crosses on top of the standing part of the line.

Pass the end up through the loop, down behind the standing part, back up over the edge of the loop, and down through the loop.

Tighten the knot, ensuring that the knot holds and the remaining loop does not slip.

Sheet Bend

A sheet bend is used to tie the ends of two lines together and is properly tied if the two ends are on the same side of the knot. If the ends are on opposite sides, the knot tends to slip. The sheet bend holds well with lines of different sizes, but is most secure if the lines are the same size.

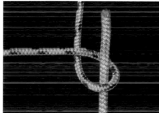  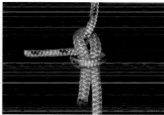 

Make a loop at the end of the smaller line with the bitter end crossing over on top. Run the larger line up through the loop.

Run the larger line under and around the standing part of the smaller line, and back through the loop again.

Tighten the knot. Both ends of the two lines are on the same side.

Shows the sheet bend from the other side.

HANDLING DOCK LINES WITH END LOOPS

Normal practice when approaching a dock is to give the person on the dock the end of the line with the loop in it and then direct him where to place the line. The line is then adjusted from the boat.

Using a Loop on a Cleat

If a loop is simply slipped over a cleat, any changes in tension and angle of the line could cause the loop to jump off the cleat. Taking a turn around the cleat with the loop reduces this possibility. Another method is to pass the loop through the opening of the cleat before putting it over the ends of the cleat. A loop on a cleat cannot be freed if it is under load.

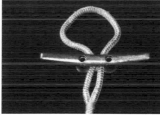  

Pass the loop through the opening in the cleat.

Then pass the loop over the ends of the cleat and tighten the line.

Taking a turn around a cleat with the loop reduces the possibility of the loop jumping off accidentally.

Making a Larger Loop

If the loop on a line is too small to fit around the piling, the line can be passed through the loop to make a larger one.

 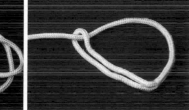

Grab the line about 18 inches below the loop and pass it through the loop.

Then pull on the line. The part of the line closest to the loop will pass completely through, forming a larger loop.

DIPPING A LOOP

If a line is to be placed around the piling and another boater has his loop already around the piling, your loop should be passed up through the other boat's loop before being placed over the top of the piling. This allows either boat to leave without removing the other loop.

Larger line

The loop of the larger line has been dipped under and inside the smaller line's loop before passing it over the piling.

COILING A LINE

When you have finished using a line, it should not be simply left in a tangled pile. Idle lines should always be coiled so they are ready to use or release.

When coiling a line, one hand makes a new loop that is fed onto the other hand holding the loops previously coiled.

- Twisted line (three strands twisted into a rope) is sensitive to clockwise and counterclockwise directions and should be coiled in round loops with no figure-8s. Most twisted lines are twisted in a right-hand direction and should be coiled in a clockwise direction; otherwise, they will kink when uncoiling.

- Braided line does not have twisted strands and has no preferred coiling direction, but will typically coil into figure-8 loops. To ensure the coils will run freely with no kinks, the loops may need to be alternated in direction or coiled in figure-8s.

When coiling twisted lines, it helps to twist or rotate the line slightly to make round loops with no figure-8s.

STOWING A COILED LINE

When a line is not being used or is stowed in a locker, it should be secured in such a way so as to prevent tangling.

Wrap the end of the line three times around the coil, then make a loop in the end and pass it through the upper hole.

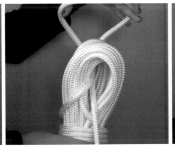

Pass the loop over the coil and bring it down to the wraps.

Pull the end of the line to tighten and secure the coil.

When coiling braided lines, they will have figure-8 loops which will run freely with no kinks.

HEAVING A LINE

When preparing to throw a line, first make sure one end is secured on your boat. Hold half of the coil in your throwing hand and the other half in your other hand. Swing and throw the coil underhand, allowing the remainder of the line to run free from your other hand. Don't throw the line right at the person, but just to the side.

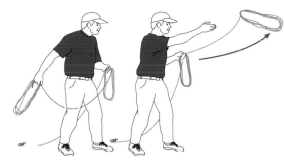

LINE-HANDLING COMMANDS

Sometimes handling dock lines may require precise instructions so that both the operator and the line handlers are on the same page and the lines are adjusted as needed. Here are some definitions of basic line-handling commands.

CAST OFF – Untie and let go lines.
TAKE IN – Untie lines from shore and bring them on board.
SLACK – Take off all tension and let the line hang slack.
EASE – Let line out until tension is eased but line is not slack.
CHECK – Hold heavy tension but not enough to part the line.
HOLD – Do not let any line out but be ready for more maneuvering.
SURGE – Momentarily release tension on a line to let a stopped boat move.
MAKE FAST – Secure a line.

SECURING A BOAT

A powerboat can be tied alongside a dock with single bow and stern lines and two spring lines, which minimize the forward and after movement of the boat, or it can be positioned in the middle of a slip with two bow lines and two stern lines.

Each dock line has a specific name and just the basics will be covered here.

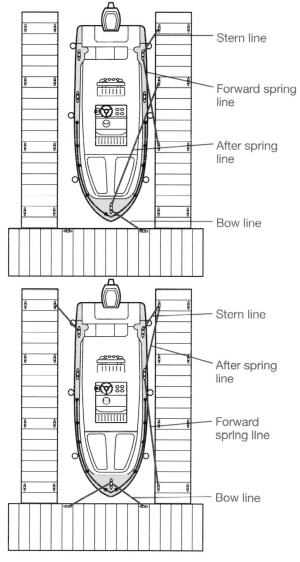

Stern line

Forward spring line

After spring line

Bow line

Stern line

After spring line

Forward spring line

Bow line

- A *bow line* is fastened to the bow of a boat and runs forward at about a 45-degree angle to the dock.

- A *stern line* is fastened to the stern of a boat and runs aft at about a 45-degree angle to the dock.

- *Spring lines* are named based on where they originate and the direction that they run from a boat. On small boats the point of origin is generally omitted from the name and this convention will be used in this book.

- An *after spring line* is fastened to either the bow or an amidships cleat (toward the center of a boat) and runs aft from the boat to the dock.

- A *forward spring line* is fastened at the stern or to an amidships cleat and runs forward from the boat to the dock.

REVIEW QUESTIONS

1. With regard to clothing, the best way to stay comfortable in changing weather conditions is to use the _____ approach.

2. Local weather conditions and forecasts can be found on the internet and television in addition to _____ marine weather reports on VHF radio.

3. The Local Notice to Mariners is a good source for information on _____.
   a. navigation plans
   b. ship departures
   c. clothing advice
   d. local hazards

4. A float plan should not be given to the Coast Guard, but to a _____ or _____.

5. Due to its ability to stretch more than other types of line, the line generally preferred for anchor and docking lines is _____.
   a. Dacron
   b. nylon
   c. polypropylene

Answers:
1) layered
2) NOAA
3) d. local hazards
4) friend; relative
5) b. nylon

Chapter 5

BOAT-HANDLING CONCEPTS

KEY CONCEPTS

- ▶ Putting a boat in motion
- ▶ Stopping
- ▶ Wheel & tiller steering
- ▶ Steering with a joystick
- ▶ Steering with directed thrust
- ▶ Steering with a rudder
- ▶ Prop walk

- ▶ Steering with twin screws
- ▶ Boat's pivot point
- ▶ Minimum control speed
- ▶ Holding position
- ▶ Balance & trim
- ▶ Use of spring lines

PUTTING A BOAT IN MOTION

Putting a boat in motion involves shifting into FORWARD or REVERSE gear at a low throttle setting and then adjusting the throttle to achieve the desired speed. *The key concept to remember when shifting to FORWARD, NEUTRAL or REVERSE is that it should be done at idle rpm* to prevent damage to the engine or transmission.

STOPPING

Since a boat has no brakes, the throttle and gearshift controls are used to stop it. Reducing the throttle to idle speed and shifting into NEUTRAL will eliminate thrust from the propeller or jet, but the boat will still keep moving until its momentum is dissipated. The faster the boat is moving, the more time and distance it will take to lose momentum and come to a stop.

COASTING STOP

Reduce the throttle gradually, then shift into NEUTRAL. You can stop without using REVERSE, but you need to allow distance for coasting to a stop. Less coasting distance is needed if you stop heading into the wind. Larger and heavier boats carry more momentum and coast farther than small boats. The larger the boat, the more distance it will coast.

WIND

A coasting stop requires more distance when the wind is behind the boat.

QUICK STOP

If a boat needs to be stopped more quickly in a shorter distance:

1 Gradually reduce throttle to idle rpm.

2 Shift into NEUTRAL and pause briefly (do a 1-2-3 count) or until boat is no longer planing.

3 Shift into REVERSE and increase throttle slightly to overcome forward momentum and stop boat.

4 Bring throttle to idle rpm and shift into NEUTRAL.

USING A WHEEL OR TILLER TO STEER

On boats with wheel steering, turn the wheel (*helm*) in the direction you want to turn just as you would a car. For boats with tiller steering, move the tiller opposite to the direction you want to turn.

STEERING WITH A JOYSTICK

Joystick steering can be programmed to work with multiple drive types. In close quarters, they allow an operator to move the boat in ways that cannot be obtained through the wheel and throttles. Joysticks send a computer signal to the engines and drives, allowing them to steer and accelerate independently of each other. The thrust directed independently from each drive allows the boat to rotate and maneuver in any direction. For example, to move the boat sideways, the signal from the joystick turns the drives in opposite directions and puts one in reverse and the other in forward, creating thrusts that move the boat sideways.

To operate a joystick, move the joystick lever in the direction that you want the boat to move.

- To go forward, move the joystick toward the bow.

- To go backward, move the joystick toward the stern.

- To move sideways, move the joystick to port or starboard. Note that the bow of the boat will remain pointed in the same direction (e.g., forward) while the boat moves laterally sideways.

- Moving the joystick at an angle (e.g., forward and to starboard) will move the boat in the corresponding direction (forward and to starboard).

- To rotate the boat, twist the joystick clockwise or counterclockwise in the direction that you want the boat to rotate.

- It is possible to rotate and move forward, backward, or sideways at the same time.

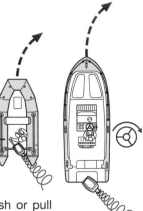

Push or pull the tiller in the opposite direction of the turn.

Turn the wheel in the direction of the turn.

Lateral Maneuvers

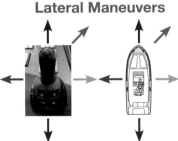

Move the joystick in the direction you want the boat to move.

Rotational Maneuvers

Twist the joystick in the direction you want the boat to rotate.

KEY POINTS

- *Operating a vessel by joystick only changes how a boat is controlled. It's important to remember that the boat is still subject to uncontrollable forces like wind and current.*

- *Joysticks are throttle responsive. The farther you push or rotate the joystick in any given direction, the higher the thrust output. Don't confuse the operation of a joystick with the operation of a bow thruster lever, which is either full power on or off.*

- *When docking in a crosswind or current, prevent the boat from accelerating out of control by using a light, two-finger grip on the joystick. Push, pull or twist the joystick in a gentle and progressive manner. This is far more effective than taps or a quick burst in the desired direction.*

- *Since the drives are at the stern of the boat, joysticks do a good job of controlling the stern. Bow thrusters do a better job of controlling the bow in a crosswind and can be used in conjunction with a joystick to help keep the bow aligned.*

- *To stop the momentum of a maneuver, use gentle pressure on the joystick in the opposite direction until the motion of the boat stops.*

STEERING WITH DIRECTED THRUST

All boats with outboard motors, stern drives and jet drives use the directed thrust of the propeller or jet to steer the boat. To generate directed thrust, the propeller has to be turning (in FORWARD or REVERSE gear) or the jet drive has to be pumping water through it. If the engine or jet drive is in NEUTRAL, the boat cannot be steered.

When the outboard motor is turned, the directed thrust from the propeller swings the stern of the boat, causing the boat to turn. To make a tighter turn, turn the outboard motor all the way and increase the amount of thrust by increasing the throttle.

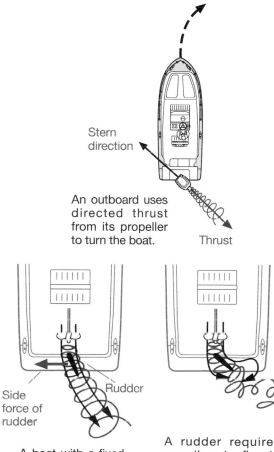

Stern direction

An outboard uses directed thrust from its propeller to turn the boat.

Thrust

Side force of rudder

Rudder

A boat with a fixed propeller uses a rudder to turn the boat.

A rudder requires smooth water flow to function. Turning the rudder too sharply can stall flow.

STEERING WITH A RUDDER

Boats with a fixed propeller drive use a rudder to produce a sideways force to turn the boat. Water must be flowing past the rudder to create this steering force. This flow is produced by the boat's motion through the water and by the propeller. As a boat moves faster, the steering ability of the rudder improves because the side force it generates increases as the speed of the water flow increases. To increase the effectiveness of a rudder in forward motion, it is normally placed behind the propeller to take advantage of the additional flow of water generated by the propeller (called *prop wash*). At very slow forward speeds you can use a momentary pulse of prop wash by briefly increasing the throttle to increase the flow of water passing the rudder, which increases the turning force without noticeably increasing the speed of the boat. This is a technique often used when maneuvering at slow speeds in a confined area.

STEERING WITH PROP WALK (WHAT IS PROP WALK?)

Prop walk is a side force produced by the rotation of the propeller. This side force causes your boat to turn slightly rather than go in a straight line. Prop walk is most noticeable when the engine and propeller are operating in reverse on boats with a fixed propeller and rudder. A right-hand propeller in reverse walks the stern to port. A left-hand propeller in reverse will walk the stern to starboard. Increasing the throttle will increase the amount of prop walk, which will swing the stern even more.

This tendency can be put to good use if you anticipate which way it will move your boat. You can test your prop walk direction by putting the boat in reverse while still tied to the dock. Center the wheel and compare the amount of water flow (wash) on both sides of the boat. The stern will move away from the side with the greatest flow when in reverse.

Prop walk can be used to your advantage in docking when the propeller is operating in REVERSE gear. You will want to approach the dock along the side of your boat that walks toward the dock. As you reach the dock, reverse your engine and let the stern walk alongside.

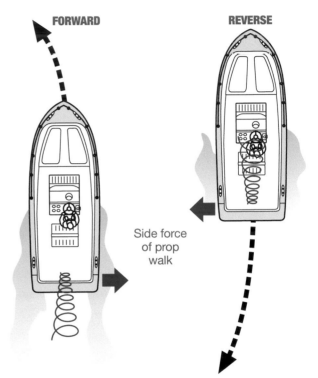

The side force of prop walk will make a boat turn slightly in forward and reverse.

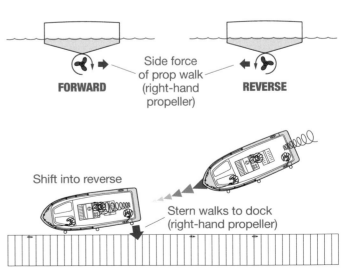

STEERING WITH BOW & STERN THRUSTERS

Bow thrusters have become standard equipment on many large powerboats and are becoming increasingly popular on more moderate-sized boats. Thrusters are used to increase a boat's maneuverability by moving either the bow of the boat sideways with a bow thruster or the stern sideways with a stern thruster. Both types of thrusters typically use one or two propellers contained in a tunnel to generate sideways thrust. They are either electrically or hydraulically powered.

STEERING WITH TWIN SCREWS (PROPELLERS)

Propellers on twin-screw powerboats typically rotate in opposite directions to counteract each other's side force (prop walk). If both throttles are set at the same rpm, the prop walk effect is negated and the boat will go forward and backward in a straight line.

A boat can use thrust from an individual propeller or a combination of both for turning. When the port propeller turns in FORWARD gear and the starboard propeller is in NEUTRAL, thrust will turn the boat to starboard in a wide turn. To make an even tighter turn, put one propeller in FORWARD gear and the other in REVERSE. If one throttle is advanced more than the other, the corresponding propeller will create more thrust and prop walk, causing the boat to turn.

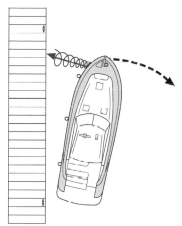

Thrust from the bow thruster rotates the bow away from the dock.

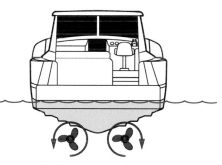

Typical rotation in forward gear

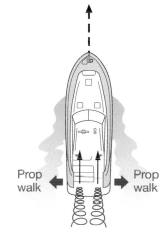

Prop walk ◄   Prop walk ►

With throttles set at same rpm, the thrust and prop walk from each propeller is equal and opposite and the boat will run in a straight line.

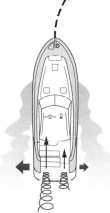

With one throttle set at higher rpm, that propeller produces more thrust and prop walk, causing the boat to turn.

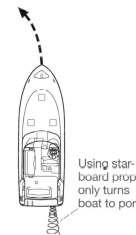

Using starboard prop only turns boat to port.

Boats with twin screws can use port or starboard props individually to produce turning thrust.

PIVOT POINT

A boat's pivot point is the point around which it appears to turn. This point is normally located from 25 to 40 percent aft from the bow. As the boat starts to move forward, the pivot point starts forward and then moves aft as speed increases. When a boat turns, the relationship of the turning thrust at the stern to the pivot point causes the bow to rotate toward the direction of the turn and the stern to swing away from it.

When backing, the pivot point starts forward but then appears to move aft considerably, causing the bow to swing in a wider arc than the stern. Many good drivers imagine they are steering just the pivot point. They visualize the path they wish their pivot point to take over the water and then steer the point along that path. When a boat makes a turn, the first part of the turn will be wider than the rest of the turn.

TURNING CONCEPTS

When making a turn, a key concept to remember is that a boat rotates around a pivot point, which causes the stern to swing out wide of your turning path. Keep this in mind when passing close to an object in the water. While your boat's bow and pivot point may clear the object, your stern could hit it.

At low speeds with reduced thrust from a propeller or jet, wind and current will have a greater effect on steering control and turning maneuvers. In tight maneuvering situations, it may be necessary to use intermittent pulses of increased thrust by briefly advancing the throttle to improve turning control or make a tighter turn.

WINDAGE

Wind will have an important effect on almost all of your boat-handling maneuvers, especially when you operate at lower speeds in moderate to strong wind conditions. The wind's impact varies with the amount of the boat's surface area (windage) that the wind pushes against. Boats with high topsides, cabins and flying bridges have greater windage than boats with lower profiles.

When drifting, the wind will usually cause the bow to fall off until the boat lies across the wind or even with the stern toward the wind. This tendency to turn away from the wind is an important consideration when holding a boat in position.

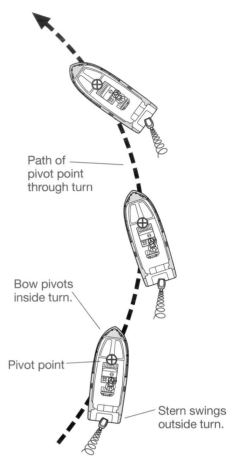

Path of pivot point through turn

Bow pivots inside turn.

Pivot point

Stern swings outside turn.

WIND DIRECTION CLUES

- *Smoke from a smokestack*
- *Flags onshore*
- *Boats on moorings (usually point into the wind unless being affected by current)*
- *Ripples or waves*
- *Wind on your face (boat has to be stopped)*

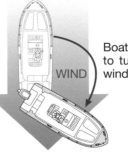

WIND

Boats have a tendency to turn away from the wind.

TURNS INTO & AWAY FROM THE WIND

When turning into the wind, windage on the boat resists the turn which results in a larger turning arc and more distance to complete the turn. When turning away from the wind, the bow's tendency to fall off will result in a tighter turn and a shorter distance to complete the turn.

UNDERWATER HULL SHAPE

A boat's underwater hull shape will affect its steering characteristics. Boats with minimal underwater profile, such as soft inflatables, will tend to skid or sideslip along the surface of the water as they turn, thereby increasing the turning arc. Turning this type of boat in windy conditions in a confined area is a true boat-handling challenge.

MINIMUM CONTROL SPEED

Minimum control speed is the slowest speed at which you can operate and still maintain steering control. This is less than the speed produced when the engine is continuously in gear and the throttle is set at idle rpm, or slightly more. It is accomplished by the use of intermittent power by shifting into NEUTRAL intermittently. With the throttle at idle rpm, shift from NEUTRAL to FORWARD and back to NEUTRAL. This produces a short, gentle pulse of power to maintain steering control. Repeat this technique to keep the boat under control and moving slowly. Minimum control speed is used in many situations such as docking and operating in confined areas. It is shown in the illustrations by ▶▶▶▶.

To make turns at minimum control speed, position the helm in the desired direction while in NEUTRAL, then shift into FORWARD gear at idle rpm to start the turn, then back to NEUTRAL near the end of the turn. As a result of the directed thrust from the propeller (or increased water flow over the turned rudder), the boat will turn but not accelerate significantly. When using intermittent power to turn, avoid oversteering and using too much throttle to prevent loss of steering control.

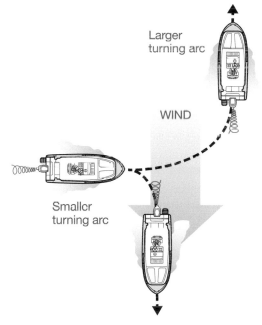

Larger turning arc

WIND

Smaller turning arc

When a boat turns into and away from the wind, there will be a difference in the turning arcs and distances that complete the turn.

MINIMUM CONTROL SPEED TIP
When steering at minimum control speed, turn the helm to the desired direction while in neutral, then shift into gear.

HOLDING POSITION

There are times when you may have to hold your boat in a specific location such as helping a boat in trouble, waiting for a bridge to open, or waiting for room at a dock. The key to holding position is to anticipate boat drift and make small, gentle corrections early rather than large powerful corrections late. Always position the helm in the direction you want to go before applying power.

HOLDING THE BOW INTO WIND

Since the bow will usually have a tendency to turn away from the wind, you will have to compensate for this by periodically shifting into FORWARD gear and making slight steering corrections to bring the bow back into the wind. Don't let the bow fall off too much. When the bow is pointed into the wind, shift back to NEUTRAL and drift back to your holding position. If the boat drifts downwind of the position, shift into FORWARD gear to bring it back in position. Repetitive small adjustments must be made to maintain a holding position, especially as the wind increases. When current has more influence than wind, hold position with the bow or stern into the current, not the wind.

HOLDING THE STERN INTO WIND

Because the bow wants to turn downwind, it is usually easier to hold position with the stern into the wind, provided waves don't come over the transom. Shift into REVERSE to keep the stern headed into the wind and to compensate for drifting. In windy conditions, you may have to switch to holding the bow into the wind to avoid exposure to exhaust gases or taking water over the back of the boat.

BALANCE & TRIM

Boat balance and trim affect not only boat speed and fuel consumption, but also steering.

BALANCE

A boat that leans to one side will be out of balance and will tend to turn. The most effective way to correct this problem is to move passengers, gear and portable fuel tanks to level the boat while it is stationary. If the condition is not corrected, it could result in loss of steering control, increased pounding of V hulls, and a risk of capsizing for smaller boats.

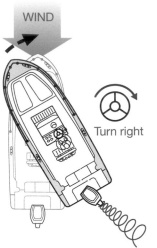

Holding Bow Into Wind

WIND

Turn right

Turn prop small amount and shift to forward to bring bow back into wind.

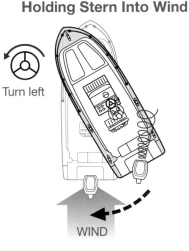

Holding Stern Into Wind

Turn left

WIND

Turn prop small amount toward wind and shift to reverse.

Left side is lower.

This boat is not balanced from side to side and will turn.

TRIM

A boat with too much bow-down or bow-up trim will lose speed and is less responsive to steering. Too much bow-down trim may also bring the propeller too close to the water surface, sucking air onto the blades, and causing it to lose thrust. When this happens there will be a sudden increase in engine rpm and a sudden slowing in the boat.

A boat's fore and aft trim can be controlled by adjusting the UP/DOWN trim angle of the propeller or by adjusting trim tabs. A hydraulic trim control is used on larger outboards to adjust propeller angle.

TRIM TIPS

An outboard motor or trim tabs trimmed down can get a boat on a plane more quickly. Once on a plane, the outboard or trim tabs should be trimmed up until the boat is at optimum speed and rpm. When encountering choppy waves, trim down to lower the bow and allow the boat to drive through the waves.

When the outboard motor is trimmed down, it trims the bow down.

When the outboard motor is trimmed up, it trims the bow up.

The outboard motor is trimmed to get level trim.

SPEED MODES

When a planing boat is moving, it will be operating in one of three speed ranges or speed modes:

DISPLACEMENT SPEEDS

The boat rides through the water at almost level trim and is easy to steer and maneuver. As it approaches the semi-displacement mode, the stern squats and the bow rises as the boat's bow wave increases in size.

SEMI-DISPLACEMENT SPEEDS

Most boats operate very inefficiently with high resistance at this speed. They have bow-high trim with the bow riding up the bow wave, producing maximum wake, poor visibility and a higher risk of collision. They are sluggish to steer and maneuver. It requires a lot of throttle to counteract the high resistance of the bow wave. In shallow waters, the stern will squat more, producing greater wake and the possibility of striking the bottom.

BALANCE DEFINITION

Balance is the athwartship (sideways) orientation of a boat to the water's surface. A boat is in balance when it is level and out of balance when it heels (leans) to a side.

BALANCE TIPS

- *Move passengers, gear and portable tanks to reduce heeling to a side and level the boat.*

- *For smaller heeling angles caused by propeller torque or wind, adjust the trim tab down on the low side and up on the high side.*

TRIM DEFINITION

Trim is the forward and aft orientation of a boat to the water's surface. When stationary, a boat should float level to its waterline.

Trim tabs are used to keep boat level and running straight. Keep tabs fully up when backing or boat is not in use.

In displacement mode, a boat glides smoothly in level trim with minimum wake.

In semi-displacement mode, the boat labors in bow-up trim. Maximum wake is produced.

PLANING SPEEDS

The boat rides on top of the water at close to level trim, supported by dynamic lift. Its wake has decreased in size, speed has increased significantly, and the boat responds quickly to small steering changes. Hydraulic trim controls can be adjusted to achieve optimum speed for a fixed-throttle setting.

CHANGING SPEEDS

In planing mode, boat rides level on top of water with less wake.

INCREASING SPEED

The speed modes help to explain how a boat's operating characteristics change as power is added or reduced. As a boat increases speed, the bow raises and forward visibility is reduced. Collisions are often the result of one or both boats operating in this semi-displacement mode. Before opening the throttle, always check to make sure your course is clear of hazards, and your passengers are aware and prepared. Whenever increasing speed raises the bow, stand up if the boat has a standup steering station or console, and adjust the trim tabs and/or trim angle of the outboard or stern drive to lower the bow and maintain your close-ahead vision.

REDUCING SPEED

When slowing down from a planing speed to a displacement speed, the boat will transit through the semi-displacement range again, generating increased wake.

BOAT WAKE

Be considerate about the wake produced by your boat. Adjust your speed to reduce your wake when passing:

- boats tied to a dock or slip or rafted alongside each other.

- boats in a mooring area or at anchor.

- boats with people fishing.

- smaller watercraft or sailboats.

CHANGING SPEED SAFETY TIPS

- *Always check to make sure your course is clear of hazards before opening the throttle.*

- *Always check to make sure your passengers are aware and prepared before any abrupt acceleration or deceleration.*

- *Adjust trim tabs and/or trim angle of the outboard or stern drive to lower the bow for close-ahead vision.*

- *Stand up if the boat has a stand-up steering console or station for better vision when increasing speed raises the bow.*

WAKE TIPS

- *Reduce wake by operating at slow displacement speeds (preferred) or planing speed (unsafe to do in anchorages due to higher risk of collisions).*

- *Change speed to reduce wake well in advance since it takes at least several boat lengths for your wake to decrease.*

SPRING LINES

A spring line is a dock line that can work as a lever to turn a boat or bring it alongside a dock, when you motor against it. It is used when leaving or returning to a dock or slip in adverse wind or current conditions.

USING AN AFTER SPRING LINE TO TURN

Motor against it to rotate the stern away from a dock.

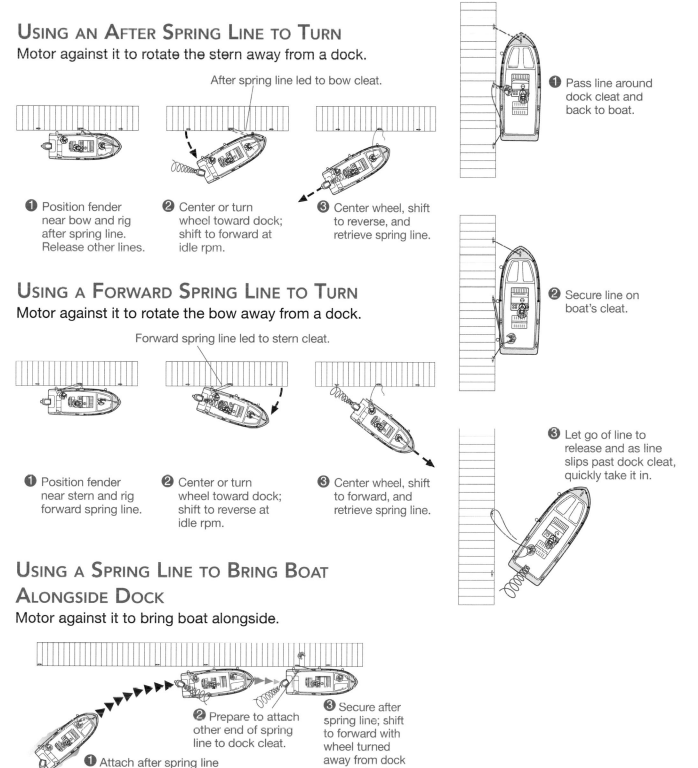

After spring line led to bow cleat.

❶ Position fender near bow and rig after spring line. Release other lines.

❷ Center or turn wheel toward dock; shift to forward at idle rpm.

❸ Center wheel, shift to reverse, and retrieve spring line.

USING A FORWARD SPRING LINE TO TURN

Motor against it to rotate the bow away from a dock.

Forward spring line led to stern cleat.

❶ Position fender near stern and rig forward spring line.

❷ Center or turn wheel toward dock; shift to reverse at idle rpm.

❸ Center wheel, shift to forward, and retrieve spring line.

USING A SPRING LINE TO BRING BOAT ALONGSIDE DOCK

Motor against it to bring boat alongside.

❷ Prepare to attach other end of spring line to dock cleat.

❶ Attach after spring line close to boat's pivot point or *amidships,* and rig fenders.

❸ Secure after spring line; shift to forward with wheel turned away from dock to bring boat alongside dock.

DOUBLING A LINE TIP

Doubling a dock line allows you to release a line from aboard the boat without any assistance from a person on the dock.

❶ Pass line around dock cleat and back to boat.

❷ Secure line on boat's cleat.

❸ Let go of line to release and as line slips past dock cleat, quickly take it in.

REVIEW QUESTIONS

1. With the engine in NEUTRAL, outboard motors, stern drives and jet drives have _____ steering.
   a. poor   b. good   c. excellent

2. The sideways force generated by a propeller is called _____.

3. Steering a boat at minimum control speed requires _____ of power.
   a. no pulses   b. gentle pulses   c. strong pulses

4. A boat will produce maximum wake in the _____ mode.

5. A line running from a bow cleat to a cleat on the dock near the stern of a boat is called a/an _____ spring line and when you motor against it the boat's _____ will swing away from the dock.

Answers:
1) a. poor
2) prop walk
3) b. gentle pulses
4) semi-displacement
5) after; stern

Chapter 6

BOAT HANDLING - DIRECTED THRUST

KEY CONCEPTS

▶ Leaving & returning   ▶ Turning maneuvers

LEAVING A DOCK

KEY POINTS

- *Make sure everyone understands what to do with dock lines and fenders.*

- *Check that no lines are in the water before starting the engine.*

- *Start the engine using the manufacturer's recommended procedure.*

- *Stow dock lines and fenders once clear of the dock.*

- *An injury could occur when using a hand or foot to push a boat away from a dock. If you have to push off, sit or stand in the cockpit and use a boat hook (pole).*

During a forward departure from a dock, the stern can swing into the dock, preventing the boat from completing its turn.

BACK-AWAY DEPARTURE

Backing away from a dock usually offers the best maneuvering control. It also avoids a problem inherent to forward departures when the boat starts to turn and its stern swings into the dock, preventing the boat from departing cleanly.

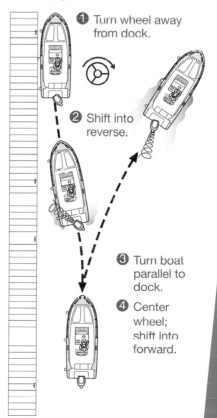

❶ Turn wheel away from dock.

❷ Shift into reverse.

❸ Turn boat parallel to dock.

❹ Center wheel; shift into forward.

❶ Turn wheel away from dock, which rotates propeller away from dock. If using a tiller, move it toward dock.

❷ Shift into REVERSE; stern swings away from dock as boat backs away. To avoid scraping the bow against dock, keep your turn small until bow clears dock.

❸ When clear of dock, turn wheel or tiller in opposite direction to turn boat parallel to dock.

❹ Center wheel or tiller, pause briefly in NEUTRAL, then shift into FORWARD.

STRAIGHT-AHEAD DEPARTURE

This method is often used when a boat is positioned near the end of a dock and can clear the dock with little, if any, turning. It can also be used if a crosswind or crosscurrent will make the boat drift clear of the dock. Remember that when turning, your stern will swing outside your intended track and could hit the dock.

1 Center outboard, release dock lines.

2 Shift into FORWARD gear and steer a straight course until clear of dock.

3 Turn when stern is clear of dock.

LEAVING A SLIP

1 Center wheel (or tiller) and shift into REVERSE, slowly backing straight out.

2 Turn boat once bow is clear of slip.

3 Center wheel (or tiller) and shift into FORWARD after pausing briefly in NEUTRAL.

TURNING MANEUVERS

AVOIDANCE TURN

This maneuver is used to prevent the stern of your boat from swinging into an obstacle when you've turned too late or too close. The initial turn away from the object positions the boat's pivot point away from it, and the turn back pivots the stern away from the object and avoids a collision.

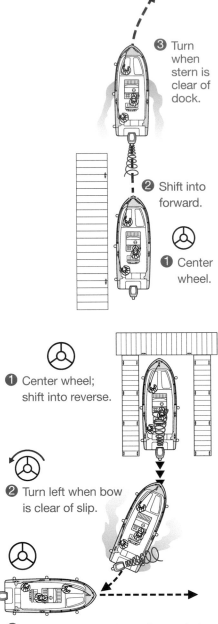

3 Turn when stern is clear of dock.

2 Shift into forward.

1 Center wheel.

1 Center wheel; shift into reverse.

2 Turn left when bow is clear of slip.

3 Center wheel; shift into forward after pausing briefly in neutral.

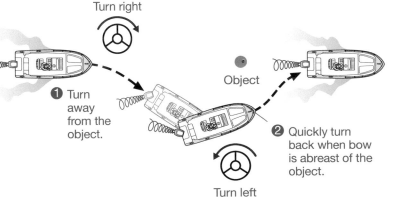

Turn right

1 Turn away from the object.

Object

2 Quickly turn back when bow is abreast of the object.

Turn left

TURNING SAFETY TIPS

- *Always look around for other boats and hazards before turning.*

- *Warn your passengers before turning or making a sudden course change.*

Pivot Turn

This is a maneuver frequently used in marinas or other very confined spaces to rotate a boat within a space of one to two boat lengths.

1 Starting at rest, turn wheel hard over to one side and shift into FORWARD gear at idle rpm to initiate pivot turn.

2 Shift into NEUTRAL and turn wheel hard over in opposite direction.

3 Shift into REVERSE at idle rpm to continue turn.

4 Shift into NEUTRAL and turn wheel hard over in opposite direction.

5 Repeat until boat has completed its turn.

NOTE: To rotate the boat in the opposite direction, just reverse the direction of the wheel listed in the steps.

DRIVING BACKWARD

Key Points

- *Wind direction: the bow will tend to turn downwind.*

- *Sea conditions: backing smaller outboard boats into waves may result in water coming over the transom and flooding the well or cockpit. If this starts to happen, abandon this maneuver.*

- *The pivot point will move aft in reverse, and depending on the boat's underwater shape and windage, it may move essentially to the propeller. This is particularly true for outboards or stern drives.*

- *Steering control: when backing and turning in reverse, use small steering adjustments. Too large or too fast adjustments can lead to a loss of control.*

Backing Downwind

It may be more difficult to maintain your course when backing downwind. If the bow falls off too much, you will lose steering control. Before this happens, shift to FORWARD gear and bring the boat back on course. Then back up again with perhaps a slight steering correction to compensate for the wind's effect.

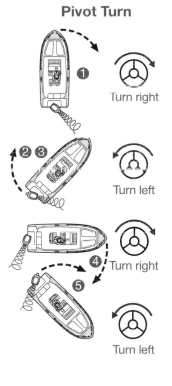

Pivot Turn

1 — Turn right

2 3 — Turn left

4 — Turn right

5 — Turn left

Backing Downwind

WIND

Turn right

When bow falls off, shift into forward and steer boat back on track.

BACKING TOWARD THE WIND

The combination of windage and pivot point will help you hold your course.

HIGH-SPEED MANEUVERS

When running at higher speeds, a boat is less affected by wind. Other considerations become important, such as sea conditions, wake from other boats and semi-submerged objects in the water. Hard impact at high speed can cause loss of steering control, damage to the hull, and possible injury to occupants. Any gear that is not carefully stowed or secured can take flight when maneuvering at high speeds. Constant alertness, a safe attitude and quick responses by the driver are at a premium. To be able to respond promptly, keep a hand on the throttle at all times.

REDUCING SPEED

When slowing down rapidly, steering control will initially be reduced because the boat's speed is not slowing as quickly as thrust is being reduced. In fact, if a boat traveling at high speed suddenly cuts its power, steering control may be lost completely. Whenever possible, put your boat on a straight course before slowing down.

TURNING MANEUVERS

During turning maneuvers, thrust from the propeller causes the boat to roll on its longitudinal axis. As the speed and tightness of a turn increases, the amount of roll increases. In a sharp turn with the boat rolled at a substantial angle, propellers on outboards and stern drives are closer to the water surface, which can result in air being drawn into its blades (sometimes referred to as *ventilation*). If the drive unit is trimmed up too much, it can aggravate this problem. When this occurs, there will be a sudden increase in engine rpm and loss of propeller power. To avoid possible damage to the engine and drive system, the rate of turn and/or speed should be reduced immediately.

Prior to making a high-speed turn, check to see that it is clear and safe to turn, and alert your passengers. Turn the wheel gradually and deliberately to maintain control throughout the maneuver. The greater the speed, the wider and more gradual the turn should be. If the turn is too sharp, the propeller will ventilate and turning control will be lost.

HIGH-SPEED STOP IN EMERGENCY MODE

While it's recommended to gradually reduce boat speed before stopping, you may be faced with a situation where you need to stop quickly. If you are stopping to avoid an obstruction, the forward momentum of the boat could result in a collision. Also with this sudden decrease in speed, you

Backing Toward the Wind

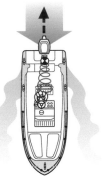

When backing a boat, use small steering adjustments to keep it under control.

HIGH-SPEED SAFETY TIPS

- *All occupants should be in seats and/or have a secure grip on boat.*

- *Attach emergency engine cutoff switch lanyard to driver, if applicable.*

- *Keep one hand on the throttle and the other on the steering wheel.*

- *Maintain an alert lookout; don't get distracted.*

- *Use moderate and measured steering adjustments.*

- *Warn occupants of sudden changes in speed and direction.*

- *Avoid abrupt stops.*

- *If in doubt, slow down.*

Emergency High-Speed Stop

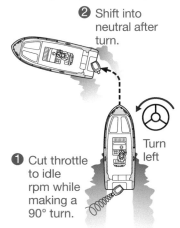

❷ Shift into neutral after turn.

Turn left

❶ Cut throttle to idle rpm while making a 90° turn.

may lose steering control momentarily and the boat's wake could come over the transom and flood the well or cockpit.

RETURNING TO A DOCK

To master this important maneuver you need to be aware of how your powerboat steers and reacts to changes of throttle and gearshift in different wind and current conditions. Here, your ability to maneuver at minimum control speed will play an important role. A common mistake, especially with boats that use directed thrust steering, is to oversteer at slow speeds, which results in loss of control of direction. It is far better to use small steering adjustments at minimum control speed with only an occasional brief, small increase in throttle to make a sharper turn. The critical time for a safe and successful docking usually starts as you make your final turn to come alongside the dock and ends as you reverse to stop the boat. You will need precise adjustment and coordination of throttle, gearshift and wheel (or tiller).

KEY POINTS

- *Place fenders at dock level and prepare dock lines before making the final approach.*

- *Be sure everyone knows in advance what to do with the dock lines. Line handlers on the bow or deck should hold on or brace themselves against unexpected changes in direction or speed.*

- *Whenever possible, come alongside the dock with the bow pointing into the wind or current, whichever is stronger.*

- *Make your approach at minimum control speed, which will avoid or minimize damage should reverse suddenly not be available.*

SMALL-ANGLE APPROACH

This is the easiest approach to use because it requires only small adjustments of steering and power controls. It also accommodates temporary changes in wind conditions (unlike an approach parallel to the dock, which requires more precision and is less tolerant of changing conditions).

1. Approach dock slowly at a 20 to 25-degree angle. If approach speed is too fast, shift into NEUTRAL to slow boat and use intermittent power to maintain minimum control speed.

2. When bow is about 1/2 to 1 boat length away from dock, make a smooth turn to bring boat parallel and close to dock. As bow starts to turn, shift into NEUTRAL.

3. Center wheel or tiller (or turn wheel toward dock if stern needs to be pulled in) and shift into REVERSE to stop boat.

4. Shift into NEUTRAL. After boat is tied to dock, turn off engine.

DOCKING TIPS

- *Minimum control speed allows you to make a smooth easy turn.*

- *Faster approach speeds require a more abrupt turn and timing becomes more critical.*

- *Always have an escape plan in case you misjudge your approach.*

Small-Angle Approach

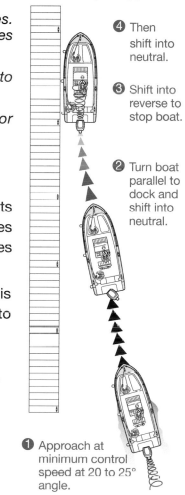

4. Then shift into neutral.

3. Shift into reverse to stop boat.

2. Turn boat parallel to dock and shift into neutral.

1. Approach at minimum control speed at 20 to 25° angle.

LARGE-ANGLE APPROACH

In a situation where the wind pushes the boat away from the dock during its approach, you should increase your approach angle to head more into the wind. This increased angle will result in a tighter turn, which will increase the momentum of the swinging stern. If the stern swings too fast, you can prevent it from hitting the dock with a small turn of the wheel away from the dock as you reverse to stop the boat. As you come alongside, the wind will try to blow the boat away from the dock, so it is important to stop quickly and pass a line to the dock without delay. The best line to use is an after spring line fastened to the boat halfway (*amidships*) between the bow and stern and led aft to a dock cleat. If the boat starts to drift away before the other dock lines are tied, you can put the boat in FORWARD gear at idle rpm with the wheel turned away from the dock and the spring line will bring the boat alongside the dock again and hold it there. As the velocity of the wind increases, the power required to maintain minimum control speed will have to be increased to overcome the increased drag from windage, which reduces the forward speed of the boat.

❶ Approach dock at approximately a 45-degree angle at a minimum control speed that maintains steering control against the wind.

❷ When bow is close to dock, turn boat almost parallel to dock, but maintain a small angle to compensate for the wind's tendency to push bow downwind.

❸ When bow is a couple of feet from dock, shift briefly into NEUTRAL and turn wheel toward dock, then shift into REVERSE and use a small amount of throttle to bring stern in as the boat stops.

❹ As soon as boat is alongside, shift into NEUTRAL and quickly tie after spring line. Then shift into FORWARD with wheel turned away from the dock to hold boat alongside until other dock lines are secured. After boat is tied up, shift into NEUTRAL and turn off engine.

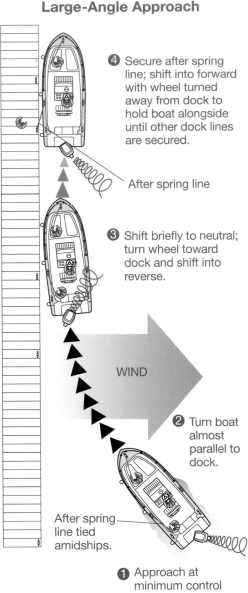

Large-Angle Approach

❹ Secure after spring line; shift into forward with wheel turned away from dock to hold boat alongside until other dock lines are secured.

After spring line

❸ Shift briefly to neutral; turn wheel toward dock and shift into reverse.

WIND

❷ Turn boat almost parallel to dock.

After spring line tied amidships.

❶ Approach at minimum control control speed at 45° angle.

Downwind Docking

With the wind (or current) from astern, any use of the engine for steering may cause a faster approach speed, which will require more distance and reverse power to stop the boat. An increase in wind magnifies the problem. Once alongside the dock, the boat may drift rapidly down the dock or its stern may spin out unless an after spring line fastened amidships on the boat is quickly looped over a dock cleat. If the line were led to the bow cleat, it could cause the stern to spin out from the dock.

RETURNING TO A SLIP

Downwind Approach

Usually you will have more control going bow first into the slip. Controlling your speed will be your main concern as you will need to counteract the wind's effect of increasing the speed of the boat into the slip.

Upwind Approach

With this approach you can use the wind to help slow the boat as you bring it into the slip. Have dock lines ready to help stop the boat from moving forward or backward too much in the slip.

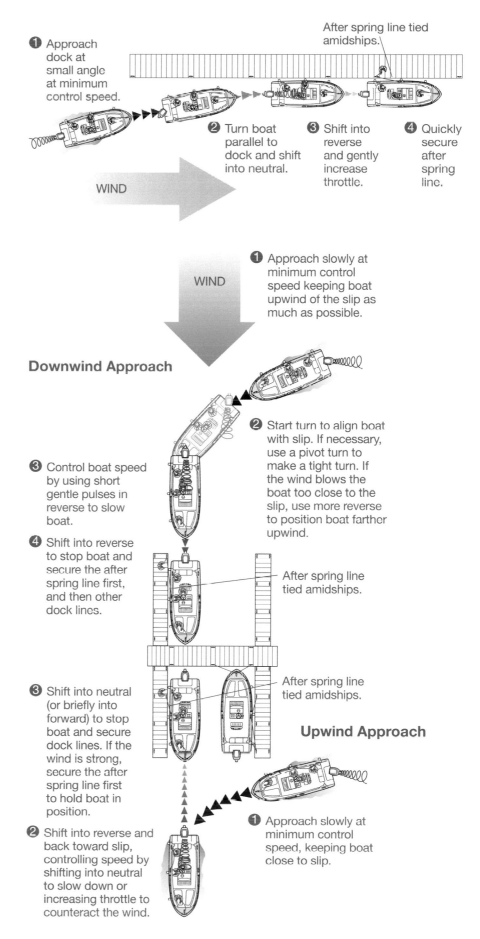

❶ Approach dock at small angle at minimum control speed.

After spring line tied amidships.

❷ Turn boat parallel to dock and shift into neutral.

❸ Shift into reverse and gently increase throttle.

❹ Quickly secure after spring line.

WIND

Downwind Approach

WIND

❶ Approach slowly at minimum control speed keeping boat upwind of the slip as much as possible.

❷ Start turn to align boat with slip. If necessary, use a pivot turn to make a tight turn. If the wind blows the boat too close to the slip, use more reverse to position boat farther upwind.

❸ Control boat speed by using short gentle pulses in reverse to slow boat.

❹ Shift into reverse to stop boat and secure the after spring line first, and then other dock lines.

After spring line tied amidships.

After spring line tied amidships.

Upwind Approach

❸ Shift into neutral (or briefly into forward) to stop boat and secure dock lines. If the wind is strong, secure the after spring line first to hold boat in position.

❷ Shift into reverse and back toward slip, controlling speed by shifting into neutral to slow down or increasing throttle to counteract the wind.

❶ Approach slowly at minimum control speed, keeping boat close to slip.

1 Turn wheel to port and briefly shift into FORWARD, just enough to swing stern to starboard without moving forward. Shift into NEUTRAL and allow pivoting momentum to continue until boat has pivoted enough to offset prop walk in reverse.

2 Turn wheel to starboard and shift into REVERSE, slowly backing out. If prop walk swings boat too close to slip, repeat steps **1** and **2**.

3 Turn boat once bow is clear of slip.

4 Center wheel; shift into FORWARD after pausing briefly in NEUTRAL.

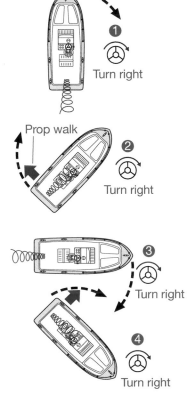

Move fender to protect hull at bow.

1 Turn left
2 Turn right
3 Turn left
4 Center

TURNING MANEUVERS

When turning in close quarters, prop walk, wind and current need to be taken into account. If you have to make a turn through the wind, the direction of your turn could affect the turning arc and whether the boat's position ends up downwind or not. If your boat has a bow thruster, it can be used to tighten your turn. When making a tight pivot turn with a bow thruster, a touch of FORWARD or REVERSE during the turn will hold your position in relation to the wind.

KEY POINTS

- *Prop walk exists when the engine is in REVERSE or FORWARD gear.*

- *Water must be flowing past the rudder to create a rudder force.*

Clockwise Pivot Turn (Right-Hand Propeller)

1 Turn right
Prop walk
2 Turn right
3 Turn right
4 Turn right

PIVOT TURN USING POSITIVE PROP WALK

Whenever possible you should make your turn in the direction that makes prop walk work for you—not against you. Turn clockwise for a boat with a right-hand propeller where the stern walks to port (clockwise) in reverse; and turn counterclockwise for a boat with a left-hand propeller which walks to starboard (counterclockwise) in reverse. You'll use a combination of prop walk and rudder force in your turn. Remember, water must be flowing past the rudder to generate a rudder force, and when you shift into FORWARD gear, this generates water flow.

1 Turn wheel hard over to starboard throughout the maneuver and shift into FORWARD gear, adding a small, gentle amount of throttle to generate water flow over rudder to initiate turn.

2 Before gaining headway, shift into REVERSE after pausing briefly in NEUTRAL. Prop walk will swing the stern to port.

3 Shift into FORWARD after pausing briefly in NEUTRAL.

4 Shift into REVERSE and use prop walk again. Repeat steps until boat has completed its turn.

Note: For left-hand propellers, turn wheel hard over to port throughout maneuver and rotate counterclockwise.

64

K-Turn Using Opposing Prop Walk

You want to avoid this situation where prop walk is fighting your turn. You won't have to use a K-Turn if you have a bow thruster. If you have to make this turn, allow more space for this K-Turn maneuver.

1 For right-hand propeller, turn wheel hard over to port and shift into FORWARD gear, adding a small punch of throttle to drive water over the rudder to start the boat turning to port.

2 Shift into REVERSE, after pausing briefly in NEUTRAL, and keep wheel to port. Watch the rotation of the bow closely as prop walk slows the turn.

3 When the bow stops rotating to port, turn wheel to starboard and continue reversing as space allows.

4 Shift to NEUTRAL, center wheel and shift into FORWARD to slow boat's movement astern.

5 Just before boat stops moving astern, turn wheel hard to port and give another punch of throttle. Repeat the sequence as necessary to complete the turn.

DRIVING BACKWARD

When you are operating in close quarters, at some point you may have to back your boat. For boats with no bow thruster, the effect of prop walk will make steering a straight line difficult. You can use the rudder to counteract the turning tendency of prop walk, but with some boats prop walk will dominate. The following technique uses prop wash over the rudder created by momentary pulses in FORWARD gear to keep the stern pointing in the direction you're aiming for. The illustration depicts a boat that walks to port in reverse.

1 If the boat is aligned in the direction you want to back, turn the wheel hard over to starboard and shift into REVERSE. As the boat moves astern, water flowing over the rudder will try to turn the stern to starboard, but prop walk may overpower the rudder's turning force.

2 If there is room and enough momentum, shift to NEUTRAL to stop prop walk and allow the boat to steer using backward momentum and rudder alone.

3 If there is not enough momentum and the direction of the boat's stern is to port of the intended direction, turn wheel to port and give a short burst of power in FORWARD—just enough to initiate the rotation in the required direction—NOT to drive the boat forward.

4 Shift to NEUTRAL and turn the wheel to starboard and REVERSE again.

5 Repeat this sequence as necessary.

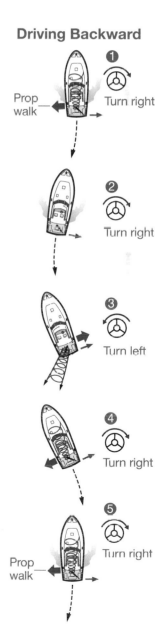

Driving Backward

Prop walk — **1** Turn right

2 Turn right

3 Turn left

4 Turn right

5 Turn right

Prop walk —

RETURNING TO A SLIP

DOWNWIND APPROACH

1 Approach slowly at minimum control speed; keep boat upwind of slip as much as possible. Start turn to align boat with slip.

2 Use a pivot turn to make a tight turn if necessary. If wind blows boat too close to slip, use more reverse to position boat farther upwind.

3 Control boat speed by using NEUTRAL and gentle applications of REVERSE.

4 Shift into REVERSE to stop boat. Secure after spring line first; then other dock lines.

UPWIND APPROACH

1 Approach slowly at minimum control speed; keep boat close to slip. Turn to align boat with slip. Use a pivot turn if there is not enough space to make a normal turn.

2 Shift into REVERSE and back toward slip, controlling speed by shifting into NEUTRAL to slow down or increasing throttle to counteract the wind.

3 Shift into NEUTRAL or briefly into FORWARD to stop the boat. Secure after spring line first to hold boat in position; then other dock lines.

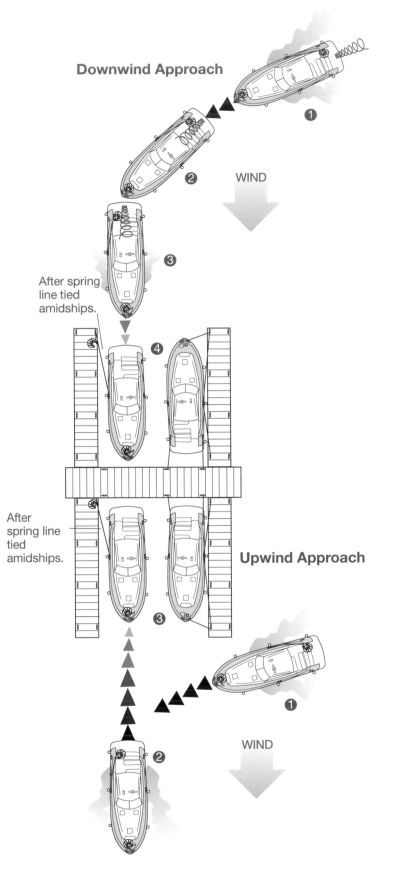

Downwind Approach

WIND

After spring line tied amidships.

After spring line tied amidships.

Upwind Approach

WIND

CROSSWIND APPROACH

This is a difficult maneuver, even for an experienced person, and should be practiced without using a bow thruster. If the wind is strong, you may find the bow thruster has little if any effect and can only be used for minor adjustments as the boat enters the slip. Another alternative is to ask for a more suitable docking space. Position fenders on both sides of the boat.

1 Position boat downwind of the slip for a backing approach and shift into REVERSE.

2 Make a backing turn toward the slip. The turn for smaller or lighter boats should be tighter than larger, heavier boats. Use rudder and gearshift to adjust for effects of prop walk and wind.

3 Continue to back toward the windward side of the slip, making small adjustments with the rudder as necessary.

4 Secure after spring line and shift into FORWARD with wheel turned to port to bring and hold boat alongside slip until starboard bow line and other dock lines are secured.

RETURNING TO A DOCK

KEY POINTS

- *Place fenders at dock level and prepare dock lines, making sure everyone knows what to do with them.*

- *Whenever possible, come alongside the dock with the bow pointing into the wind or current, whichever is stronger, making your approach at minimum control speed.*

- *In the absence of wind or current, approach the dock in a direction to take advantage of prop walk.*

SMALL-ANGLE APPROACH

1 Approach slowly at a 20 to 25-degree angle on the side that prop walk will pull your stern toward the dock in reverse.

2 When the bow is about ½ to 1 boat length from dock, shift into NEUTRAL and make a smooth turn to bring boat close to dock and almost parallel. If more water flow over the rudder is needed to turn the boat, use intermittent power by briefly shifting into FORWARD.

3 When the bow is close to dock, center wheel and shift into REVERSE to stop. Prop walk will swing the stern into dock. If stern needs to be brought in more or faster, gently increase throttle.

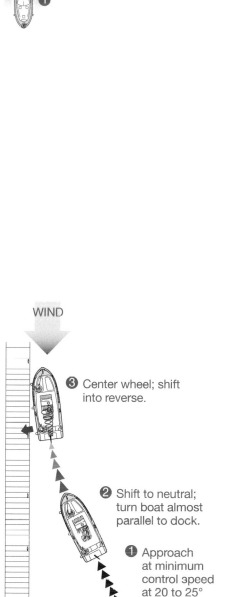

WIND

After spring line tied amidships.

WIND

3 Center wheel; shift into reverse.

2 Shift to neutral; turn boat almost parallel to dock.

1 Approach at minimum control speed at 20 to 25° angle.

CROSSWIND APPROACH WITH BOW THRUSTER

1 Approach at a small angle at minimum control speed. Use intermittent bursts of bow thruster to counteract the wind and keep boat on course.

2 Reduce speed when close to dock, using bow thruster to prevent the bow from falling away from the dock.

3 Secure the after spring line and shift into FORWARD with wheel turned away from dock to bring and hold boat alongside dock until other dock lines are secured.

CLOSE-QUARTERS DOCKING

Carefully check wind and current conditions before making this approach. If you feel uncomfortable about the dock space, look for another location. When possible, dock on the side that prop walk will pull the stern toward the dock when you reverse to stop forward momentum. Use the after spring line to bring the boat alongside as described in step **3**.

1 Approach slowly at minimum control speed at an angle to clear boat on port side.

2 When the bow is close to dock, start to turn boat and pass after spring line to person on dock. Shift into REVERSE to stop boat and swing stern to dock.

3 Secure after spring line and shift into FORWARD with wheel turned away from dock to bring and hold boat alongside dock until other dock lines are secured.

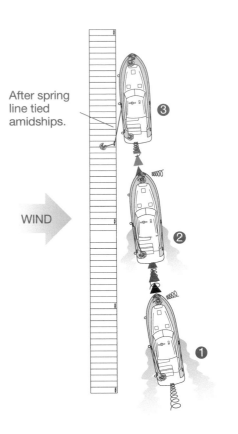

After spring line tied amidships.

WIND

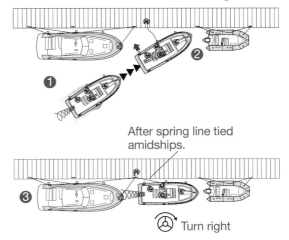

Close-Quarters Docking

After spring line tied amidships.

Turn right

REVIEW QUESTIONS

1. Prop walk occurs when the engine is in _____ or _____ gear.

2. _____ must be flowing past the rudder for it to be used for turning.

3. If a boat has a propeller where prop walk in REVERSE gear walks the stern to port, the best direction to make a pivot turn is _____.

4. When making a downwind approach to a slip, the first line to secure is the _____ spring line.

5. The preferred side to come alongside a dock is on the side of the boat that prop walk will pull the stern _____ the dock when the engine is in _____.

Answers: 1) REVERSE; FORWARD 2) Water 3) clockwise 4) after 5) toward; REVERSE

Chapter 8

BOAT HANDLING – TWIN SCREWS

KEY CONCEPTS

▶ Monohull maneuvers   ▶ Catamaran maneuvers

Twin-screw maneuvering concepts apply to both monohulls and catamarans. With a propeller in each hull of a catamaran, the distance between the two propellers is farther apart and the twin-screw advantage is increased, but catamarans are generally lighter and have different windage and underwater profiles than a monohull. All boats react differently in wind and current and it is always best to practice maneuvers before you need to use them in close quarters.

MONOHULL MANEUVERS

LEAVING A DOCK

BACK-AWAY DEPARTURE

With twin screws this is simply done by reversing the propeller closest to the dock to swing the stern away from the dock. Once the stern is clear, both propellers are reversed to back straight out. If conditions or other boats alongside the dock limit maneuvering space, then use a pivot turn (coupled with an after spring line if more control is needed) to rotate the stern until the boat can be backed straight out.

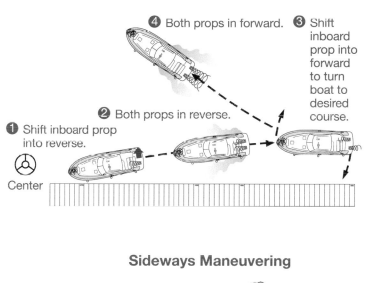

❹ Both props in forward. ❸ Shift inboard prop into forward to turn boat to desired course.

❷ Both props in reverse.

❶ Shift inboard prop into reverse.

Center

SIDEWAYS MANEUVERING

Many twin-screw boats with fixed propellers can be maneuvered sideways with varying degrees of success dependent on hull shape and configuration of propellers and rudders. The method described here may not work for all boats. Practice this maneuver to determine what works best for your boat.

Sideways Maneuvering

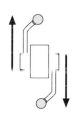

Split gearshifts with port in forward, starboard in reverse, and helm to port.

Boat moves to starboard.

Turn left

(opposite to twist direction)

If boat twists too much and doesn't move sideways, try pulling reversing propeller in neutral intermittently.

TURNING MANEUVERS

CLOSE-QUARTERS MANEUVERING

At slow speeds, gearshifts are the primary controls used to maneuver twin-screw powerboats. In close-quarters maneuvering, the rudders generally remain centered.

CONTROLLING YOUR TURN

You can vary your turn by using different combinations of gearshift and throttle. If you turn the steering wheel in the same direction as the turn, you will tighten the turn. Experiment with these controls in different wind and current conditions in open water to learn how your boat responds. Your goal is to be able to control your boat with precision when maneuvering around docks and slips.

PIVOT TURN

With its starboard propeller in FORWARD at idle rpm and its port propeller in REVERSE at close to idle rpm, a boat will make a counterclockwise pivot (or twist) turn. The throttle on the reversing prop may have to be increased slightly to compensate for its reduced performance in reverse. If the boat starts to creep ahead, either increase the throttle of the reversing propeller or put the forward propeller in NEUTRAL intermittently during the turn. If the boat creeps backward, increase the throttle of the forward propeller or shift the reversing propeller into NEUTRAL intermittently.

BACKING TURN

With its port propeller in REVERSE at idle rpm and its starboard propeller in NEUTRAL, a boat will make a backing turn to the side opposite the reversing propeller or to starboard in this situation.

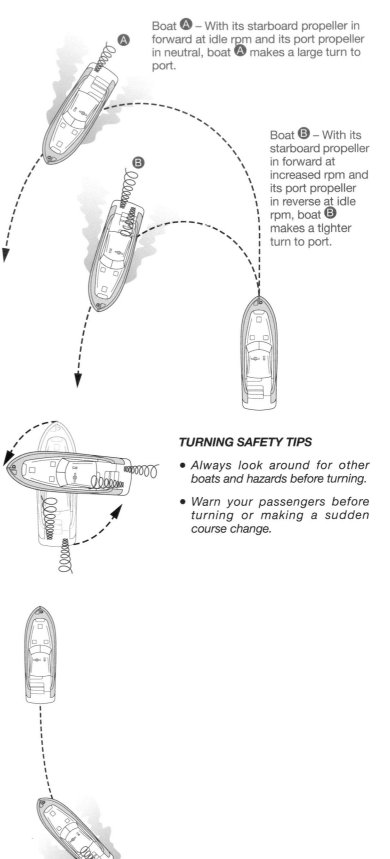

Boat **A** – With its starboard propeller in forward at idle rpm and its port propeller in neutral, boat **A** makes a large turn to port.

Boat **B** – With its starboard propeller in forward at increased rpm and its port propeller in reverse at idle rpm, boat **B** makes a tighter turn to port.

TURNING SAFETY TIPS

- *Always look around for other boats and hazards before turning.*

- *Warn your passengers before turning or making a sudden course change.*

RETURNING TO A DOCK

A twin-screw powerboat can be easily docked on either side.

1 Approach slowly at minimum control speed.

2 Make a smooth turn to bring boat almost parallel and close to dock by shifting outboard engine to NEUTRAL.

3 Shift inboard prop to NEUTRAL and outboard prop in REVERSE to swing stern and stop boat. Reverse inboard prop, if necessary.

RETURNING TO A SLIP

1 Approach slowly at minimum control speed.

2 Make a pivot turn to line up boat stern first to slip.

3 Shift both propellers into REVERSE at idle rpm and back into slip.

4 Control speed and direction by shifting propellers to NEUTRAL as needed.

5 Stop boat by briefly shifting into FORWARD.

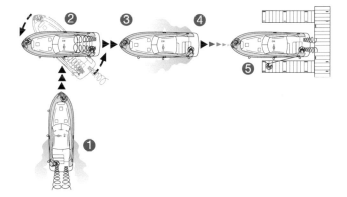

CROSSWIND APPROACH

1 Position boat downwind of the slip for a backing approach and shift into REVERSE.

2 Make a backing turn toward the slip with both engines in REVERSE and the starboard one at a higher throttle setting. Control the rate of turn with throttles and gearshifts. The turn for smaller or lighter boats should be tighter than for heavier ones.

3 Secure the after spring line and shift starboard engine into FORWARD with port engine in NEUTRAL to bring and hold boat alongside slip until starboard bow line and other dock lines are secured.

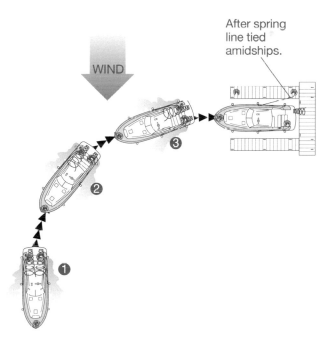

After spring line tied amidships.

WIND

CATAMARAN MANEUVERS

CONCEPTS

MANAGING THE FOUR CORNERS

In a catamaran, the operator is managing a four-cornered box with two bows and two sterns and visibility can be a problem sometimes. The steering station may be located in several positions. Some are low and the person steering may be looking around parts of the cat. Others are higher, making it easier to see at least one side of the cat. In most cases, the person steering is not likely to have a good view of all four corners. It is very helpful to have a person serving as a lookout at these blind spots.

BOAT-HANDLING CONSIDERATIONS

Catamarans move forward and backward quite easily due to their long, narrow hulls. Their high topsides and cabins create a lot of windage and they don't coast very far into the wind. In fact, they could be considered to stop on a dime. When maneuvering in an anchorage, windage can cause a cat to slide sideways into another boat. Current also has a significant effect on catamarans because they have two hulls. In close-quarters maneuvering, gearshifts are typically the primary controls while rudders remain centered.

EFFECT OF DOMINANT FORCE

If the dominant force of current or wind is on the bow or forward of the beam when leaving or returning to a dock, it is best to make a forward departure or return. If the dominant force is on the stern or aft of the beam, it is best to make a reverse departure or return. If the current and wind are in opposite directions, the one that has the dominant effect will determine whether it will be a forward or reverse departure or return.

LEAVING A DOCK

A catamaran can be easily pivoted from a dock by using opposite thrust with one engine in FORWARD and the other in REVERSE. When pivoting, use a fender at the point of rotation on the hull to avoid damage. If there is no wind or current, simply put the engines in opposite thrust and use the rudders to walk the catamaran sideways.

Dominant Force Effect

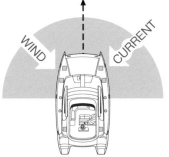

When the dominant force is forward of the beam, make a forward departure or return to the dock.

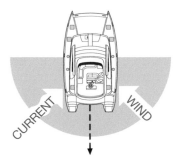

When the dominant force is aft of the beam, make a reverse departure or return.

FORWARD DEPARTURE

If the current (or wind) is strong, use a forward spring line to hold the cat in position while other dock lines are released.

1 Pivot bow from dock by shifting inboard engine in FORWARD and outboard engine in REVERSE.

2 Shift outboard engine in FORWARD; adjust throttles as needed and stow fenders.

REVERSE DEPARTURE

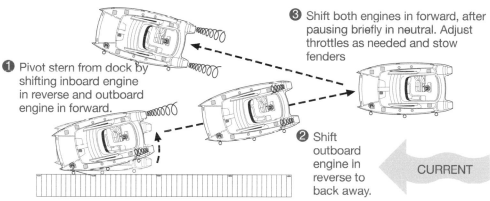

1 Pivot stern from dock by shifting inboard engine in reverse and outboard engine in forward.

3 Shift both engines in forward, after pausing briefly in neutral. Adjust throttles as needed and stow fenders

2 Shift outboard engine in reverse to back away.

CURRENT

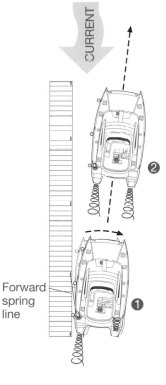

Forward Departure

CURRENT

Forward spring line

TURNING MANEUVERS

To develop a mental picture of how a catamaran will respond to steering with twin engines, remember that if the driver pushes one of the throttles FORWARD, that hull will move forward. Likewise, a throttle pulled into REVERSE will make that hull move backward. It may be helpful to picture turning someone by taking hold of the shoulders from behind, and pulling on one while pushing on the other.

PIVOT TURN

Because the engines are so far apart, it is easy to pivot a catamaran. With one engine in forward and the other in reverse, the cat will pivot in its own length.

TURN AROUND A HULL

By varying the amount of power of each engine, it is possible to pivot a catamaran around either hull.

Pivot Turn

Rotation point

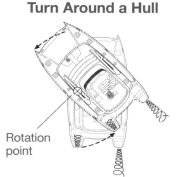

Turn Around a Hull

Rotation point

CLOSE-QUARTERS MANEUVERING

These pivoting characteristics make it easy to maneuver a catamaran. On most cats, the rudders will have little steering effect at low speeds and you will steer with the engines. Strong winds have a great effect on a cat because of its shallow draft and high topsides. Just as on other boats, the bows will blow away from the wind, often quickly. In close quarters, going forward may require more speed than is safe or comfortable, and the best way (sometimes the only way) in strong winds may be to back up towards the objective. When backing, keep the speed low and a firm hand on the wheel to prevent the rudders from accidentally turning hard over.

RETURNING TO A SLIP

REVERSE APPROACH

Unless the dominant force dictates otherwise, the preferred method is to back into a slip. It is much easier to disembark from the steps at the stern and twin-engine catamarans are just as maneuverable in reverse as they are with forward propulsion. Rig fenders on both sides and position the line handlers at the four corners to handle dock lines and serve as lookouts for clearance with the slip.

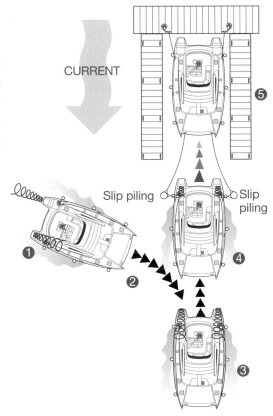

❶ Approach at minimum control speed; keep catamaran close to slip.

❷ Make a tight turn to line up with slip. If necessary to counteract set of current, increase throttle of reversing engine.

❸ Shift both engines into REVERSE and back toward the pilings, increasing the throttles or shifting into NEUTRAL as necessary for speed and steering control.

❹ Put loop end of bow lines over the pilings (or pick up line attached to each piling) and continue to back toward the slip.

❺ Pass stern lines and adjust bow and stern lines. Rig other dock lines if necessary.

RETURNING TO A DOCK

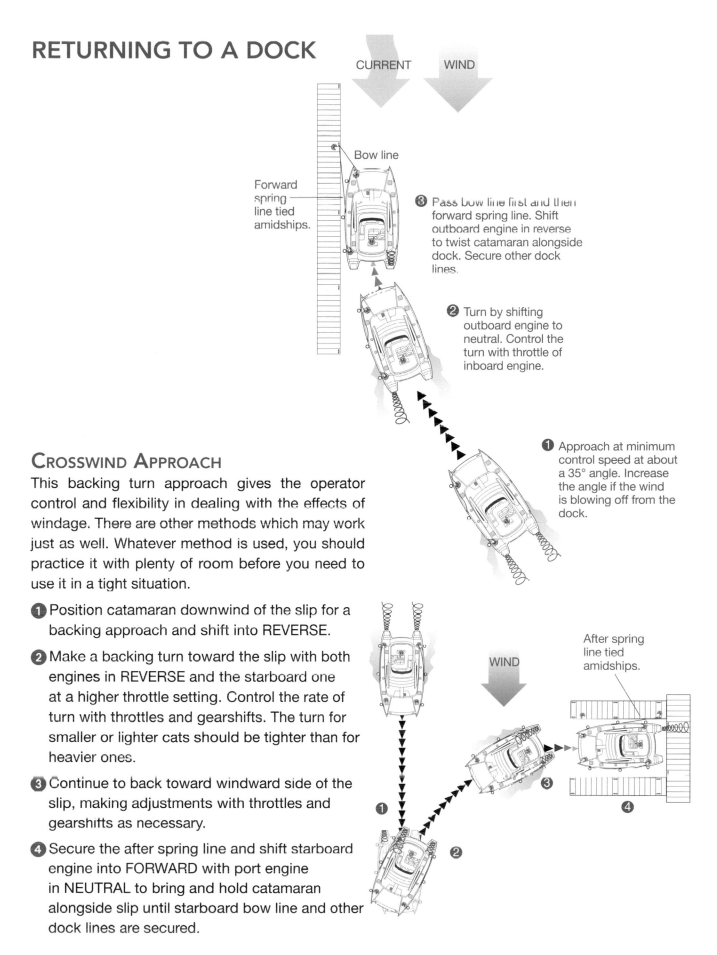

CURRENT WIND

Bow line

Forward spring line tied amidships.

❸ Pass bow line first and then forward spring line. Shift outboard engine in reverse to twist catamaran alongside dock. Secure other dock lines.

❷ Turn by shifting outboard engine to neutral. Control the turn with throttle of inboard engine.

❶ Approach at minimum control speed at about a 35° angle. Increase the angle if the wind is blowing off from the dock.

CROSSWIND APPROACH

This backing turn approach gives the operator control and flexibility in dealing with the effects of windage. There are other methods which may work just as well. Whatever method is used, you should practice it with plenty of room before you need to use it in a tight situation.

❶ Position catamaran downwind of the slip for a backing approach and shift into REVERSE.

❷ Make a backing turn toward the slip with both engines in REVERSE and the starboard one at a higher throttle setting. Control the rate of turn with throttles and gearshifts. The turn for smaller or lighter cats should be tighter than for heavier ones.

❸ Continue to back toward windward side of the slip, making adjustments with throttles and gearshifts as necessary.

❹ Secure the after spring line and shift starboard engine into FORWARD with port engine in NEUTRAL to bring and hold catamaran alongside slip until starboard bow line and other dock lines are secured.

WIND

After spring line tied amidships.

75

REVIEW QUESTIONS

1. *When maneuvering a twin-screw boat in close quarters, _____ are the primary steering controls while _____ remain centered.*

2. *To make a pivot turn in a counterclockwise direction, shift the starboard engine in _____ and the port engine in _____.*

3. *To make a backing turn to starboard, shift the _____ engine in REVERSE and the _____ engine in NEUTRAL.*

4. *If the dominant force is forward of the beam of a catamaran, you should make a _____ departure when leaving a dock.*

5. *The preferred method for a catamaran to return to a slip is to _____ into it unless wind or current dictates otherwise.*

Answers:
1) gearshifts; rudders
2) FORWARD; REVERSE
3) port; starboard
4) forward
5) back

Chapter 9

ADVANCED BOAT HANDLING

KEY CONCEPTS

▶ Anchoring
▶ Mooring
▶ Coming alongside
▶ Rafting alongside

▶ Heavy-weather maneuvers
▶ Bridges
▶ Locks

Advanced boat handling builds on the fundamental skills introduced in the previous chapters and enables you to deal with more challenging boating situations.

ANCHORING

There will be times when you will want to anchor at a destination or during an emergency. Here are some procedures for setting and retrieving an anchor as well as factors to consider when selecting a suitable anchoring location.

How well an anchor holds is determined by three primary factors:

- anchor type and size,

- bottom type (e.g., mud, sand, clay), and

- the amount of scope, which is the ratio of length of rode to water depth plus height of bow (*freeboard*).

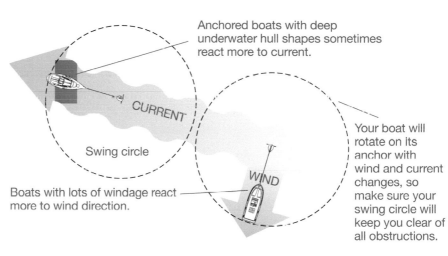

Anchored boats with deep underwater hull shapes sometimes react more to current.

CURRENT

Swing circle

Boats with lots of windage react more to wind direction.

WIND

Your boat will rotate on its anchor with wind and current changes, so make sure your swing circle will keep you clear of all obstructions.

ANCHORING TIPS

- *Check the water depth on a chart. If there is tide, make sure there is enough depth at low tide and enough rode (anchor line and chain) at high tide.*

- *Make sure there are no obstructions above or below the water that your boat could hit when it swings on its anchor.*

- *Try to anchor in calmer protected waters by choosing a location in the lee (downwind) of land or a breakwater.*

- *Check your chart to avoid grassy or rocky bottoms which are difficult for setting lightweight anchors.*

- *Do not anchor in channels, high traffic areas or near underwater cables.*

- *Take a pass around the intended anchoring area to check for any uncharted hazards.*

SCOPE

More scope increases holding ability. While a ratio of 5:1 may be adequate for an all-chain rode, or a nylon rode with a short length of chain for lunch in a sheltered spot with a good holding bottom, you'll want to increase it to 7:1 or more for strong wind and sea conditions.

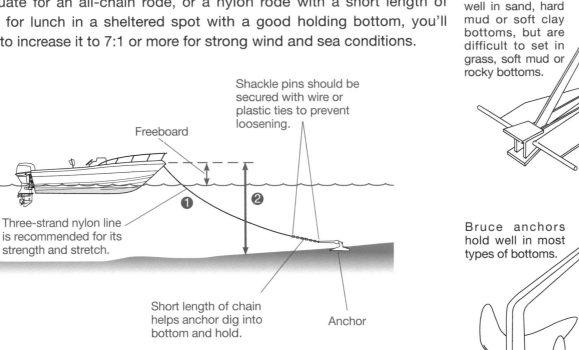

Freeboard

Shackle pins should be secured with wire or plastic ties to prevent loosening.

Three-strand nylon line is recommended for its strength and stretch.

Short length of chain helps anchor dig into bottom and hold.

Anchor

EXAMPLE

If water depth plus freeboard ❷ = 7 feet and if you let out 35 feet of rode ❶,

$$\text{Scope} = \frac{35 \text{ feet}}{7 \text{ feet}} = \frac{5}{1} \text{ or } 5:1$$

If the tide rises 3 feet, scope $= \dfrac{35 \text{ feet}}{10 \text{ feet}} = \dfrac{3.5}{1} \text{ or } 3.5:1$

and your anchor may drag unless you let out more line.

ANCHOR & RODE INSPECTION
☐ Check anchor line for worn or frayed areas.
☐ Check chain for damaged links.
☐ Check that shackles are in good condition and pins are securely fastened.
☐ Check condition of anchor.

Anchor Types

Lightweight-type anchors such as a Danforth hold well in sand, hard mud or soft clay bottoms, but are difficult to set in grass, soft mud or rocky bottoms.

Bruce anchors hold well in most types of bottoms.

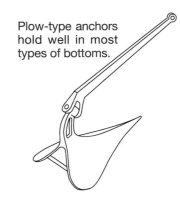

Plow-type anchors hold well in most types of bottoms.

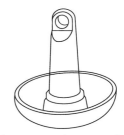

Mushroom anchors are best for mud and silt bottoms. Unlike other anchors shown here, it depends primarily on its weight for holding.

Setting an Anchor

When anchoring, a boat should be anchored at the bow. Anchoring at the stern could result in waves coming over the transom and possibly swamping smaller boats; plus there is a danger of carbon monoxide poisoning if the engine is running.

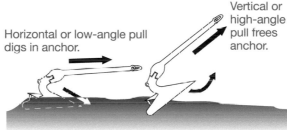

Horizontal or low-angle pull digs in anchor.

Vertical or high-angle pull frees anchor.

Most anchors dig into the bottom and hold best when pulled at a low angle to the bottom. A more vertical angle of pull can prevent the flukes from burying or even break the anchor free.

① After checking area, approach anchoring spot slowly, heading into wind or current, whichever is the dominant force on the boat.

② Stop boat and lower anchor over bow—do not throw it. The end of the rode should be attached to boat before releasing anchor.

③ Let out rode as boat drifts downwind. If wind has too little effect, back boat very slowly while letting rode run out freely. Avoid backing too fast, which could cause anchor to bounce along bottom.

④ When a scope of 5:1 has been let out, secure the rode and reverse slowly against it until it becomes taut. Once anchor is set, let out additional rode as needed. To check whether anchor has set, hold a hand on the rode while reversing to feel for any chatter or vibration from anchor dragging or bouncing along bottom.

CATAMARAN SETTING AN ANCHOR

Bridles used for anchoring and mooring in their stowed position while underway.

CURRENT

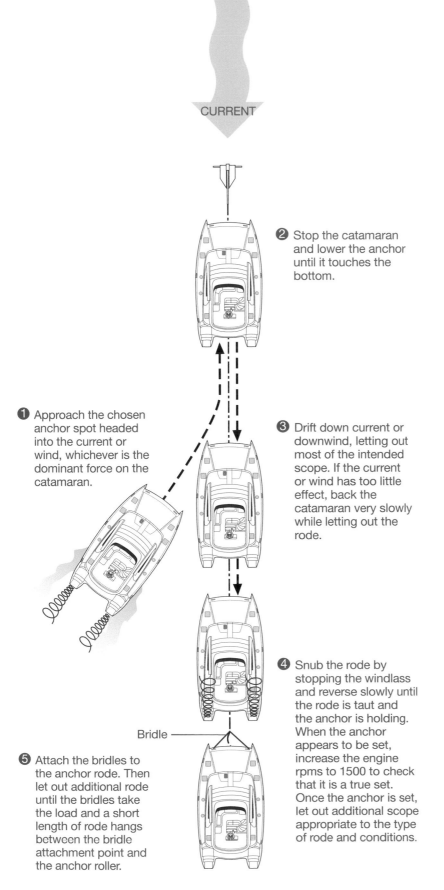

❶ Approach the chosen anchor spot headed into the current or wind, whichever is the dominant force on the catamaran.

❷ Stop the catamaran and lower the anchor until it touches the bottom.

❸ Drift down current or downwind, letting out most of the intended scope. If the current or wind has too little effect, back the catamaran very slowly while letting out the rode.

❹ Snub the rode by stopping the windlass and reverse slowly until the rode is taut and the anchor is holding. When the anchor appears to be set, increase the engine rpms to 1500 to check that it is a true set. Once the anchor is set, let out additional scope appropriate to the type of rode and conditions.

Bridle

❺ Attach the bridles to the anchor rode. Then let out additional rode until the bridles take the load and a short length of rode hangs between the bridle attachment point and the anchor roller.

80

RETRIEVING AN ANCHOR

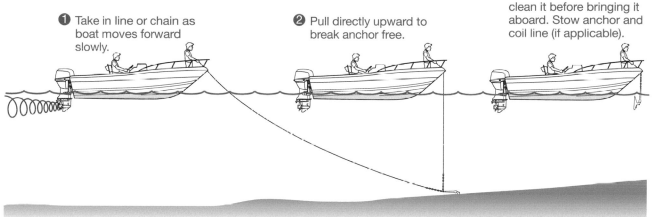

❶ Take in line or chain as boat moves forward slowly.

❷ Pull directly upward to break anchor free.

❸ Pull anchor to surface and clean it before bringing it aboard. Stow anchor and coil line (if applicable).

WINDLASS

Larger boats usually use a windlass for raising the anchor, which can handle both line and chain. Powerboats typically use electric windlasses operated by a button in the windlass or deck, or by a hand control. It's a good idea to run your engine while using an electric windlass to avoid running down the batteries. When lowering the chain, use the brake to stop it, not your hand.

Keep clothing, hair and other body parts clear of the windlass. Never put a hand on the chain while the windlass power is on.

HAND SIGNALS

The noise of engine, wind and waves makes it difficult to communicate by voice. Hand signals are a good alternative, but the driver and bow person should review them beforehand.

Control button

A windlass should be used to raise the anchor and its rode, not to break the anchor free.

Raise left arm with hand pointing to port to indicate steer to port.

Raise right arm with hand pointing to starboard to indicate steer to starboard.

Raise arm and motion forward to indicate go straight ahead.

Raise arm with closed fist to indicate stop.

Raise arm with palm facing aft to indicate reverse.

MOORING

Moorings typically have a large buoy that is attached to an anchor on the bottom with chain. They often have a floating line (*pendant*), sometimes rigged with a pickup pole, which you can grab to bring the pendant aboard. If there is no pole or you cannot reach it, you will need a boat hook. Some moorings may not have a pendant and you'll need to tie a stout line to the chain or the ring on the bottom of the buoy, using two round turns to reduce chafe. Buoys may have a ring on top, but before tying onto it make sure a metal rod connects it to the bottom ring. A ring attached only to the buoy's surface could rip off.

Picking Up a Mooring

The driver should approach the mooring with it on his side of the boat to keep it in sight throughout the approach. If the driver loses sight of the mooring, the bow person should use hand signals or a boat hook to direct the driver.

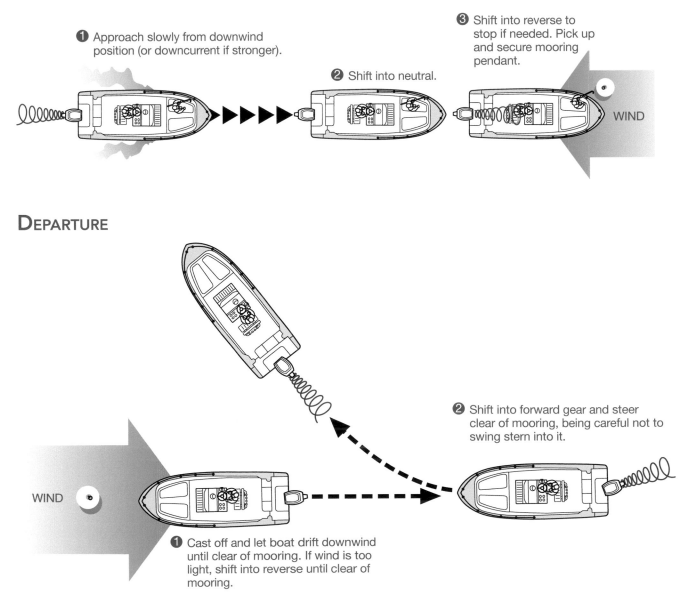

❶ Approach slowly from downwind position (or downcurrent if stronger).

❷ Shift into neutral.

❸ Shift into reverse to stop if needed. Pick up and secure mooring pendant.

WIND

Departure

❷ Shift into forward gear and steer clear of mooring, being careful not to swing stern into it.

WIND

❶ Cast off and let boat drift downwind until clear of mooring. If wind is too light, shift into reverse until clear of mooring.

PICKING UP A MOORING
BOW APPROACH

WIND

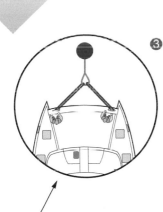

❸ Pass a bridle line from each bow through the eye splice of the pendant and lead it back to the bow from which it came. Adjust the bridles as necessary.

❷ Stop the catamaran, and a line handler picks up the mooring pendant with a boat hook.

❶ Approach the mooring into the wind (or current, whichever one is the dominant force) on the side closest to the driver.

PICKING UP A MOORING
STERN APPROACH

WIND   CURRENT

❻ Adjust the length of both lines as necessary.

❺ The free end of the first bow line is cleated to the bow cleat on the steering station side. Both ends of the second bow line are cleated to the bow cleat on the opposite side.

❹ Allow the boat to drift back as both line handlers walk forward with the lines.

❸ Pass the end of the first bow line through the ring (or pendant) and hand it to the other line handler. Pass the second bow line through the ring (or pendant), keeping both ends on board.

❷ Approach the mooring on the steering station side by backing into the wind or current, whichever one is the dominant force. Once the cat is lined up with the mooring and getting close to it, use the engine farther away from the mooring to make the final approach to keep the pendant from fouling in the near propeller.

❶ Rig a bow line from the bow cleat on the steering station side and lead it aft outside all lifelines to the stern steps. Another line, which will become a second bow line, is on hand at the stern (it is not led from or attached to a bow cleat).

COMING ALONGSIDE AN ANCHORED BOAT

1 Determine swing behavior of anchored boat and approach slowly at an appropriate angle. When boat is about 1/2 to 1 boat length away, make smooth turn to bring boat parallel to anchored boat and shift to NEUTRAL.

2 Reverse to stop boat. If necessary, increase throttle to accelerate swing, especially if anchored boat starts to swing away. Shift to NEUTRAL and tie up.

EFFECT OF WIND SHIFTS ON COMING ALONGSIDE

Generally, anchored boats point into the wind unless the current is dominant. Determine the amount and quickness of the anchored boat's oscillations and adjust your approach angle accordingly.

Large-Angle Approach: this approach easily compensates for oscillations in moored boat's swinging motion.

Small-Angle Approach: if boat swings any farther, you will have to stop and hold position until it swings back.

Straight Approach: will have to stop and hold position until boat swings back.

RAFTING ALONGSIDE

Always wait to be invited and use your own fenders.

1 First boat sets anchor.

2 Bring the second boat alongside with fenders in place, and secure to the first boat with spring, bow and stern lines.

3 Set additional anchors as needed. If a wind shift is anticipated, set an anchor at a 60-degree angle to the first anchor from the second boat.

Rafting lines should be secured so they can be easily removed in case of an emergency.

RAFTING CHECKLIST
☐ Place fenders high enough to protect topsides.
☐ To cross over boats, get onto a boat at its maximum beam location, then walk around the foredeck to get to the maximum beam on the other side of the boat.
☐ Be considerate of other people's quiet hours after dark.
☐ Inform other boats of your departure plans.

HEAVY-WEATHER MANEUVERING

Smaller outboards are usually designed for use in relatively sheltered waters. If caught unexpectedly in bad weather or rough seas, position people and equipment as low and as close to the center of the boat as possible. Don't let water accumulate in the cockpit or bilge. A cockpit half full of water in severe sea conditions is a cause for concern.

Keep in mind that you want to work your boat through the waves while always maintaining control and minimizing stress on the boat. Avoid driving into breaking crests, slamming into waves, or falling off their crests by making adjustments in direction and throttle to anticipate and react to changing wave conditions. Remember, one hand on the wheel and one hand on the throttle.

RUNNING AGAINST WIND & WAVES

As waves increase in size, it is usually better not to pound straight into them, but to cross them at an angle to produce an easier ride for the boat and its occupants. This angle will vary from 10 degrees to 45 degrees, depending on the size of the waves. Often waves seem to come in a recurring pattern with a couple of smaller ones followed by a larger one, then a couple of smaller ones followed by a larger one, etc. Sometimes, it is just a matter of slowing down a little to let the boat ride over the large wave. Other times, you may have to increase your angle to the large wave and slow down. Once it passes, you can go back to your previous direction and throttle setting.

RUNNING WITH WIND & WAVES

When strong winds and large waves are coming from behind, there is a risk of running down the front side of a wave and burying the bow in the backside of the next wave. This could cause the boat to suddenly turn and roll sideways (*broaching*) with a risk of capsizing. To avoid this situation, run at a slower speed to match the speed of the waves, maintaining a position on the backside of a wave.

SAFETY TIP FOR INLETS

Large waves are frequently encountered in inlets, especially with an outgoing (ebbing) current and wind blowing onshore. If the inlet is too rough, it is best to remain offshore and wait for slack water or less wind.

Running Against Wind & Waves

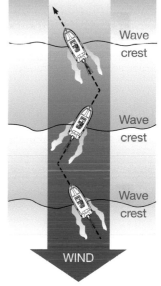

If your destination is directly upwind in heavy seas, you can tack (zig-zag) across waves for a smoother ride.

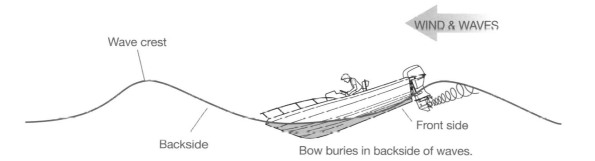

Wave crest

Backside

Bow buries in backside of waves.

Front side

WIND & WAVES

Another risk of running faster than the speed of waves is jumping off wave crests and making a hard and dangerous landing. If you have to run faster, throttle back as you approach the crests and angle down them to soften landing. Work your way through the waves by powering up the backside and throttling back and angling over the crest. If approaching a breaking wave, slow down to avoid it.

RUNNING SIDEWAYS TO WIND & WAVES

Find a suitable speed and heading to ride in the trough or on the backside of a wave. If set to leeward of your course, pick a set of smaller waves to angle upwind. Avoid breaking waves by adjusting your speed.

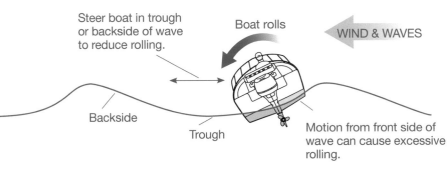

Steer boat in trough or backside of wave to reduce rolling.

Boat rolls

WIND & WAVES

Backside

Trough

Motion from front side of wave can cause excessive rolling.

BRIDGES

LIGHTS

Bridges are lighted from sunset to sunrise and during reduced visibility. Red lights typically indicate unsafe areas, and green lights indicate areas safe for navigation.

Fixed bridges are marked as follows:

• Two green lights mark the center of a navigable channel.

• A red light marks each margin of a navigable channel or each pier if it limits the channel margin.

• Three vertical white lights directly above each green light marks the main channel span if there are two or more spans over a navigable channel.

Bridges that can be opened are marked as follows:

• Red lights mark a closed bridge and the piers of a bridge.

• Green lights mark a bridge when it is open.

Running With Wind & Waves

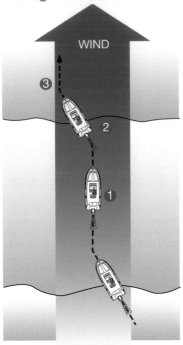

WIND

❶ Steer up the backside of a wave.

❷ As you near the wave top, throttle back and steer at an angle to stay in contact with the wave as you pass over it.

❸ As you start to climb the backside of the next wave, straighten your course and add power as needed.

Note: Timely adjustments of throttle will be vital while running faster than the waves. Techniques will vary for different boats and sea conditions. Experiment to determine the techniques most suitable for your boat.

Drawbridges may open on a fixed schedule or on demand. Some may have VHF radio and will have signs indicating the calling and working channels for opening the bridge. A request for an opening can be made by sound signals.

- One prolonged blast and one short blast indicates a request to open a bridge. If the bridge can be opened immediately, the bridge tender will respond with one prolonged blast and one short blast.

- Five short blasts by the bridge tender indicates the bridge cannot be opened immediately or, if opened, will be closed promptly.

BRIDGE TIPS

- *Vertical and horizontal clearances are depicted on nautical charts.*

- *Operation schedules and VHF channels are listed in the U.S. Coast Pilot and many commercial waterway guides.*

LOCKS

Locks are a means of allowing a boat to pass around a dam or from a different water level to another. Many locks have an on-duty lockmaster who controls all movement through the locks, sometimes using horn or light signals or VHF radio.

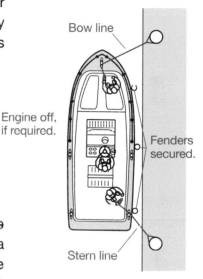

Maintain tension on bow and stern lines as the water level in the lock changes.

Light Signals		Horn Signals	
Green	= enter lock	**One long blast**	= enter lock
Yellow	= prepare to move into lock (often flashing)	**One short blast**	= leave lock
Red	= do not enter		

A boat entering a lock should have fenders in place and adequate lengths of line ready to use. Boats may lock through alongside a lock wall or in the center of the chamber tied off on both sides. Once secured, lock instructions may require that the engine be turned off. With large changes of water level, the water in the lock may become quite turbulent when the water rises in the lock. Never use hands or feet to hold onto or fend off the lock wall.

REVIEW QUESTIONS

1. *Your boat has a two-foot freeboard. You wish to anchor on a windy day in 18 feet of water. Your anchor rode (line plus chain) should be at least _____ feet long.*

2. *When setting an anchor, you should let out the _____ as the boat drifts downwind. If the wind has too little effect, back the boat very _____.*

3. *Large waves are frequently encountered in inlets, especially with a/an _____ (outgoing) current and onshore wind. If the inlet is too rough, it is best to wait for _____ water or less wind.*

4. *A _____ light at a lock signals do not enter the lock.*

5. *Two _____ lights on a fixed bridge mark the _____ of a navigable channel.*

Answers: 1) 140 2) rode; slowly 3) ebbing; slack 4) red 5) green; center

Chapter 10

EQUIPMENT & REQUIREMENTS

KEY CONCEPTS

▶ Registration, documentation & numbering

▶ Hull identification

▶ Maximum capacities

▶ Safety equipment

▶ Federal regulations

▶ Pollution

▶ Accident reporting

Part of preparation is ensuring that you have equipment on board that works properly and conforms to federal and state requirements. Once you leave the dock, you'll be sharing the waters with other boaters and enjoying the natural environment. Safety and seamanship includes knowing and observing the regulations that help protect the waters and govern safe operation.

REGISTRATION, DOCUMENTATION & NUMBERING

REGISTRATION & DOCUMENTATION

Powerboats must either be registered in their state of principal use or federally documented. Some states also require non-motorized boats to be registered. The certificate of number (registration) or certificate of documentation must be aboard the vessel when it is operated and must be produced if requested by a law enforcement officer. If documented, the hailing port must be displayed on the stern and the documentation number must be permanently affixed to the inside of the hull. If registered, the state registration number must be displayed on each side of the bow of the boat in block letters at least three inches high and have a contrasting color from the background color.

HULL IDENTIFICATION NUMBER (HIN)

Boats manufactured after November 1, 1972 are required to display a Hull Identification Number in two locations on the boat. The primary number must be near the top on the starboard side of the transom. In 1984 a second location of the HIN was required and it is located somewhere in the interior of the boat or beneath a fitting or hardware. The HIN is also on the certificate of registration or documentation, but keep a record of this number to identify your boat in case it is stolen.

LAWS & REGULATIONS

State and local laws and regulations may differ from federal regulations. Check with your state and local boating contacts for more information.

State Registration Numbers

State decal: its location will vary by state.

State registration number

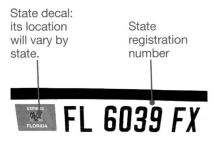

State registration numbers must be on both sides of the bow and lettering must be at least three inches high. The space between groupings of letters and numbers is equal to a letter width (except for "I" or "1").

MAXIMUM CAPACITIES LABEL OR PLATE

All powerboats (except inflatables) smaller than 20 feet in length built after October 31, 1972 must have a legible Maximum Capacities label permanently displayed and visible to the operator. For boats less than 20 feet with no capacities label/plate, check with the manufacturer or use a rough guide for the maximum number of people by multiplying the length (in feet) by the beam (in feet) and dividing by 15.

REQUIRED EQUIPMENT

The Federal Boating Safety Act of 1971 and subsequent regulations specify the equipment a powerboat must carry based on a boat's overall length. You should also check your state's boating regulations.

LIFE JACKETS

At least one U.S. Coast Guard approved life jacket appropriate for the intended use and sized for each person on board is required. Under federal regulations, children under 13 years of age are required to wear an approved life jacket while underway unless below deck or in an enclosed cabin. States may have different age requirements which should be observed while operating in state waters. Life jackets must be readily accessible, not buried under other gear, sealed in plastic bags or locked in compartments. Boats 16 feet and longer must carry at least one throwable (flotation) device which should be readily available. Life jackets are required to be in good serviceable condition. They should be checked regularly to make sure there is no loose stitching, rips, frayed straps or fabric, jammed zippers, or waterlogged or damaged flotation. Inflatable life jackets must have a full CO_2 cylinder and their status indicators must indicate they can inflate. To check their air-holding condition, orally inflate them and then deflate and repack. Replace any that are no longer in good condition.

Factors to consider when selecting a life jacket include: U.S. Coast Guard approval, amount of buoyancy which affects how high you will float in the water, its ability to turn a person face up, water conditions and how long it will take to be rescued, type of boating activity (for example,

Maximum Capacities Label/Plate

Maximum persons or their weight (weight controls)

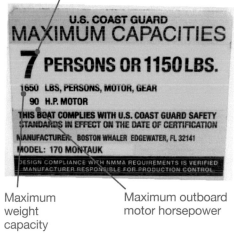

Maximum weight capacity

Maximum outboard motor horsepower

Type Designation Approval Label

❶ Type
❷ Size
❸ Weight & chest size
❹ USCG approval

Canada/US Harmonized Standard Approval Label

❷ Size ❶ Level ❸ Weight & chest size
❹ Limitations of use
❺ USCG approval

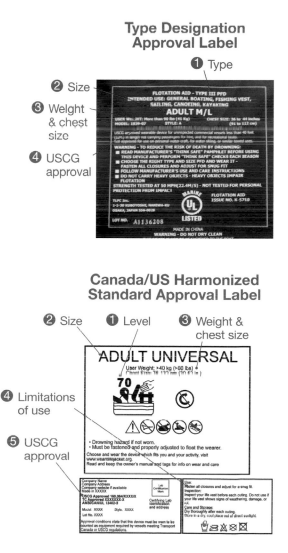

some life jackets are not appropriate for towed water sports), user's weight and chest size, and if you need leg or crotch straps to prevent the jacket from riding up. Some of this information can be found on the life jacket labels.

A life jacket that is comfortable to wear and thus worn is far more likely to save a life. It is very hard to put on a life jacket in an emergency, especially if you are already in the water.

LIFE JACKET LABELS

There are generally two kinds of labels: 1) written labels that refer to a Type designation; and 2) the newer, icon-based Canada/US Harmonized Standard labels. The legacy Type designation labels use Types I, II, III and V and writing to indicate expected performance and usage. The new Harmonized Standard labels use icons to depict the relative performance with a number: 50, 70, 100, 150, and 275. A lower level number generally offers greater mobility, comfort and style with good flotation for most people. A higher level number generally offers greater flotation, turning and stability in the water. The higher levels are appropriate for offshore use where rough water conditions and longer rescue times are likely. Separate icons also show turning ability, and any limitations of use. Both labels indicate whether the life jacket is U.S. Coast Guard approved, the user's weight and chest size ranges, and any limitations of use such as not designed for PWCs, waterskiing or tubing.

Offshore Life Jacket
(Level 100 or 150/Type I)

OFFSHORE LIFE JACKET (LEVEL 100 OR 150/TYPE I)

This life jacket is designed to turn an unconscious person from a face down position to face up and maintain that position. It is suitable for all waters and where rescue is not imminent, but is the bulkiest and most uncomfortable to wear.

Near-Shore Life Jacket
(Level 70/Type II)

NEAR-SHORE LIFE JACKET (LEVEL 70/TYPE II)

This life jacket is designed to turn some unconscious people over, but the turning action is not as reliable or as pronounced as the Offshore life jacket. It is suitable for calm, near-shore waters and if rescue is nearby, but is relatively uncomfortable to wear.

Flotation Aid
(Level 70/Type III)

FLOTATION AID (LEVEL 70/TYPE III)

This life jacket is not designed to turn an unconscious person over and is used in a variety of sports such as boating, waterskiing, hunting and kayaking.

It comes in a wide variety of shapes, sizes and colors and is a popular and comfortable type of life jacket. It is suitable for a conscious person in calm, sheltered waters where fast rescue is possible.

Inflatable Life Jacket

INFLATABLE LIFE JACKETS

Most of these are designed to inflate automatically when immersed, but some must be activated manually. Be sure you know which one you are wearing and that it is appropriate for the activity. Once inflated their performance level may be 70, 100, or 150 as noted on the Harmonized Standard labels or they may carry a Type designation. A person must weigh more than 80 pounds and be at least 16 years old to use one. Hybrid inflatables have an amount of inherent (foam) flotation so they will perform as buoyancy aids, and the additional inflated buoyancy raises the performance level as indicated on the label. Inflatables are considered the most comfortable of all life jackets, but are not recommended for non-swimmers.

Belt Pack Inflatable
Life Jacket

THROWABLE DEVICES (TYPE IV)

These are designed to throw to a person in the water to hold onto (not worn) until rescued. This type includes boat cushions, life rings and horseshoe buoys.

SIGNALING EQUIPMENT

Throwable Device
(Type IV)

VISUAL DISTRESS SIGNALS (VDS)

All boats operating in U.S. coastal waters, the Great Lakes, territorial seas and those waters connected directly to them up to a point where they narrow to less than two miles, are required to carry USCG approved visual distress signals. Powerboats less than 16 feet or boats participating in organized events are not required to carry day signals but must carry night signals when operating from sunset to sunrise.

SAFETY TIP
If visual distress signals are not legally required for your area, it is good seamanship to carry them on board in case an emergency arises.

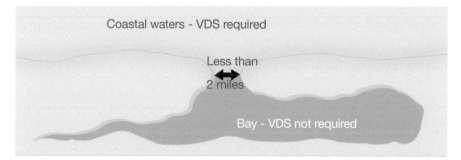

Coastal waters - VDS required

Less than
2 miles

Bay - VDS not required

There are a variety of visual distress signals available for day use, night use and for both. If pyrotechnic devices (e.g., flares, smoke signals and meteors) are selected, a minimum of three signals for day use and three signals for night use, or three signals approved for both day and night are required. All distress flares must not have exceeded their service life and must be kept in an accessible location. A watertight red or orange container labeled "Distress Signals" is recommended.

DISTRESS SIGNALS

The following signals can only be used to indicate a vessel is in distress and requires assistance. If a vessel has a life-threatening emergency, it can use a Mayday call on a VHF radio as a distress signal. Chapter 11 describes how to make a Mayday call.

A watertight flare kit is recommended to meet visual distress signal requirements.

Day Use Only
- orange smoke signal
- continuous sounding of fog horn
- orange distress flag (black square & black circle on orange
- slowly raising & lowering arms
- international code flags N over C
- square flag above or below a ball

Night Use Only
- electric automatic SOS distress light (ordinary flashlight does not meet requirement)

Day & Night Use
- hand-held red flare
- parachute red flare
- red-star meteor shells

SIGNALS TO ATTRACT ATTENTION

Light and sound signals may be used to attract attention as long as they cannot be mistaken for distress signals, limited visibility signals or signals used when meeting another vessel (see Chapter 13 for information on these signals). A searchlight may also be aimed in the direction of danger.

SOUND SIGNALING DEVICE

You are required to carry a sound signaling device that is capable of making an efficient sound signal. If your boat is 39.4 feet (12 meters) or longer, you must carry a bell as well as a whistle.

NAVIGATION LIGHT EQUIPMENT

Any boat operating between sunset and sunrise, and during restricted visibility, must display lights. Lighting requirements vary considerably with the size and type of vessel (see Chapter 13 for more information).

FIRE EXTINGUISHERS

Fire extinguishers are classified by the type of fire they are designed to extinguish and by their size. The letter indicates the type of fire: A for combustible solids like wood, paper, cloth, rubber and some plastics; B for flammable liquids such as gasoline, diesel, oil, grease and alcohol; and C for live electrical fires. Some extinguishers can be approved for several different types of fire and are labeled accordingly. The Roman numeral, which follows the letter, designates the size of the extinguisher: I being the smallest and V the largest. U.S. Coast Guard approved fire extinguishers are required if any of the following conditions exist:

Fire extinguishers should be readily accessible and mounted away from possible sources of fire.

- inboard engine installed

- closed compartments or under-seat compartments where portable fuel tanks may be stored

- double bottoms not sealed to the hull or not completely filled with flotation material

- closed living spaces

- closed stowage compartments in which combustible or flammable materials are stored

- permanently installed fuel tank(s) which could not be moved in the event of a fire or other emergency

The minimum number of hand-portable fire extinguishers (B-I or B-II) required on a recreational boat is based on the overall length of the boat.

Length (feet)	No Fixed System	With Approved Fixed System*
Under 26	one B-I	None
26 to under 40	two B-I or one B-II	one B-I
40 to 65	three B-I, or one B-I & one B-II	two B-I or one B-II

*An approved fixed system is a U.S. Coast Guard approved pre-engineered fire extinguishing system installed for the protection of the engine compartment.

Inspect fire extinguishers monthly to ensure: seals are intact; there is no physical damage; and that indicators are functional and reading in the desired range. Fire extinguishers should be placed where they are readily accessible and away from possible sources of fire.

ADDITIONAL EQUIPMENT

In addition to the required equipment, most boats will need other items suitable to the intended use of the boat and available stowage space, such as:
☐ Anchor & rode
☐ Towline
☐ First aid kit
☐ Heaving line
☐ Bailer/bilge pump
☐ Oars/paddles (for small powerboats)
☐ Tool kit
☐ Spare parts
☐ Boat hook
☐ Chart of area
☐ Boarding ladder
☐ Compass
☐ Flashlight
☐ VHF radio and/or mobile phone
☐ Spotlight
☐ Fenders
☐ Binoculars
☐ Dock lines
☐ GPS

VENTILATION

All boats with gasoline engines are required to have a natural ventilation system for each compartment that contains an engine or fuel tank. A natural ventilation system consists of a supply duct for fresh air flow and an exhaust duct. A powered ventilation system with one or more exhaust blowers is required for each compartment that has an inboard gasoline engine with a starter motor. Boats required to have an exhaust blower will have a warning label close to the ignition switch stating that before starting the engine, the blower must be operated for at least four minutes.

Air Circulation in Bilge and Engine Compartment

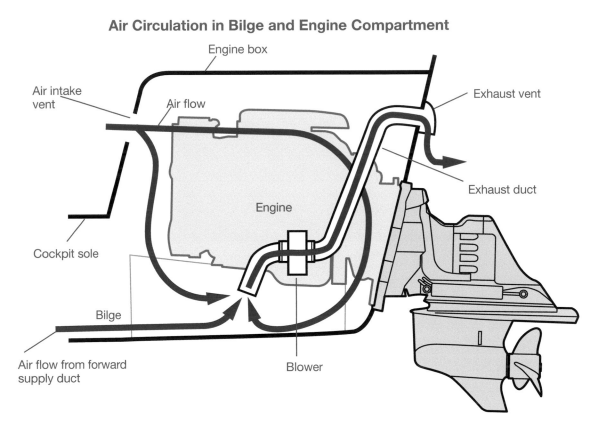

Engine box

Air intake vent

Air flow

Exhaust vent

Exhaust duct

Engine

Cockpit sole

Bilge

Blower

Air flow from forward supply duct

BACKFIRE FLAME ARRESTORS

All inboard gasoline engines must have a U.S. Coast Guard approved carburetor backfire flame arrestor on each carburetor to prevent the risk of fire if a backfire occurs. These flame arrestors should be routinely cleaned or replaced.

A flame arrestor controls a backfire flame should it occur. Use only a flame arrestor suitable for marine use.

MINIMUM REQUIRED SAFETY EQUIPMENT

Equipment	Class A < 16 ft.	Class 1 16 < 26 ft.	Class 2 26 < 40 ft.	Class 3 40-65 ft.
Life Jackets	One U.S. Coast Guard approved wearable life jacket for each person on board or being towed on water skis, plus one throwable device for boats 16 feet and over.			
Whistle or a sounding device, such as a horn	Vessels less than 39.4 ft. (12 meters) must carry an efficient sound-producing device.		Vessels 39.4 ft. (12 meters) or longer must carry a whistle.	
Bell	Not required on Class A, Class 1 or Class 2 vessels.			Vessels 39.4 ft. (12 meters) or longer must carry a bell.
Fire Extinguishers	One B-I extinguisher. Not required on outboard boat less than 26 feet, or boat is open construction and has no permanent or enclosed fuel tanks.		Two B-I fire extinguishers, or one B-II fire extinguisher.	Three B-I fire extinguishers, or one B-I and one B-II fire extinguishers.
Visual Distress Signals (coastal waters only)	Required only when operating at night.	Signals for day and night use are required. Examples are: orange smoke signal (day) and S-O-S electric light (night); or three red flares (day/night).		

WATER POLLUTION

The Refuse Act of 1899 prohibits throwing, discharging or depositing any refuse matter of any kind (e.g., trash, garbage and oil) into the waters of the United States.

GARBAGE MANAGEMENT

Under the Provisions of MARPOL, Annex V, limitations are placed on the discharge of garbage from vessels. It is illegal to dump plastic anywhere in the ocean or navigable waters of the United States. It is illegal to discharge garbage in the navigable waters of the United States including the inland waters and the Great Lakes. States and local laws may have additional restrictions. Vessels 26 feet or longer must display, in a prominent place, a durable placard of at least 4 inches by 9 inches notifying passengers and crew of these restrictions. Offshore vessels 40 feet or longer with a galley and berths must have a written waste management plan and a designated person responsible for it.

DISCHARGE OF GARBAGE

U.S Navigable Water to 3 Miles From Shore:
Illegal: Plastic; any garbage

Legal: Greywater (shower, sinks); dishwater

3 to 12 Miles From Shore:
Illegal: Plastic. If 1 square inch or larger: food, waste, paper, rags, glass, crockery, metal, dunnage

Legal: Greywater; dishwater. If smaller than 1 square inch: food, waste, paper, rags, glass, crockery, metal

12 to 25 Miles From Shore:
Illegal: Plastic; dunnage

Legal: Greywater; dishwater; food waste; paper; rags; glass; crockery; metal

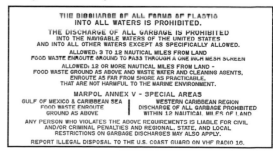

A placard with restrictions on garbage discharge must be displayed on vessels 26 feet or longer.

OIL OR HAZARDOUS MATERIAL POLLUTION

The Federal Water Pollution Control Act prohibits the discharge of oil or hazardous substances that may be harmful to U.S. navigable waters. All mechanically powered vessels are required to retain oily mixtures on board and draining oil or oily waste into the bilge is prohibited. Spilled or leaking oil usually end up in the bilge and it is against the law to pump bilge water overboard if it is contaminated. Acceptable methods of retention of oily or hazardous mixtures for disposal at a reception facility ashore include: oil absorbent pads or sheets, buckets, bailers and plastic bags. Vessels 26 feet or longer must display an Oil Discharge Prohibited placard of at least 5 inches by 8 inches in machinery spaces or at the bilge pump station.

If a vessel discharges oil or a hazardous substance in the water, the operator or owner must immediately notify the U.S. Coast Guard at this toll-free number: 800-424-8802. The following information must be reported: location, source, substance, description, color, size, date and time observed.

SEWAGE POLLUTION

The Clean Water Act prohibits the discharge of untreated or inadequately treated sewage into the navigable waters of the United States, which includes coastal waters up to three miles offshore. The Act established No-Discharge Zones (NDZs) where the discharge of any treated and untreated sewage is prohibited. Freshwater lakes and reservoirs are NDZs. The EPA maintains a list of no-discharge zones, which is available online.

Installed toilets (*heads*) on all vessels must be U.S. Coast Guard approved Type I, II or III marine sanitation devices (MSDs), which are designed to treat, discharge or retain sewage. This requirement does not apply to portable toilets. Type I MSDs are restricted to boats 65 feet long or less and treat the sewage to specified standards before being discharged overboard. Type II MSDs are required for vessels greater than 65 feet and have higher treatment standards for the discharged effluent than Type I units. Type III MSDs prevent the overboard discharge of treated or untreated sewage by pumping it into a holding tank. U.S. Coast Guard approved Type I and II MSDs are identified with certification labels. No label is required for holding tanks that hold sewage at ambient temperatures and pressures.

Pumpout stations are used to empty holding tanks and toilet dump stations are available for portable toilets. Information on the availability of these locations varies considerably from state to

DISCHARGE OF OIL PROHIBITED
An Oil Discharge Prohibited placard must be displayed on vessels 26 feet or longer, stating the following:

The Federal Water Pollution Control Act prohibits the discharge of oil or oily waste upon or into any navigable waters of the United States. This prohibition includes any discharge that causes a film or discoloration of the surface of the water, or causes a sludge or emulsion beneath the surface of the water. Violators are subject to substantial civil and/or criminal sanctions, including fines and imprisonment.

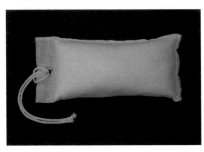

Oil absorbent pad

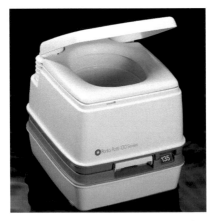

Portable toilets are often the choice for small powerboats. They can be easily carried on and off the boat.

state. In some cases locations are posted on websites. Some nautical almanacs, such as Reed's, include pumpout station locations. You can also check with your local U.S. Coast Guard District or state boating office for the latest information on pumpout station locations and no-discharge zones.

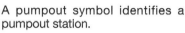

A pumpout symbol identifies a pumpout station.

NEGLIGENT OPERATION

Negligent or grossly negligent operation of a vessel that endangers lives and/or property is prohibited by law. Grossly negligent operation is a criminal offense and an operator may be fined up to $5,000, imprisoned for one year, or both. Examples that may constitute negligent or grossly negligent operation include:

- Operating a boat in a designated swimming area

- Operating a boat while under the influence of alcohol or drugs

- Excessive speed in the vicinity of other boats or in regulated waters

- Hazardous waterskiing or other water sports practices

- Bowriding or riding on the seatback, gunwale or transom.

SPEED REGULATIONS

Boats must be operated within posted speed limits at all times. When no limits are posted, a boat must be operated at a speed so it will not endanger others. This includes proceeding at a speed below wake-producing speeds (below 5 mph) when passing marinas, docks with boats tied alongside, restricted anchorages and swimming areas. You are responsible for any damage caused by the wake of your boat. Navigation Rule 6 defines *safe speed* as a speed that will allow a vessel to take proper and effective action to avoid collision and be stopped within a distance appropriate to the prevailing circumstances and conditions.

TERMINATION OF USE ACT

This act gives the Coast Guard the authority to board a vessel at any time without permission or a warrant. If an unsafe condition is found, the boat operator must follow the directions of the Coast Guard Boarding Officer to take immediate steps necessary for the safety of those aboard. These steps may include direction to: (a) correct the unsafe condition immediately; (b) proceed to a mooring, dock or anchorage; or (c) suspend further use of the boat until the condition is corrected.

For the purpose of the Act, an unsafe condition includes:

- insufficient number of U.S. Coast Guard approved life jackets

- improper display of navigation lights

- insufficient fire extinguishers

- an overloaded boat

- fuel leakage or fuel in bilges

- improper ventilation of fuel tanks and engine spaces

- improper backfire flame control

- an obvious unsafe situation

BOATING ACCIDENTS

The highest incidents of accidents occur in good weather, in the mid-to-late afternoon, and during peak boating periods. Most non-fatal boating accidents result from collisions with other boats, but the predominance of fatalities occur because of capsizing and falling overboard.

A formal accident report must be submitted within 48 hours if a person dies or disappears or there are injuries requiring more than first aid. A formal report must be submitted within ten days for accidents involving more than $2,000 damage or the complete loss of a vessel. Accident report forms may be obtained at any office where boats are registered. State requirements for reporting boating accidents may be more stringent than federal requirements. Check with local marine patrol or the state Boating Law Administrator.

ALCOHOL ABUSE

Boating accident statistics continue to show a high correlation between boating fatalities and alcohol use. Even in small amounts, ingestion of alcohol impairs vision, coordination, balance, awareness and judgment, and increases effects of sun and fatigue. It also hastens the body's heat loss thus shortening survival time in the water.

Because of alcohol-related boating accidents, most states have enacted operating under the influence laws. A blood alcohol content of 0.08 (0.10 in some states) or greater constitutes being legally intoxicated. Most of these laws also allow an officer to make a determination of intoxication based on observation of an operator's behavior. Refusal to submit to toxicological testing is automatic presumption of intoxication.

ACCIDENT REPORTING

Immediate notification is required if a person dies or disappears as a result of a recreational boating accident. The following notification should be provided to the nearest state boating authority.

- *Date, time and location of the accident*

- *Name of each person who died or disappeared*

- *Number and name of the vessel*

- *Name and address of the owner and the operator*

WARNING

Operating a boat while under the influence of alcohol, a controlled substance, or a combination of drugs and alcohol impairs the ability to operate a boat safely, causes accidents, and is illegal.

RENDERING ASSISTANCE

A person in charge of a vessel is required by the Navigation Rules to assist any individual in danger at sea if it can be done without seriously endangering the vessel or those on board. Failure to render assistance will result in a fine of up to $1,000 or imprisonment up to two years. A person rendering assistance in good faith to others who do not object is not liable for damages if he or she acts reasonably and prudently.

SAFETY & SECURITY ZONES

These zones were established to prevent attacks on U.S. Naval vessels, commercial ships and critical infrastructure. You should not operate your boat near military vessels, cruise ships, commercial ships, commercial port operations, power plants and facilities for military and petroleum operations. Additionally, you should not stop or anchor under bridges or in shipping channels. Violations of these zones could result in legal action or injury.

NAVAL VESSEL PROTECTION ZONE

This zone has specific restrictions. You must not approach within 100 yards of any U.S. Naval vessel, and you must operate at minimum speed within 500 yards. If you need to pass within 100 yards to ensure a safe passage in accordance with the Navigation Rules, you must contact the U.S. Naval vessel or the U.S. Coast Guard escort vessel on VHF radio (Channel 16) for authorization. Violations of the Naval Vessel Protection Zone are a felony offense, punishable by up to 6 years in prison and/or up to $250,000 in fines.

REVIEW QUESTIONS

1. A wearable type of life jacket that is not designed to turn an unconscious person over from a face down position to face up is a/an_____.
   a. Offshore life jacket   b. Flotation aid   c. Near-Shore life jacket

2. All boats operating in U.S. coastal waters, the Great Lakes, territorial seas and those waters connected directly to them up to a point where they narrow to less than _____ are required to carry U.S. Coast Guard approved visual distress signals.
   a. 2 miles   b. 5 miles   c. 10 miles

3. The minimum number of hand-portable fire extinguishers required on a recreational boat is based on the _____ of the boat.

4. No-Discharge Zones prohibit the discharge of any _____ and _____ sewage.

5. A person in charge of a vessel is required by law to provide assistance to any individual in danger at sea if it can be done without seriously _____ the vessel or those on board.

Chapter 11

ONBOARD SYSTEMS

KEY CONCEPTS

▶ Electrical systems

▶ Marine VHF/DSC radio

▶ Bilge systems

▶ Marine Sanitation Devices (MSDs)

▶ Fresh water systems

▶ Sumps

▶ Stoves

▶ HVAC systems

This chapter covers the basics of essential systems you will encounter on board most powerboats, but we suggest you also read and study manufacturers' manuals for more complete information on the specific systems used on your boat.

ELECTRICAL SYSTEMS

Powerboats are capable of hosting two types of electrical systems: direct current (DC) and alternating current (AC). The DC system powers the general operation of the boat. Common examples are the starter motor to turn on the engine, lights, pumps, stereo and VHF radio. The AC system uses 120 volts or 240 volts to power the larger, house-type fixtures and appliances such as the HVAC system, TV, microwave and power tools. When these two systems are present on a boat, they are separate and do not crossover. While some onboard refrigerators may be capable of accepting both AC and DC power, marine systems will use one or the other.

DIRECT CURRENT SYSTEM

Direct current begins and ends with the battery. From the battery, current flows first to the battery selector switch and then to the starting system and a DC breaker panel. In smaller boats, there is generally one battery used for both starting and other electrical circuits, while larger boats may have multiple batteries and multiple battery switches to separate starting batteries from house or domestic batteries. In both cases, the battery switch acts as the first gate between the battery and the rest of the DC system. When in the OFF position, electricity cannot flow. The automatic bilge pump and safety alarms (e.g., bilge water level, smoke, propane leakage) are usually wired separately to the battery allowing them to continue to operate.

DC breaker panel

Whenever you start an engine, turn on lights or other equipment, power is drained from the batteries. Two primary methods by which to charge the batteries are: the alternator; and an AC converter or battery charger. When the engine is running, its alternator creates DC electricity and charges the batteries. The AC converter requires an AC electrical source like shore power or a generator to convert alternating current into direct current and thereby charge the batteries.

Most battery switches have four positions: 1, 2, ALL (BOTH) and OFF. To start the engine, set the battery switch to either 1 or 2. If the charge is too low to turn over the engine, first switch to the other battery; if this doesn't work, switch to ALL (BOTH). In the case of boats with two or more engines, a parallel switch (or emergency start button) will allow access to the combined charge from two or more batteries to get one engine and its alternator running.

ALTERNATING CURRENT SYSTEM

AC electricity is the same type of electricity found in American homes. Boats with an AC system are equipped with a shore power inlet that allows you to connect to a dock's AC power supply with a shore power cord. When away from the dock, boats equipped with an AC generator (genset) or power inverter can create AC electricity without being plugged into shore power, allowing for full use of the AC system.

AC electricity is distributed to the boat through an AC breaker panel, very similar to and often located near the DC breaker panel. If more than one AC power source is available to the boat an AC selector switch will be present, allowing you to choose which AC source you'd like to use so as not to overload the system. Once a source has been selected it's important to take note of the warning light labeled Reverse Polarity. The reverse polarity system monitors the electricity coming into the boat to ensure that it is exclusively fed through the hot wire and returning through the neutral wire. Any other combination of feed and return will activate the reverse polarity light, warning that this power supply is not safe to use. If the light is not lit, then it is safe to use that AC power to the various fixtures, appliances and receptacles using the provided breakers.

SWITCHING FROM SHORE POWER TO GENERATOR

When switching from one AC source to another, it's important to fully unload one source by turning off the electrical outlets, then their breakers and lastly the main switch for the source and then slowly add load to the new source by reversing the sequence. Generators prefer to run under load powering multiple circuits such as the battery charger, refrigerator,

Battery switch allows management of multiple batteries.

AC breaker panel

Shore power outlets provide electricity for charging batteries if the boat's electrical system has an AC converter or battery charger. The prongs of a shore power cord are keyed so that you can only connect to a supply that matches your boat's AC needs.

GENSET TIPS

- *Run engine room blower for at least four minutes before starting a gasoline-powered genset.*

- *Some gensets need to be preheated.*

- *Check exhaust outlet for consistent water flow. If no water, immediately turn off the genset.*

TV and HVAC. It's not advisable to exclusively run small receptacles like the battery charger on the genset.

Battery Inspection

- Batteries and their boxes are secured and should always have a cover to avoid shorting the terminals inadvertently.

- Batteries should not be located in a confined space where accumulated battery gases may be exposed to an electrical spark and cause an explosion.

- Make sure battery terminals have no corrosion and cables are securely attached.

- Check the fluid levels of the batteries, if possible.

- Insulation on electrical wires is in good condition with no cracks or worn spots.

Start Powerboating Right!

BATTERY TIPS

- *Keep your batteries charged.*

- *Turn off electrical fixtures and equipment when not in use.*

- *Leave battery switches in the OFF position when leaving your boat.*

- *Don't reposition the battery switch with the engine running without first checking the electrical system manual to see whether this can cause a problem.*

MARINE VHF/DSC RADIO

The marine VHF radiotelephone system is a line-of-sight, Very High Frequency system and provides local marine weather forecasts, two-way voice communication with nearby boats and marinas, and access to emergency assistance. The VHF radio is limited by horizon, typically 10 to 15 miles for ship-to-ship communication and 20 to 30 miles for ship-to-shore, depending on the height of the antennas. At the low-power setting, these ranges are reduced. Hand-held VHF radios typically have ranges of only a few miles.

Digital Selective Calling (DSC)

DSC allows boaters to send or receive distress, urgency, safety and routine radiotelephone calls to or from any similarly equipped vessel or shore station. You can direct dial and call vessels with DSC and others can call you without broadcasting the call to all radios. Users of a VHF/DSC radio must obtain a Maritime Mobile Service Identity (MMSI) number which is available from BoatUS, the FCC, Sea Tow or the United States Power Squadrons. When the Distress button is activated, an automatically formatted distress alert will be instantly sent to the U.S. Coast Guard and any DSC radio within range. This alert will send the following information: your MMSI number; latitude and longitude position (radio must be connected to a GPS); and the nature of distress if entered. The U.S. Coast Guard's response to your distress alert will automatically switch your radio to Channel 16 for voice communication.

Distress button   Squelch

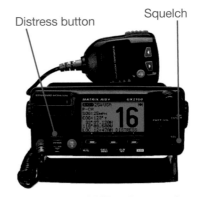

Fixed-mount VHF radios use the boat's battery for power and are required to have DSC if made after 1999. Adjust the squelch control by turning it down just under the crackling sound.

CHANNEL DESIGNATIONS

Each channel is authorized for a specific purpose. Check your nautical almanac or go to the U.S. Coast Guard Navigation Center website for a complete list of channel designations.

The channels of greatest interest to the recreational boater are:

Channel		Purpose
WX1-WX7	**Weather**	Provides continuous local marine weather forecasts, including storm warnings and watches.
09	**Boater Calling**	Is a supplementary calling channel for recreational boaters to relieve congestion on Channel 16. It is NOT an emergency channel. In some states, it is used for bridge openings.
13, 67	**Navigation Safety**	Used to communicate navigational information between vessels, such as meeting and passing situations. Vessels greater than 20 meters (65.6 feet) long maintain a listening watch on Channel 13 in U.S. waters (67 for lower Mississippi River). Channel 13 is used at some drawbridges.
16	**Distress, Safety & Calling**	Used in emergencies, or to get attention for calling another station. Except in an emergency, upon receiving a response, advise the other boat to switch to a non-commercial channel. Routine radio checks are prohibited on this channel.
1022 (or 22A*)	**U.S. Coast Guard Liaison and Maritime Safety Information Broadcasts**	Is the principal channel for communication with the Coast Guard, except for distress and safety calls on Channel 16. It is monitored constantly and is the source for marine information broadcasts.
68, 69, 71 & 1078 (or 78A*)	**Non-commercial**	Used for intership (boat-to-boat) and ship-to-shore communication for recreational boaters. Switch to one of these channels after initiating on Channel 16 (or 09).
70	**Digital Selective Calling**	Restricted to Digital Selective Calling (DSC) communication.
72	**Non-commercial**	Restricted to only intership (boat-to-boat) communication for recreational boaters.

*Channel number on old VHF radios. To use, set U/I/C switch to U for U.S. setting.

Most hand-held VHF radios do not have DSC with GPS capability, but this one does. Note display of the latitude/longitude position.

Radio Communication Basics

- The high/low power switch on a VHF radio allows the user to select a power transmitter setting. Most communications should be attempted on the low power setting and only switched to high if needed.

- Use only those channels identified for recreational boating.

- Radio communication is public and shared. Speak clearly, be brief, and don't use profanity.

- Any vessel calling in an emergency always has priority.

- To make an intership (boat-to-boat) call:

  1. Initiate the call on Channel 16 or 09 if it is the designated calling channel for your area. Note: DSC Channel 70 may be used for intership when MMSI of vessel being called is known.

  2. Identify the boat you're calling, then identify your boat by saying "This is" followed by your boat's name. **Example:** *"Resolute, Resolute, Resolute. This is Sabino. Over."* Over indicates this is the end of my transmission and a response is desired.

  3. Once contact is made, you must switch to a non-commercial channel if both of you are recreational boaters.

- The procedures for calling a shore station are the same, except if the shore station has an assigned operating channel, call them on that frequency instead of Channel 16 or 09.

- To end a call:

  1. Each boat must give its name followed by the word "Out." Out indicates this is the end of my transmission and no response is desired or required. Do not use "over" or "over and out." **Example**: "This is *Resolute*. Out." and "*Sabino*. Out."

  2. Both boats switch back to Channel 16.

- DSC Distress alerts or Mayday distress calls are made when a vessel or person is threatened by grave and imminent danger requiring immediate assistance. To send a DSC Distress alert, push and hold the Distress button until a beep is heard (don't push it more than once). When the Coast Guard receives your distress call your VHF automatically switches to Channel 16, and you should be prepared to answer their questions about your situation. To make a Mayday distress call, repeat Mayday three times followed by "This is" and repeat your boat's name three times. **Example: "Mayday, Mayday, Mayday**. This is *Lead Balloon, Lead Balloon, Lead Balloon*." This is followed by your distress message—remember the three Ws: WHO you are, WHERE you are, and WHAT is your type of distress, assistance desired, and any other information to help with the rescue. **Example: "Mayday, Mayday, Mayday**. This is *Lead Balloon, Lead Balloon, Lead Balloon*. We are one nautical mile east of Cape May. We are on fire and sinking. Two people are severely injured. Request immediate assistance. There is a total of five people on board. Boat is a 40-foot powerboat with white deck and topsides. Sending up red parachute flares and activating EPIRB. Over."

- Pan-Pan (pahn-pahn) urgency calls are made when there is a very urgent message concerning the safety (but is not life-threatening) of a vessel or some person on board or within sight. Use "**Pan-Pan, Pan-Pan, Pan-Pan**" instead of "**Mayday, Mayday, Mayday**."

- Sécurité (see-cur-ee-tay) calls are used to send a message concerning the safety of navigation or giving important meteorological warnings. Sécurité is spoken three times.

BILGE SYSTEMS

The bilge is where water collects from leaks, rain, waves or wash downs in the bottom of a boat. Many powerboats have a drainage system that drains water from the bilge through drain holes in the transom when the boat is hauled out of the water. These are closed with drain plugs, which are either screwed in or locked in place using a lever. *Make sure these plugs are secured before launching your boat.*

This lever-type drain plug can be easily removed to drain the bilge and secured in place to prevent loosening from vibration.

Boats that have a battery system for lights and electrical equipment usually have an electric bilge pump. These pumps can be manually activated but often have a float switch that turns on the pump when water in the bilge reaches a certain level. Boats with electric pumps should also carry buckets or manual pumps for emergencies.

There are drainage systems on some small boats that allow bilge water to exit the stern when the boat is at planing speed. Boats with this system will have drain plugs or valves accessible from inside the boat.

Electric bilge pumps Ⓐ can be automatically activated by a float switch Ⓑ.

BILGE SYSTEM INSPECTION

- Check the bilge regularly for water or oil. If there is any oil, it cannot be pumped overboard and must be collected for disposal ashore.

- Carry extra drain plugs.

- Stow manual bilge pumps or pump handles in an accessible location.

- Keep intake screens on bilge pumps free of debris.

- Make sure float switch on electric pump operates freely.

MARINE SANITATION DEVICES (MSDs)

Marine heads generally do not have the capacity of toilets in the home. They tolerate less toilet paper and NO foreign objects. Raw water (seawater) is pumped into the bowl and the discharge is pumped into a holding tank or treatment device. With an electrically operated head, a push button is used to flush it. Manually operated heads have a hand or foot lever or a twist knob that is used to let water into the bowl while a pump handle is used to pump the water in and out of the bowl. Whatever head type is used, always make sure the raw water seacock is open before using, and close the valves, seacock(s) and seat lid when finished.

MSD TIPS

- *Make sure all valves and seacock(s) are open before using.*

- *Stop pumping if you encounter resistance.*

- *Don't put anything in the head except a small amount of toilet paper and human waste.*

- *Close valves and seacock(s) after using.*

- *Leave area clean for the next person.*

MSD System

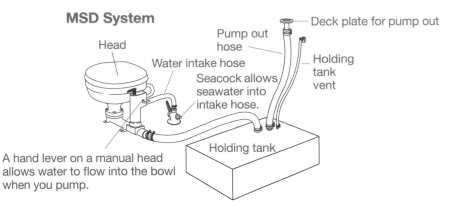

A hand lever on a manual head allows water to flow into the bowl when you pump.

Manual heads may have a foot lever instead of a hand lever or twist knob. Depress the pedal to let water in and release it to stop.

FRESH WATER SYSTEM

Boats carry a limited amount of fresh water in one or several water tanks, depending on the size of the boat. As a result, water conservation is always a consideration, especially if you cannot conveniently refill tanks. To help conserve water, a boat may have a manual water pressure system which you pump either with your hand or foot to get water from a faucet. Larger powerboats with several tanks and a sufficient battery system usually have a pressurized system powered by an electric pump so that water comes out of a faucet whenever you turn it on.

MANUAL HEAD
OPERATION TIPS

- *Open raw water seacock.*

- *Pump a small amount of water into the bowl before using.*

- *After flushing, pump additional strokes to make sure the discharge line is clear.*

- *Close seacock after use.*

FILLING FRESH WATER TANKS

1. Close sink faucets so water doesn't run out when filling.

2. Run the water hose for 30 seconds to clear debris before filling tanks.

3. Check the deck fill plate to see it's labeled WATER before filling.

4. After filling, tighten deck fill cap securely so water tank does not get contaminated.

Larger boats often have a pressurized water system with on/off faucets (above) and may also have a manual pump water system (operated by black handle above) to conserve water. Some manual pumps are operated by pumping a foot lever.

There is usually a deck fill cap for each water tank. Be sure you fill the one marked WATER, not WASTE or FUEL.

SUMPS

Drains from showers and iceboxes are usually below the surface of the outside seawater. They typically drain into a sump tank in the bilge that is emptied by a sump pump. If the tank is not pumped out and it fills up, water will not drain from the shower or icebox. The intake on the sump pump should be inspected and cleaned regularly to prevent clogging by debris and hair. To avoid reverse flow in the discharge line due to siphoning, the line will frequently be looped above the seawater surface with an air breaker valve at the top of the loop or exit through the hull above the seawater. Keep the air breaker valve clean. If it gets clogged, the discharge line may siphon seawater into the sump and flood the shower. Sinks are normally positioned higher than the seawater level and will usually drain directly overboard.

Shower Sump Diagram

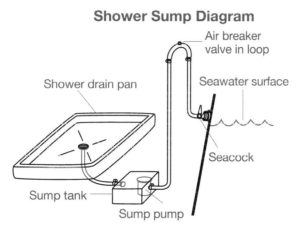

STOVES

Stoves on cruising powerboats come in several sizes and types. They can range from portable single-burner butane stoves and two-burner alcohol stoves (on smaller boats) to propane gas or electric stoves (on larger boats).

ELECTRIC STOVES

Cruising powerboats are usually equipped with electric stove tops and microwaves or a combination microwave convection oven. Due to the greater electrical load requirements, these run on the 120/240v AC system powered by the genset or shore power instead of the DC house batteries. If these galley appliances are operating while other high load appliances are running (e.g., air conditioning), you may have to manage the load between your AC power supplies.

ELECTRIC STOVE SAFETY TIPS

• *Don't overload the AC system.*

• *Stove tops can look like counter space. Don't store things on top of them.*

• *It may not be readily apparent that a stove top may still be hot after it is turned off.*

• *Fire extinguishers should be readily accessible in case of a fire.*

Keep an electric stove top clear of items, and avoid overloading the AC system when using it.

PROPANE STOVES

Stoves and ovens that use propane are commonly found on older boats. If your boat has one, it needs to be used with care because propane is heavier than air. Leaking gas can settle in the bilge and might be ignited by a spark. These systems have a solenoid which is an electrically controlled valve that will turn on or shut off the gas supply from a remote location.

When starting to cook:

1 Turn on the tank valve and then the solenoid switch.

2 Strike the match or starter before turning on the burner control.

When finished cooking:

1 Turn off the solenoid and then the burners to burn off excess fuel.

2 Check that all controls, including the oven, are off.

Propane stoves need to be used carefully. A solenoid switch allows quick shutoff of propane fuel.

Portable gas and charcoal grills may be used for barbecuing. Be considerate of others by not letting smoke from your grill drift downwind into their boats.

PROPANE STOVE SAFETY TIPS

- *Fire extinguishers should be readily accessible in case of a fire.*

- *Shut off fuel when stove is not in use.*

- *Don't leave burner oven controls on after you turn off the fuel supply.*

- *Close the tank valve when leaving the boat.*

Propane Safety System

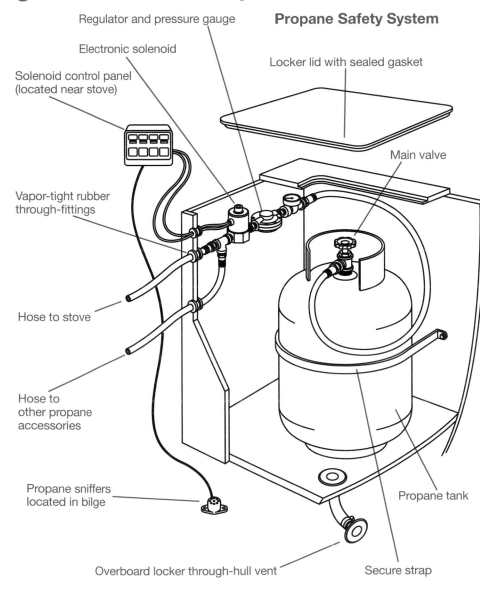

Regulator and pressure gauge

Electronic solenoid

Solenoid control panel (located near stove)

Locker lid with sealed gasket

Main valve

Vapor-tight rubber through-fittings

Hose to stove

Hose to other propane accessories

Propane sniffers located in bilge

Propane tank

Overboard locker through-hull vent

Secure strap

108

HEATING, VENTILATION & AIR CONDITIONING SYSTEMS

Powerboats with living accommodations are often equipped with heating, ventilation and air conditioning systems, also known as HVAC. HVAC systems typically draw AC power due to their high electrical demand and are water-cooled by pumping raw water from outside the boat through the unit's condenser. When using HVAC systems, make sure the seacock is open and the raw water filter is clear of debris. Additionally, the HVAC breaker and HVAC pump breaker (if present) must be turned on.

Modern HVAC systems are controlled using a wall-mounted keypad much like that of a home's thermostat. Similarly, a boat's thermostat can be set to a specific temperature to automatically regulate the system's heating and cooling output to match the set temperature. Thermostats equipped with a dehumidification mode can reduce the moisture in the air by intermittently cycling the HVAC unit, which avoids overloading the system by running nonstop.

HVAC SYSTEMS TIPS

- *Do not cover up the return air vent with pillows or blankets.*
- *Check HVAC unit's exhaust outlet for consistent water flow. If no water, immediately turn off the HVAC system.*
- *Turn off HVAC system when not on board, unless it is capable of running in dehumidification mode*
- *Dehumidification mode helps preserve the boat's interior when no one is aboard.*
- *HVAC pumps are not self-priming and may need to be burped or bled after the boat is launched.*
- *The condensation tray under the HVAC unit is prone to algae growth and requires regular cleaning. Allowing growth to build up may add an unpleasant odor to the air coming from HVAC vents.*

HVAC keypad

REVIEW QUESTIONS

1. *The type of electrical system most powerboats use for starting, instruments, bilge pumps and lights is a* _____.
   a. 6-volt DC   b. 9-volt DC   c. 12-volt DC

2. *Except for distress and safety calls, when contacting the U.S. Coast Guard on a marine VHF radio, the preferred channel to use is* _____.
   a. 16   b. 1022 (or 22A)   c. 71

3. *When a person or vessel is in grave and imminent danger, the VHF distress call is preceded by the word* _____ *spoken three times.*

4. *Before using a manual or electrical pump on a marine toilet, make sure the raw water* _____ *is open.*

5. *Propane gas must be handled with care because it is* _____ *than air and can settle in the bilge.*

This chiller in the engine room is part of a chilled water HVAC system used on larger powerboats which uses fresh water instead of a refrigerant to cool or heat the cabin spaces.

Answers: 1) c. 12-volt DC
2) b. 1022 (or 22A)
3) Mayday
4) seacock
5) heavier

Do not cover up HVAC air vents with pillows or other items.

Chapter 12

THE ENVIRONMENT

KEY CONCEPTS

▶ Weather

▶ Winds

▶ Thunderstorms

▶ Tides & currents

Weather, tides and currents play an important role in the success and enjoyment of a trip or a day's outing. Current weather conditions and forecasts are found in newspapers, on the radio, television and the internet. Additionally, weather applications with real-time information and alerts can be downloaded onto your smartphone, and many chart plotter systems provide real-time weather data.

Get in the habit of keeping track of the weather to get a picture of upcoming weather. While on the water, be constantly aware of what is happening in the sky and periodically check weather broadcasts on your VHF radio or smartphone.

WEATHER

North American weather systems generally move from west to east. The speed at which these systems move depends on many factors. These include their strength, the location of the jet stream and the time of year. Typically, weather a couple of hundred miles to the west of you can be your weather for tomorrow.

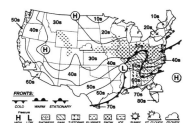

This newspaper weather map shows high and low pressure systems, fronts, types of precipitation, sky conditions and temperatures.

A high pressure system (H) usually indicates dry, sunny weather with cooler air and lighter winds than low pressure systems.

A low pressure system (L) is usually accompanied by a warm or cold front and inclement weather with stronger winds, rain and sometimes storms.

A weather chart downloaded to a smartphone.

A front develops when colder, dry air meets warmer, moist air.

Warm fronts occur when lighter, warmer air rides up over heavier, cooler air. This front usually moves more slowly (about half the speed) than a cold front and brings overcast skies, rain and bad weather with the possibility of thunderstorms and strong winds. High cirrus clouds are first seen as the front approaches. After a warm front has passed, the air will be warmer. *TIP: Remember the symbol for a warm front as boiling bubbles.*

Cold fronts occur when heavier, cooler air pushes under lighter, warmer air. It moves rapidly and is often accompanied by towering cumulus or cumulonimbus clouds, rain, strong winds and possible thunderstorms. After a cold front has passed, the air will be cooler. *TIP: The symbol for a cold front can be remembered as icicles on a wire.*

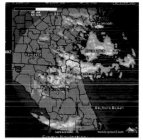

An example of a radar image from a smartphone.

Observation	Prediction
Sun and clear sky in the morning	Onshore winds during the day and offshore winds (land breezes) during the night, usually dying in the morning.
Thermal sea breeze	Increasing strength during the day as the land heats up and decreasing or dying at night as the land cools. Expect the wind to veer clockwise as velocity increases. In some parts of the country, increasing sea breezes will be accompanied by growing cumulus clouds.
Calm, overcast days	Continued calm and overcast, unless the sun comes out.
Cold and warm fronts	Showers or rain, changing air temperature, winds shifting in a clockwise direction. Cold fronts usually move faster than warm fronts.
High cirrus clouds	A warm front with rain and changing winds should appear in a couple of days. Clouds will get lower and more dense as the front gets closer.
Cumulus clouds growing taller (cumulonimbus)	Thunderstorms and strong winds
Dark clouds approaching	A squall or storm

Barometers help predict weather by measuring atmospheric pressure. Usually, a rising barometer signals good weather; a falling one warns of poor weather.

Wispy, thin cirrus clouds often mean good weather for the day, but also predict an approaching change in the weather.

White, puffy cumulus clouds are often an indicator of good weather, and are typically seen after a cold front has passed through.

Towering cumulonimbus clouds, or thunderheads, are usually accompanied by heavy rain, strong winds and lightning.

Bays and harbors can be shrouded in fog when warm, moist air from the land meets cold water and cools below its dew point.

PERSONAL OBSERVATION

Recognizing the patterns of weather systems and local conditions is an important part of your preparation and awareness on land and on the water. Be observant and learn to recognize the signals of impending weather from changes in wind direction, cloud patterns, air temperature and atmospheric pressure.

THUNDERSTORMS

The familiar afternoon forecast of a 20% chance of thunderstorms can sound routine, but few weather phenomena can threaten boaters as quickly and as dramatically as a thunderstorm. They often advance on the heels of a sea breeze and, if not detected early, can overtake you before you can reach safe haven. The first clue of their approach might be a distant, high altitude arc of cirrus clouds that often forms above cumulonimbus clouds. Any change in the color, shape or size of clouds means some change in weather is coming. The more pronounced the change, the more significant the weather. As a thunderstorm develops, the top part of the thundercloud becomes anvil-shaped and streams in the direction that the storm is moving. The wind ahead of a thunderstorm can be variable or steady, and may weaken and die as the storm approaches. When the roll cloud passes overhead, the wind will shift and blow violently with gusts that can exceed 50 knots. Heavy rain begins just behind the roll cloud.

A distant cumulonimbus cloud with a clearly visible anvil is probably going to pass to the side of you, but a rapidly growing cumulonimbus cloud with no visible anvil may be headed in your direction. Many storms develop erratic paths so their direction could suddenly change. The rough distance to a storm may be determined by timing the interval between a lightning flash and the associated thunderclap. Divide the time in seconds by five for the distance in statute miles.

Squalls often accompany cold fronts and bring strong winds. If you see a squall line developing, it's time to seek shelter.

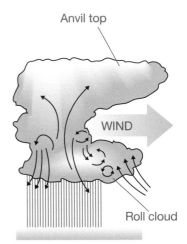

The anvil top of a thundercloud streams in the direction that the storm is moving.

BAD WEATHER SIGNALS

- *Increase in cloud cover and darkening skies*
- *Sudden decrease or increase in wind velocity*
- *Change in wind direction*
- *Lightning nearby or in the distance*
- *Thunder in the distance*
- *Gusty wind conditions*

Both sides of cloud Ⓐ are moving to the right of the boat; the storm should miss and pass to your right.

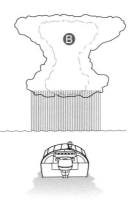

The left side of cloud Ⓑ is moving to the left and the right side to the right; this indicates you are in its path.

WINDS

Winds are created from pressure differences in the atmosphere, blowing from higher to lower pressure. Winds can be generated by major weather systems or local conditions.

WINDS AROUND A LOW PRESSURE SYSTEM

In a low pressure system, the pressure decreases as you move toward its center, which will cause air to blow inward toward the center. The rotation of the earth will make this air spiral inward in a counterclockwise direction in the northern hemisphere.

WINDS AROUND A HIGH PRESSURE SYSTEM

In a high pressure system, the pressure increases as you move toward its center, which will cause air to blow outward from the center. However, the turning of the earth causes this air to spiral out in a clockwise direction in the northern hemisphere.

ONSHORE/SEA & OFFSHORE/LAND WINDS

Local winds can be caused by the differences in air temperature over land and water. Onshore sea breezes are formed as warm air rises above the land, drawing in cooler air from over the water. As the land heats up in the afternoon, the velocity of these winds will increase. Local offshore land winds often occur at night or in the morning when the land has cooled and the warmer air over the water rises, drawing cooler air from over the land.

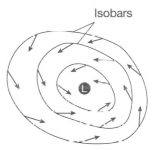

Wind spirals inward and counterclockwise around a low pressure system **L** generally following the concentric lines on the map called isobars. Tightly spaced isobars indicate strong winds.

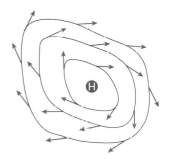

Wind spirals outward and clockwise around a high pressure system **H**.

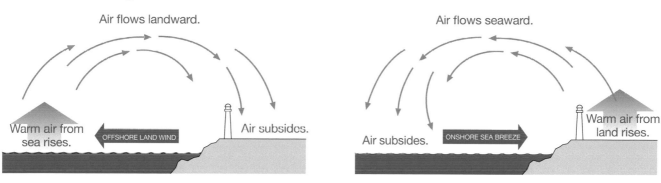

TOPOGRAPHIC EFFECTS ON WINDS

Wind direction and strength can be affected by local topography. For instance, on rivers surrounded by elevated land, the wind will tend to funnel down or up the river, following bends in the river.

TIDES

Tides are the vertical movement (rise and fall) of water and are caused by the gravitational effects of our planet and the moon, and to a lesser degree by the sun. As the moon rotates around the earth, it affects the rise and fall of water. Tides are also influenced by topography, geography and weather patterns. The frequency of high and low tides and their heights will vary by location because of the combination of these factors. But with a watch, a tide table and chart, you can determine the depth of the water in which you will be motoring or anchoring at any given time.

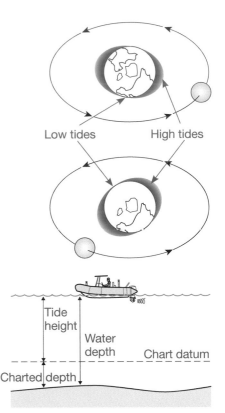

Low tides   High tides

TIDE TABLES & GRAPHS

These give daily information regarding the times of high and low tides and their heights. They are depicted in graphical and tabular formats and can be downloaded from the internet. The heights from the tide table or graph are added (unless they have negative sign, in which case they are subtracted) to the depth shown on the nautical chart to determine the actual water depth at a particular location at high or low tide. Choose a tide station specific for your location and note what time is used (e.g., Daylight Savings Time, Standard Time or Greenwich Mean Time).

To determine the actual depth of water at low or high tide, add the height from the tide table or graph to the depth on the nautical chart. If the height has a negative sign, then subtract it.

Tide Predictions - Tabular Format

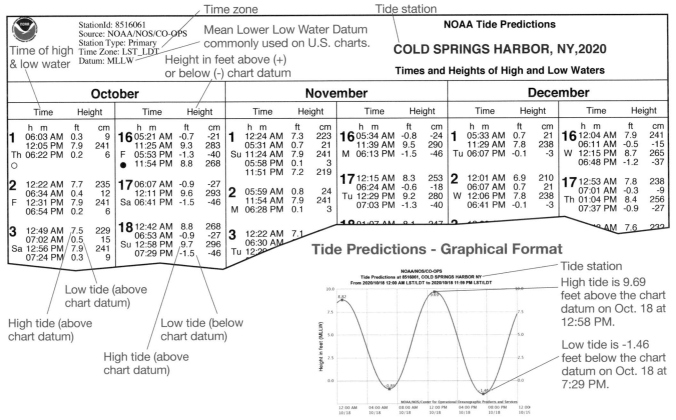

Time zone

Tide station

Time of high & low water

StationId: 8516061
Source: NOAA/NOS/CO-OPS
Station Type: Primary
Time Zone: LST_LDT
Datum: MLLW

Mean Lower Low Water Datum commonly used on U.S. charts.

Height in feet above (+) or below (-) chart datum

NOAA Tide Predictions

COLD SPRINGS HARBOR, NY,2020

Times and Heights of High and Low Waters

	October								November								December						
	Time	Height			Time	Height			Time	Height			Time	Height			Time	Height			Time	Height	
	h m	ft	cm		h m	ft	cm		h m	ft	cm		h m	ft	cm		h m	ft	cm		h m	ft	cm
1 06:03 AM	0.3	9	**16** 05:21 AM	-0.7	-21	**1** 12:24 AM	7.3	223	**16** 05:34 AM	-0.8	-24	**1** 05:33 AM	0.7	21	**16** 12:04 AM	7.9	241
12:05 PM	7.9	241	11:25 AM	9.3	283	05:31 AM	0.7	21	11:39 AM	9.5	290	11:29 AM	7.8	238	06:11 AM	-0.5	-15
Th 06:22 PM	0.2	6	F 05:53 PM	-1.3	-40	Su 11:24 AM	7.9	241	M 06:13 PM	-1.5	-46	Tu 06:07 PM	-0.1	-3	W 12:15 PM	8.7	265
○			● 11:54 PM	8.8	268	05:58 PM	0.1	3							06:48 PM	-1.2	-37
						11:51 PM	7.2	219										
2 12:22 AM	7.7	235	**17** 06:07 AM	-0.9	-27				**17** 12:15 AM	8.3	253	**2** 12:01 AM	6.9	210	**17** 12:53 AM	7.8	238
06:34 AM	0.4	12	12:11 PM	9.6	293	**2** 05:59 AM	0.8	24	06:24 AM	-0.6	-18	06:07 AM	0.7	21	07:01 AM	-0.3	-9
F 12:31 PM	7.9	241	Sa 06:41 PM	-1.5	-46	11:54 AM	7.9	241	Tu 12:29 PM	9.2	280	W 12:06 PM	7.8	238	Th 01:04 PM	8.4	256
06:54 PM	0.2	6				M 06:28 PM	0.1	3	07:03 PM	-1.3	-40	06:41 PM	-0.1	-3	07:37 PM	-0.9	-27
3 12:49 AM	7.5	229	**18** 12:42 AM	8.8	268	**3** 12:22 AM	7.1		**18** 01:07 AM	8.1	247	**3**			AM	7.6	232
07:02 AM	0.5	15	06:53 AM	-0.9	-27	06:30 AM												
Sa 12:56 PM	7.9	241	Su 12:58 PM	9.7	296	Tu 12:2												
07:24 PM	0.3	9	07:29 PM	-1.5	-46													

High tide (above chart datum)

Low tide (above chart datum)

High tide (above chart datum)

Low tide (below chart datum)

Tide Predictions - Graphical Format

NOAA/NOS/CO-OPS
Tide Predictions at 8516061, COLD SPRINGS HARBOR NY
From 2020/10/18 12:00 AM LST/LDT to 2020/10/18 11:59 PM LST/LDT

Height in feet (MLLW)

8.82   9.69

-0.89   -1.46

NOAA/NOS/Center for Operational Oceanographic Products and Services

12:00 AM 04:00 AM 08:00 AM 12:00 PM 04:00 PM 08:00 PM 12:00 AM
10/18   10/18   10/18   10/18   10/18   10/18   10/19

Tide station

High tide is 9.69 feet above the chart datum on Oct. 18 at 12:58 PM.

Low tide is -1.46 feet below the chart datum on Oct. 18 at 7:29 PM.

CURRENTS

Current is the horizontal movement of water, and can be caused by a river's flow, tides, wind or ocean movements. When motoring from one point to another, a powerboat's speed over the bottom and time to its destination can be affected by the strength and direction of the current.

CURRENT TABLES & GRAPHS

These give daily information on the times of slack water and maximum ebb and flood as well as their speeds in knots (1 knot = 1 nautical mile per hour).

Tidal Current Predictions - Graphical Format

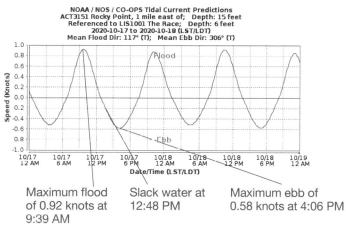

NOAA / NOS / CO-OPS Tidal Current Predictions
ACT3151 Rocky Point, 1 mile east of; Depth: 15 feet
Referenced to LIS1001 The Race; Depth: 6 feet
2020-10-17 to 2020-10-18 (LST/LDT)
Mean Flood Dir: 117° (T); Mean Ebb Dir: 306° (T)

Maximum flood of 0.92 knots at 9:39 AM

Slack water at 12:48 PM

Maximum ebb of 0.58 knots at 4:06 PM

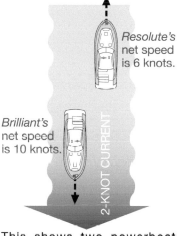

Resolute's net speed is 6 knots.

Brilliant's net speed is 10 knots.

2-KNOT CURRENT

This shows two powerboats motoring at 8 knots in a current of 2 knots. *Brilliant* has favorable current to increase its speed over the bottom (SOG) to 10 knots, while *Resolute* has to motor against the current, making only 6 knots of SOG.

Tidal Current Predictions - Tabular Format

	TIME (LST/LDT)	EVENT	SPEED (KNOTS)
2020-10-17	12:30 AM	slack	-
2020-10-17	03:42 AM	ebb	-0.52
2020-10-17	06:43 AM	slack	-
2020-10-17	09:39 AM	flood	0.92
2020-10-17	12:48 PM	slack	-
2020-10-17	04:06 PM	ebb	-0.58
2020-10-17	07:25 PM	slack	-
2020-10-17	10:09 PM	flood	0.87

Maximum flood of 0.92 knots at 9:39 AM

Slack water at 12:48 PM

Maximum ebb of 0.58 knots at 4:06 PM

EBB DEFINITION
Ebb is the direction of an outgoing current.

FLOOD DEFINITION
Flood is the direction of an incoming current.

REVIEW QUESTIONS

1. Weather generally moves from _____ to _____ in the U.S.

2. The top part of a thundercloud is an _____ shape and _____ in the direction that the storm is moving.

3. Winds rotate in a _____ direction around a low pressure system.

4. Sea breezes or onshore winds generally occur at what time of the day?
   a. morning b. afternoon c. night

5. Tides are the _____ movement of water and current is the _____ movement of water.

*Answers: 1) west; east
2) anvil; streams
3) counterclockwise
4) b. afternoon
5) vertical; horizontal*

Chapter 13

NAVIGATION RULES

KEY CONCEPTS

▶ Inland Navigation Rules

▶ International Navigation Rules

▶ Maintaining a lookout

▶ Safe speed

▶ Lights & sound signals

▶ Meeting situations

The fundamental purpose of the Navigation Rules is to help vessels avoid collisions. There are two sets of Rules. The Inland Rules apply to the navigable inland waters of the United States. These include the U.S. waters of the Great Lakes, harbors, rivers, bays and sounds on the shoreward side of the demarcation line, which defines the boundary between inland and international waters. The International Rules apply to the high seas and are known as the International Regulations for Preventing Collisions at Sea, 1972, abbreviated as 72 COLREGS. While the two sets of Rules are mostly similar, there are some notable differences in light and sound signals and situations in narrow channels. *The Navigation Rules: International-Inland* is available online, at some marine stores, or can be ordered from the U.S. Government Publishing Office.

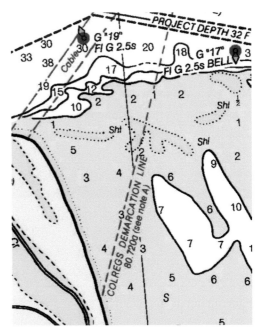

A magenta-colored demarcation line depicts the boundary where Navigation Rules change from Inland Rules to International (72 COLREGS) Rules.

MAINTAINING A PROPER LOOKOUT

A vessel shall, at all times, maintain a proper lookout by sight and hearing and any other means available.

SAFE SPEED

A vessel shall, at all times, operate at a safe speed so that proper and effective action can be taken to avoid a collision or to stop within an appropriate distance. Safe speed is determined by visibility, traffic density, the boat's maneuverability, background light at night, navigational hazards, water depth, wind, current and sea conditions.

NAVIGATION RULE 2: RESPONSIBILITY

The Navigation Rules does not exonerate any vessel, operator or crew from the consequences of:

● *any neglect to comply with the Rules or*

● *neglect of any precaution required by the ordinary seamanlike practice or by the special circumstances of the case.HVAC vents.*

Due regard shall be made to all dangers of navigation and collision, including the limitations of the vessels, which may make a departure from these Rules necessary to avoid immediate danger.

OPERATING IN NARROW CHANNELS

A boat shall keep as near to the starboard edge of a channel as possible. In shipping channels with adequate water depth outside the channel, a small powerboat should operate alongside the channel. A powerboat less than 66 feet long (20 meters) or a sailboat shall not impede passage of a vessel that can only operate in the channel. Do not anchor in a channel.

The Inland Rules require that in narrow channels or fairways on the Great Lakes and Western Rivers, a vessel under power proceeding downbound with a following current shall have right of way over an upbound vessel heading against the current. The downbound vessel shall indicate manner and place of passing with appropriate sound signals.

SOUND SIGNALS

Boats may provide information to other boats about their maneuvers through the use of sound signals. Nowadays, vessels may also use radio communication to make passing arrangements. This reduces the confusion generated by traditional sound signals in heavy traffic where it may be unclear who is being hailed. Monitoring radio communication is also an excellent way to gain awareness of vessel traffic. See Chapter 11 for information on channel designations of a marine VHF radio and their use.

LIGHTS FOR NIGHTTIME OPERATION

The Navigation Rules require running lights when operating from sunset to sunrise, during hours of restricted visibility, or whenever it is deemed necessary. These lights can take many forms, such as sidelights, sternlights, masthead lights, all-round lights and towing lights. Their location and required visibility depend on the type and size of vessel. Some typical light arrangements are shown on pages 117, 119-120. Refer to the Navigation Rules for additional light requirements for sailboats, Great Lakes vessels and vessels towing, pushing, fishing, or restricted in their ability to maneuver.

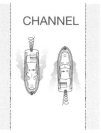

CHANNEL

Each boat shall keep near to the outer limit of a channel on her starboard side.

Sound Signals

● A short blast is about one second's duration.
— A prolonged blast is from four to six seconds' duration.

For vessels in sight of each other:
● One short blast indicates *altering* course to starboard (International), or *intending* to alter course to starboard (Inland) when meeting or crossing.

● ● Two short blasts indicate *altering* course to port (International), or *intending* to alter course to port (Inland) when meeting or crossing.

● ● ● Three short blasts indicate engine is in reverse (although vessel may still be moving forward).

● ● ● ● ● Five short blasts = danger.

Other sound signals:
— One prolonged blast is sounded by a vessel nearing a blind bend of a channel or fairway, or when departing a berth.

For other sound signals consult the *Navigation Rules: International-Inland*.

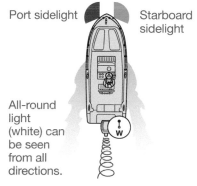

Port sidelight   Starboard sidelight

All-round light (white) can be seen from all directions.

Light requirement for a powerboat underway whose length is less than 39.4 feet (12 meters).

RISK OF COLLISION

Every vessel shall use all available means to determine if a risk of collision exists. If there is any doubt, it shall be assumed that a risk exists. To determine whether a risk exists, take a bearing of the other boat with your compass or by lining it up with a point on your boat. If the bearing remains unchanged and the distance between the boats is decreasing, a collision will occur unless there is a change in course or speed. With large vessels or a tow at close range, a risk of collision may exist even when there is an appreciable change of bearing.

Along with sight and hearing, if your boat has AIS and radar you are obliged to use them to help determine if a collision exists.

AUTOMATIC IDENTIFICATION SYSTEM (AIS)

AIS transmits vessel information on two reserved VHF channels and, depending on how the navigation equipment is set up, shows target icons on radars, chart plotters and stand-alone AIS displays. When a target or vessel is interrogated (using the cursor or touch screen), relevant information about that vessel is shared including:

• name and Maritime Mobile Service Identity (MMSI) number;

• position, size, course and speed; and

• Closest Point of Approach (CPA) and Time to CPA (TCPA) which is useful to help determine if a risk of collision exists and in what time frame.

Recreational vessels generally carry a Class B AIS transponder or an AIS receiver unit. The latter unit only receives data from another boat and does not transmit any of your boat's information, so it is important to know which one you might have.

MEETING SITUATIONS

A boat that is required to keep out of the way of another vessel is the give-way vessel. It shall alter its course in ample time and with an obvious change of course and/or speed to make it readily apparent to the other vessel that effective action is being taken. The other vessel is the stand-on vessel and should maintain consistent course and speed. However, it is every vessel's obligation to avoid a collision. If it becomes apparent that the give-way vessel is not maneuvering in time to avoid a collision, a stand-on vessel should then change course and speed.

When vessels are approaching in sight of each other, the Rules for the following situations apply: crossing, head-on, overtaking, and responsibilities between vessels.

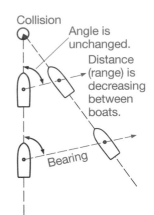

If a compass bearing of the other boat remains constant and the distance between the boats is decreasing, you are on a collision course. This is often referred to as Constant Bearing, Decreasing Range.

KEY POINTS FOR AIS

• *AIS uses various icons which an operator needs to learn to effectively use the system. These should be in your manufacturer's manual.*

• *AIS has a limited range and is generally the same as what your VHF receives and transmits.*

• *In a congested traffic area, AIS targets could cover navigational information on your chart plotter.*

• *If the data fed into the unit is incorrect, target information will be misrepresented so visual confirmation is always a must whenever possible.*

• *AIS is not a substitute for keeping a good lookout and should not be relied upon as your only means of determining a risk of collision.*

Basic Meeting Situations

Head-on

Crossing — Crossing

Overtaking

CROSSING SITUATION RULE

When two powerboats are on an intersecting course, the boat on your starboard side is the stand-on vessel, and the give-way vessel must alter course. Whenever possible, the give-way vessel should alter course to pass astern of the stand-on vessel. If the stand-on vessel must change course to avoid a collision, it shall not alter its course to port toward the give-way vessel.

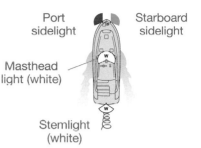

Light requirement for a powerboat (or sailboat using an engine) underway whose length is less than 164 feet (50 meters).

Give-way vessel should alter course early and substantially.

Stand-on vessel

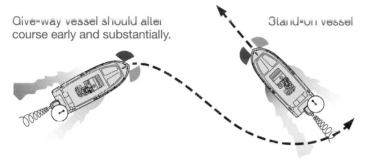

Crossing: driver of give-way vessel sees these lights at night.

Crossing: driver of stand-on vessel sees these lights at night.

TIP
To quickly determine which boat must give way remember the colors of the port (red) and starboard (green) sidelights. If you see the red side of the other boat, think of it as a red traffic light signaling stop (or change course). If you see the green side, it's the same as a green light meaning go—maintain your speed and course.

HEAD-ON SITUATION RULE

When two powerboats approach each other, they should alter course to starboard so that they pass port side to port side and signal with one short blast. If you alter to port and pass starboard side to starboard side, the signal and response is two short blasts. If there is any doubt as to whether such a situation exists, it shall be assumed to exist.

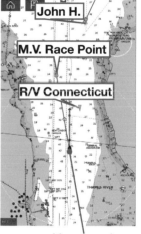

Your vessel

This is what a head-on situation would look like on an AIS screen.

Image Courtesy of Raymarine

Acknowledge agreement ●

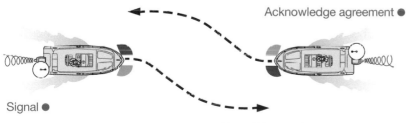

Signal ●

Note: If boats alter course to port to pass starboard side to starboard side, the signal and response is ● ●.

Head-on: drivers of both boats see these lights at night.

OVERTAKING SITUATION RULE

The overtaking boat is the give-way vessel and may pass to either side of the stand-on vessel. A vessel is overtaking when it is in the area defined by the 135-degree arc of the other vessel's sternlight.

Overtaking: driver of give-way vessel sees this light at night.

Overtaking: driver of stand-on vessel sees these lights behind him.

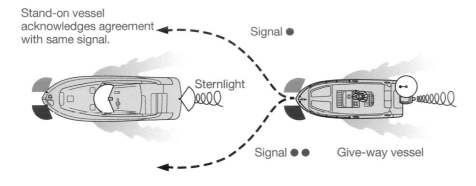

Stand-on vessel acknowledges agreement with same signal.

Signal ●

Sternlight

Signal ● ●   Give-way vessel

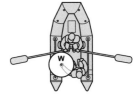

Light requirement for a boat being rowed or paddled: a flashlight is turned on in sufficient time to prevent a collision.

MEETING SITUATIONS WHEN IN RESTRICTED VISIBILITY

Restricted visibility can be caused by fog, mist, falling snow, heavy rainstorms or sandstorms. In conditions where boats cannot see one another, a distinct set of Rules exist.

- Maintain a careful lookout.

- Operate at a safe speed for the condition and be ready to maneuver immediately. A rule of thumb is to travel at a speed at which your boat can be stopped within half the distance of the prevailing visibility.

- Listen for sound signals. If you hear a fog signal from another vessel forward of your boat's beam, slow down to minimum control speed and be prepared to stop until danger of collision is over.

- If radar alone indicates another close-quarters vessel or a developing risk of collision, take avoiding action in ample time and avoid altering course to port for a vessel forward of the beam (unless overtaking it), or toward a vessel abeam or abaft the beam.

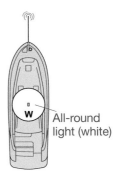

All-round light (white)

Light requirement for an anchored boat less than 164 feet (50 meters). During the day, a black anchor ball is displayed. These requirements do not apply for boats less than 23 feet anchored away from a narrow channel, fairway, anchorage, or an area where vessels normally navigate.

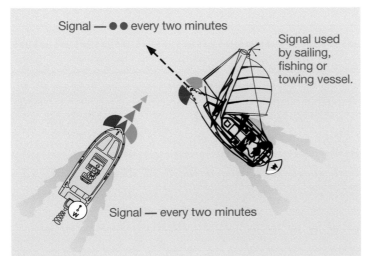

Signal — ● ● every two minutes

Signal used by sailing, fishing or towing vessel.

Signal — every two minutes

TRAFFIC SEPARATION SCHEMES

Areas with a high volume of shipping will often have traffic separation schemes, or vessel traffic lanes, that are reserved for use by large vessels and those with restricted maneuverability. You should stay clear of these schemes.

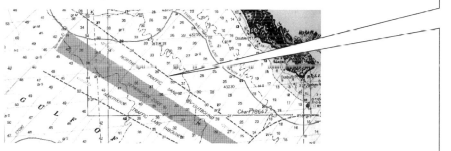

RESPONSIBILITIES BETWEEN VESSELS RULE

There are several types of vessels of which a powerboat underway shall keep clear. These are:

- a vessel not under command. Examples: a vessel on fire or one whose engines won't operate.

- a vessel which, by the nature of its work, is restricted in its ability to maneuver. Examples: a vessel dredging, or servicing a navigation mark or underwater cable.

- a vessel engaged in fishing with nets, lines or trawls that restrict its ability to maneuver. It does not include fishing with trolling lines.

- a boat using only a sail(s) for propulsion unless the sailboat is overtaking the powerboat.

YOUR DUTIES IN A TRAFFIC SEPARATION SCHEME ARE AS FOLLOWS:

- *You should keep well clear of Traffic Separation Schemes if convenient.*

- *If you need to join the traffic in a scheme, you should do so at the ends if this is reasonable.*

- *When crossing a scheme, you are obliged to cross at right angles to the traffic flow at your best speed.*

- *The separation zone must be crossed at right angles as well. Do not resume your course or run along inside it parallel to the traffic.*

- *You can go around the edge of a Traffic Separation Scheme without being subject to the above rules.*

The navigation rules contained in this course summarize basic navigation rules for which a boat operator is responsible on inland waterways. Additional and more in-depth rules apply regarding various types of waterways, such as International Waters and Western Rivers, and operation in relation to commercial vessels and other watercraft. For a complete listing of the navigation rules, refer to the document Navigation Rules and Regulations Handbook by the United States Coast Guard. For state-specific navigation requirements, refer to the state laws where you intend to boat.

REVIEW QUESTIONS

1. The fundamental purpose of the Navigation Rules is to help vessels avoid _____.

2. The boundary between inland and international waters is marked by a _____ line which is shown on _____.

3. If you are in a crossing situation, the boat on your _____ side is the give-way vessel.

4. When the bearing of an approaching boat does not change and its distance is decreasing, you are on a _____ course.
   a. separation b. safe c. collision

5. In restricted visibility, you should proceed at a speed that the boat can be stopped within _____ the distance of the visibility.
   a. quarter b. half c. twice

Answers: 1) collisions 2) demarcation; charts 3) port 4) c. collision 5) b. half

Chapter 14

BASIC NAVIGATION & PILOTING CONCEPTS

KEY CONCEPTS

▶ What is navigation?
▶ Charts
▶ Position
▶ Distance
▶ Distance, speed & time
▶ Direction
▶ Compass
▶ Aids to navigation

WHAT IS NAVIGATION?

In its simplest form, navigation is the safe movement of a vessel on the water using all available means to confirm your position and course. To navigate efficiently and safely, we require sources of information such as: our position, speed, heading, depth, sensory references (visual, auditory, smell) and additional electronic aids such as radar and AIS (covered in Chapter 13). For the operator to use these tools effectively, we will cover key concepts to help lay the foundation for navigating in daylight hours.

Today this task is made easier with the convenience and speed of modern electronic navigation equipment through which we can know our position and course to a destination. With all these great tools and their capabilities at our disposal, the one biggest limiting factor is the correct use by the operator. Having them is one thing, but understanding the limitations and correct use is where the comfort lies.

CHARTS

Charts provide information about the area in which we are boating, showing coastline, depth soundings, bridge and cable heights, submerged hazards, navigation aids (buoys and beacons), bottom characteristics and other relevant information.

Nautical charts are presented in the form of electronic or paper charts. There are two electronic chart options: raster navigational charts (RNCs) and vector/electronic navigational charts (ENCs). They both serve the purpose of delivering chart imagery but are different in look and capability. All of the chart information you see is gathered from surveys performed by hydrographic offices which is then used to produce charts. With the trend moving to a more digital-based navigation approach, paper chart production and availability are on the decline. However, paper charts should not be discarded just yet, as they provide a reliable backup. To maintain their reliability, however, they need to be periodically updated with information from the *Notice to Mariners and Local Notice to Mariners*.

ELECTRONIC NAVIGATIONAL CHARTS (ENCs)

More commonly known as vector charts, these are emerging as the preferred format on newer chart plotter systems. The main feature of a vector chart is multiple layers of information such as depth, buoys, topographical and marina information, and these are all overlaid and brought together to create the chart. One great advantage is that the latest charts can be easily obtained, downloaded and ready for use anywhere with a Secure Digital (SD) card and internet access. As with paper charts, electronic charts also need to be periodically updated by downloading and installing the latest version.

RASTER NAVIGATIONAL CHARTS (RNCs)

This was the original form for digital charts used for electronic navigation systems. The raster chart is an exact scanned image of a paper chart, digitized to be used on your chart plotter. These work well as an overview chart, as you do not lose any detail when zoomed out and can be used in conjunction with vector charts to provide the maximum amount of detail when underway.

Raster chart

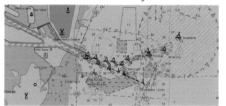

Vector chart

KEY POINTS FOR RASTER CHARTS

- *Zooming in and out does not offer more information and you can often have the "stitching" of two different scaled charts when zoomed in or out. It will also pixelate if over zoomed and detail becomes small and difficult to read when zoomed out.*

- *Scrolling over a buoy will not provide any additional information other than what can be viewed on the chart already.*

- *Information is printed on a raster chart in North-up orientation with North at the top of the chart. If you are using the chart plotter in head-up or course-up orientation, information such as depth or light characteristics may not read right side up. Think of it as rotating your paper chart to your boat's heading or course.*

KEY POINTS FOR VECTOR CHARTS

- *When zoomed out it is possible for dangers or other important information to not be visible because detail is dependent on scale. Always use correct scale to provide appropriate detail.*

- *They do not carry as much detail for buoys and land features such as headlands. To find information on a buoy or a lighthouse, you will need to move the cursor over it and click.*

- *Layers of information can be removed to see other important data as needed. If you remove a layer of information, do not forget to restore it once you are done!*

- *They carry tide and current data which can be layered onto the screen.*

- *Other information such as marina and fuel dock locations can be pulled up for planning purposes.*

PAPER CHARTS

These work much the same way as their digital counterparts in providing a picture of the area you are navigating in. Most are in the Mercator projection which allows for the Earth's spherical surface to be represented as a flat grid with longitude and latitude scales.

KEY POINTS FOR PAPER CHARTS

- *There are different scales for amount of detail, so you will require a few charts for your navigation area.*

- *Small scale (e.g., 1:200,000) = SMALL DETAIL (e.g., coastal chart)*

- *Large scale (e.g., 1:12,000) = LARGE DETAIL (e.g., harbor chart)*

- *They provide an excellent big picture view when used in conjunction with your chart plotter.*

TITLE BLOCK ON PAPER & RASTER CHARTS

The title block includes important information such as scale, chart datum and measurement units for soundings.

Scale

Chart Datum (WGS84)

Soundings in feet at MLLW

18643 • BO

Nautical Chart 18643
Mercator Projection
Scale 1:30,000 at Lat. 38°12'
North American Datum of 1983
(World Geodetic System 1984)
18th Edition, Dec. 2009
SOUNDINGS IN FEET
at Mean Lower Low Water

CHART SYMBOLS

Most chart symbols and abbreviations for navigation aids, underwater features and landmarks are self-explanatory. *U.S. Chart No. 1* is a useful reference for those that aren't obvious and can be downloaded from the NOAA nautical charts website.

On this chart, *soundings* (water depths) are in feet. Other charts may have them in fathoms (1 fathom = 6 feet), fathoms and feet, or meters. The title block indicates what units are being used on a chart. If fathoms and feet are used, the main number is in fathoms and the subscript is in feet. For example, 4_3 indicates 4 fathoms plus 3 feet for a total depth of 27 feet (4 x 6 = 24 and 24 + 3 = 27 feet).

Electronic Navigational (Vector) Chart

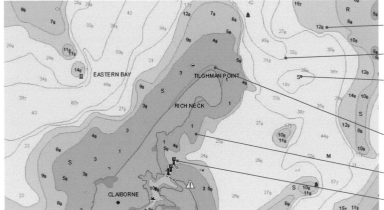

The numbers scattered throughout the water are **soundings** (depths) at mean lower low water (MLLW).

A **contour line** follows a constant water depth.

Letters indicate the type of seabed such as mud (M), sand (S), grass (Grs), rock (Rk), clay (Cy), coral (Co).

Green indicates areas that **cover and uncover with the tide**.

Darker blue tint indicates areas of **shallower water**.

These symbols are used to indicate **Aids to Navigation** (see page 131).

Raster Navigational Chart & Paper Chart

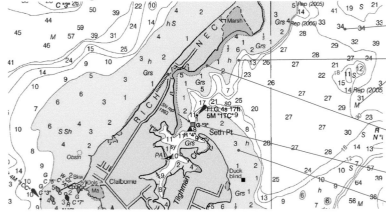

The numbers scattered throughout the water are **soundings** (depths) at mean lower low water (MLLW).

A **contour line** follows a constant water depth.

Letters indicate the type of seabed such as mud (M), sand (S), grass (Grs), rock (Rk), clay (Cy), coral (Co).

Green indicates areas that **cover and uncover with the tide**.

These symbols are used to indicate **Aids to Navigation** (see page 131).

Blue tint indicates areas of **shallower water**.

POSITION

Lines of latitude and longitude (lat/long) are used to define position on all charts. Both latitude and longitude are measured in degrees (°), minutes (') and decimals of minutes (e.g., 14'.281), or degrees, minutes and seconds ("). On a chart, minutes and seconds have nothing to do with time; they are simply subdivisions of a degree. 60 minutes equals 1 degree and 60 seconds equals 1 minute. Check to determine whether your chart is using decimals of minutes or seconds. Latitude is measured north or south from the Equator (0°) and this measurement increases towards the poles (90°). Longitude is measured east or west from the Greenwich Observatory in England (0°) and this measurement increases towards the International Date Line in the Pacific Ocean (180°).

GLOBAL POSITIONING SYSTEM (GPS)

This forms the cornerstone of our ability to secure real-time positioning, expressed as latitude and longitude on electronic navigation systems and paper charts. A network of 24 active satellites in six orbital planes circle the earth every 12 hours. These satellites relay their position and time at the speed of light to your GPS receiver. Four or more satellite signals are needed for a reliable real-time *fix* (position) on your chart plotter or mobile device.

In addition to the satellites, ground-based stations have been integrated into the GPS and is known as Differential GPS (DGPS). These earth or geostations provide greater accuracy to less than a foot by correcting slight errors from orbiting satellite signals.

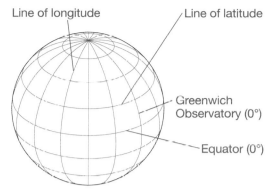

Lines of longitude are parallel on a chart, but they actually converge toward the North and South Poles.

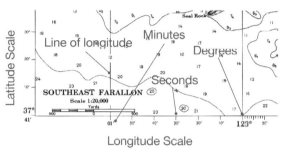

Accuracy of GPS position: 10.6 feet

Satellite #21 signal

This GPS satellite screen indicates signals are being received from nine satellites and the accuracy of the GPS position is estimated as 10.6 feet.

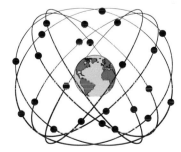

GPS depends on 4 satellites in 6 orbital planes to determine a position anywhere on our planet. The position and number of satellites will vary as the earth rotates and the satellites change their positions in orbit.

Each of the four satellite signals provides a line of position from the satellite. Their point of intersection determines your vessel's position (*fix*).

POSITION ON AN ELECTRONIC CHART

Depending on how you have manipulated the menus, the position of your vessel or the plotter's cursor can generally be read off the data boxes in a chart plotter screen. This is because, with its built-in GPS locator, the plotter already knows the location of anything on the chart it is using. Knowing the latitude and longitude of your vessel at any point in time is essential for relaying your position to emergency responders, recording in the ship's log, plotting your position on a paper chart as backup, or even marking a favorite anchorage.

POSITION ON A PAPER CHART

To plot a position of 41°13.4′ North latitude and 71°30.8′ West longitude (normally written or read out as 41 13.4N 71 30.8W), locate these positions on the latitude and longitude scales and transfer them by right angles to the position on the chart. This can be done by any suitable instruments, including a chart protractor, dividers and parallel rulers.

DISTANCE

ON A CHART PLOTTER

Almost all chart plotters will read out the distance and bearing to the cursor from the vessel, so you only need to put the cursor over your destination point to see how far it is in the data box. On some plotters, there is a function which allows you to measure distance from one point to another, separate from your boat's position.

ON A PAPER CHART

To measure distance on a paper chart, place one point of the dividers on the departure point and the other on the destination point. Move the dividers to the latitude scale (NOT the longitude scale) on the side of the chart and read off the distance in nautical miles. One minute of latitude is equal to one nautical mile.

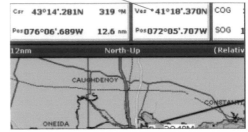

Vessel's position

The vessel's position (Ves Pos) is 41°18.370′ North latitude and 72° 5.707′ West longitude.

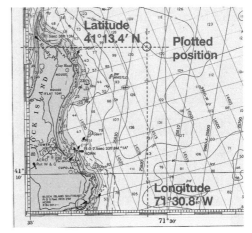

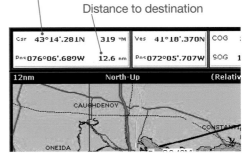

Cursor position at destination

Distance to destination

Distance to the destination is 12.6 nautical miles (nm).

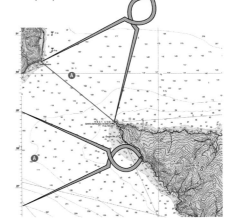

Use the latitude scale on the side of a paper chart to measure distance with dividers. Ⓐ measures 2.45 minutes or 2.45 nautical miles.

DISTANCE, SPEED & TIME

Having determined the distance to your destination point, you will want to know how long the trip will take and how much fuel you may need. Marine fuel consumption is generally measured in gallons per hour rather than miles per gallon, so you will need to take into account time and speed for that distance.

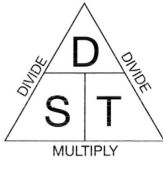

MULTIPLY

The DST Triangle is a visual reminder that when you want to determine D, you multiply S and T; and when you want to determine T, you divide D by S.

Distance (D) is measured in nautical miles (nm) where 1 nm is equal to 1.15 statute miles. Electronic devices can be set to nautical or statute miles or kilometers. Make sure you check the setting.

Speed (S) is measured in knots where a knot is defined as one nautical mile per hour (1 knot – 1.15 mph).

Time (T) is measured in hours and tenths of an hour, or in hours and minutes.

The relationship between distance, speed and time is expressed by these three formulae.

$$D = S \times T \qquad\qquad T = \frac{D}{S} \qquad\qquad S = \frac{D}{T}$$

If minutes are used, 60 converts minutes and hours. For example:

$$D - \frac{S \times T}{60} - \frac{20 \text{ knots} \times 12 \text{ minutes}}{60} - 4 \text{ miles}$$

$$S = \frac{60 \times D}{T} = \frac{60 \times 4 \text{ nautical miles}}{12} = 20 \text{ knots}$$

The DST triangle is sometimes used to visualize the relationship.

DIRECTION

All direction at sea is defined in terms of degrees by using a compass. Unlike a car, which is traveling in one direction at a given time, a boat's movement offers more choices. All are correct, but the difference is important:

• *Heading* is the direction the boat is pointing.

• *Course* is the direction in which the boat is to be steered.

• *Course Over Ground (COG or Track)* is the direction in which the boat is traveling across the seabed. In a crosscurrent, this may well be different from the boat's heading. Most plotters can show you either or both. Choose, and know which you have chosen. If in doubt, go for COG.

These are described in more detail in Chapter 15.

COMPASS

The compass is an essential piece of navigational equipment. Even with the reliance on chart plotters to provide position, your heading is crucial to safe navigation. Compasses provide a heading measured in degrees (0 to 360 degrees) and come in digital and traditional options. Nautical charts are orientated to point towards the North Pole (called True North), but a magnetic compass points to a location in northern Canada called Magnetic North.

Traditional steering compass depicts a boat's heading in degrees Magnetic.

This digital compass reading shows a heading of 230° Magnetic (M).

COMPASS VARIATION

The difference in degrees between your magnetic compass reading and True North is called variation. The amount and direction of variation will change depending on your location on the earth. The degree difference can be found on your plotter by searching through settings, or on your chart where a compass rose will indicate the amount and direction of the variation for your area.

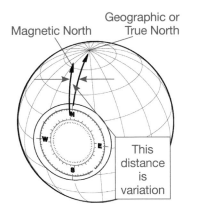

Magnetic North is not a fixed point like True North, but slowly wanders. This causes the amount of variation to change, and its predicted annual increase or decrease is shown on the compass rose. GPS units account for the change automatically.

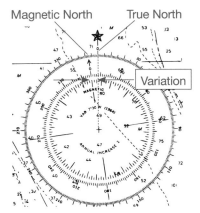

Variation can be either East or West. This example shows Magnetic North to the West of True North and is a West variation. The note inside the circles indicates a variation of 7° 30' W (West).

COMPASS STEERING TIPS

- *If a GPS or chart plotter gives your heading in degrees True, you will have to convert it to a magnetic heading for your compass by adding or subtracting the variation. Add for a West (W) variation and subtract for an East (E) variation.*

- *Motion can jostle a compass; read it when the boat is steady.*

- *Do not stare at the compass. Use it to get the boat heading in the direction you want, then use a reference to steer to, such as a buoy, a point of land or a distant cloud. Noting the wave direction relative to your course can help. If you use a cloud, stars or distant boats by which to steer, remember that they move constantly, so you will need to reset your reference periodically using the compass.*

- *Remember: the boat turns around the compass—the compass doesn't turn in the boat.*

- *Do not put magnetic objects such as phones or foghorns close to your compass.*

COMPASS DEVIATION

Your compass responds to metal objects which have magnetic properties and/or electrical interference. The difference in compass readings created by their influence is called deviation. For instance, a bag of tools accidentally placed next to the compass can cause deviation so that the compass reads 075 degrees when it should read 080 degrees. Even metal eyeglass frames can do it.

FLUXGATE COMPASS

A fluxgate compass is an electromagnetic compass and is essentially a digital version of your traditional steering compass with no moving parts. They are normally mounted lower in the boat close to the waterline and send an electronic signal to a display in the navigation station or steering area.

SATELLITE COMPASS (GPS COMPASS)

These compasses determine True North using GPS positioning and a two-or-more antenna configuration. The blending of the GPS data and an Inertial Measurement Unit provides the heading.

AIDS TO NAVIGATION

Navigation aids are nautical road signs that can be used to help you determine your position, follow a safe course, and warn of dangers. Aids to navigation may be divided into two broad categories:

1 Buoys are floating marks anchored (moored) in a fixed position. Buoy positions depicted on a nautical chart are approximate within the swing movement allowed by the scope of their mooring cable. Be aware they can sometimes drag from their position as a result of storms, ice, or impact with a ship.

2 Beacons are fixed to the sea bottom or located on shore, making them a reliable and precise aid for navigating. Beacons include daybeacons with a daymark, beacons with a light(s), lighthouses and ranges.

Buoys and beacons with lights can be identified by their color (red, green, white or yellow) and rhythm (pattern of their flashes). There is a variety of rhythms displayed by various lights. Most unlit marks have reflective tape that will be picked up by your searchlight. All marks are identified on charts. Anything floating (typically a buoy) is shown at an angle from the vertical, while fixed objects are straight up and down. NOTE: *This is not necessarily the case with vector charts.* ***Use U.S. Chart No. 1 as a reference for symbols and abbreviations.***

KEY POINTS FOR FLUXGATE COMPASSES

- *Heading is digital, so it can supply heading information to your chart plotter, autopilot and radar.*

- *They are magnetic, so are still influenced by the earth's magnetic fields (variation) and fields created by the vessel (deviation). These errors can be corrected in the chart plotter.*

- *Many are able to auto correct and provide a heading in degrees True, or you can choose to display it in degrees Magnetic. Either is fine, but you MUST know which it is, as the difference could be as much as 20 degrees.*

KEY POINTS FOR SATELLITE COMPASSES

- *They are unaffected by influences of the Earth's magnetic field.*

- *They indicate a heading in degrees True.*

- *There are no corrections needed as with a fluxgate compass.*

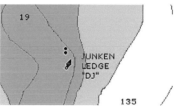

Here's a buoy on a chart plotter. For more details, place the cursor over it and click ENTER.

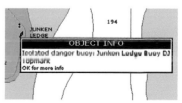

After clicking ENTER on the buoy, a box pops up with additional information.

CAUTION
It is illegal to tie onto an aid to navigation or be in a position that prevents other vessels from seeing it.

There are four navigation marking systems used in U.S. waters:

1 The U.S. Aids to Navigation System (USATONS) is used on all navigable waters in the U.S., with the exception of the Mississippi River and its tributaries and the Intracoastal Waterway.

2 The Information and Regulatory Markers System is used on navigable state waters and non-navigable internal state waters.

3 The Intracoastal Waterway System is used on the Intracoastal Waterway from New Jersey through Texas.

4 The Western River System is a variation of the U.S. Aids to Navigation System and is used on the Mississippi River and its tributaries.

U.S. AIDS TO NAVIGATION SYSTEM (USATONS)

LATERAL MARKS

A system of lateral marks is used to indicate on which side a mark should be passed when returning from seaward. In U.S. waters, red marks are kept on your starboard side and green ones on your port side. Remember this orientation by the "3 Rs" of RED, RIGHT, RETURNING (from seaward). When an approach from seaward cannot be determined, the Conventional Direction is used, which is a clockwise rotation around the U.S. land mass and northerly and westerly in the Great Lakes, except for southerly in Lake Michigan.

The Conventional Direction for lateral marks is a clockwise rotation around the U.S.

PORT LATERAL MARKS
Color: **GREEN**
Shape: **CANS** or **SQUARES**
Character: **ODD NUMBERS**
Light: **GREEN** (if lighted)

STARBOARD LATERAL MARKS
Color: **RED**
Shape: **NUNS** or **TRIANGLES**
Character: **EVEN NUMBERS**
Light: **RED** (if lighted)

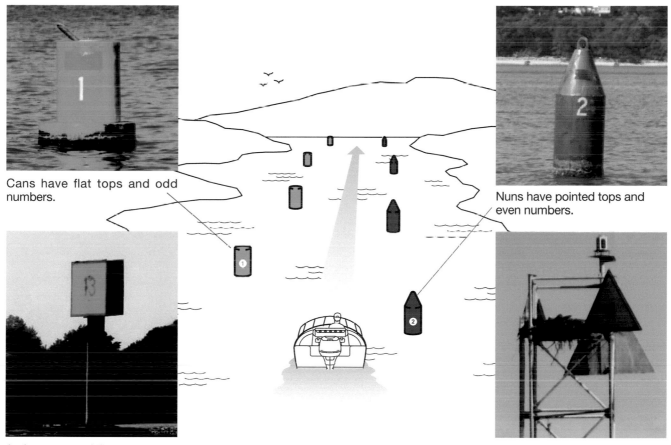

Cans have flat tops and odd numbers.

Nuns have pointed tops and even numbers.

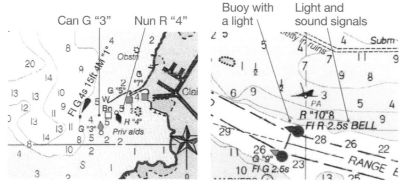

A beacon with a square daymark and odd number marks the left side of a channel.

A beacon with a triangle daymark and even number marks the right side of a channel.

Can G "3"   Nun R "4"

Buoy with a light   Light and sound signals

On raster and paper charts, red buoys have an R indicating their color, while some greens may not have a G. Note the odd number (G "3") on the green can and the even number (R "4") on the red nun. If a red or green buoy has a light and/or sound signal, this is indicated (Fl R 2.5s BELL).

Click on this lighted buoy for information.

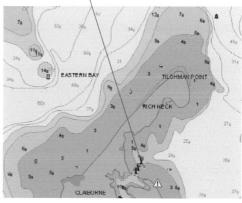

On vector charts, you will need to click your cursor on the buoy or beacon for information about it.

PREFERRED CHANNEL MARKS

When channels divide, one will be preferred for deeper draft vessels or as part of a continuing waterway. It may or may not be the one you want, but at the division you will find a preferred channel buoy. This may be passed on either side but will exhibit a preferred side based on the color of the uppermost band. If the main channel is to your left, when returning from seaward, the top band will be red indicating the buoy is to be passed on your starboard side. If the top band is green that indicates the preferred channel is to the right and the buoy is to be passed on your port side.

Color: red and green horizontal bands

Shape: cans, squares, nuns and triangles

Character: letter(s)

Light: same color as uppermost band (if lighted) and is a group flashing light [e.g., Gp Fl (2+1) 6s (2 flashes and 1 flash every 6 seconds)]

Green top band indicates the preferred channel should be passed on your port side to take the preferred channel.

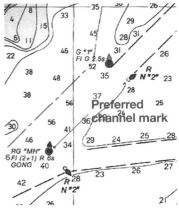

This preferred channel buoy with a light is identified on this raster/paper chart by RG "MH" Fl (2+1) R 6s. The RG symbol indicates that the top band is red (R), which tells us that the preferred channel is to the left. We can also identify the buoy by the letters MH on it.

SAFE WATER MARKS

These marks denote navigable (safe) water on all sides. They are frequently used to identify the middle of a channel or an offshore approach point to a channel.

Color: red and white vertical stripes

Shape: sphere or buoy with a red spherical topmark

Character: letter(s)

Light: white (if lighted) and flashes the Morse code (Mo) signal for the letter A (1 short flash followed by 1 long flash)

This lighted safe water buoy at the seaward approach to the Winyah Bay channel is identified by the symbols RW (red and white stripes) and Mo A (light flashes Morse code A). WB indicates it is the safe water mark for the Winyah Bay entrance.

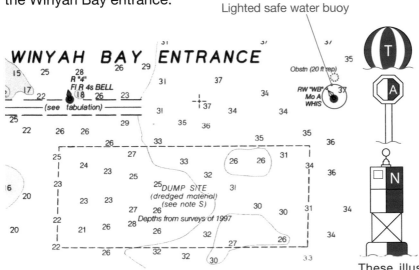

These illustrations show a variety of safe water marks.

ISOLATED DANGER MARKS

These are placed near an isolated danger with navigable water all around. They have black and red horizontal bands with a topmark of two black spheres. If lighted, they display a group flashing of two white flashes every 5 seconds.

SPECIAL PURPOSE MARKS

These are not navigation marks, but are used to alert you to a special feature or area such as turning basins, anchorages, weather buoys, pipelines, traffic separation schemes, spoil areas and jetties. These marks can be identified by their yellow color with black letter(s). If lighted, they display a yellow fixed or flashing light. You will have to refer to a chart, *Notice to Mariners, Coast Pilot* or *Light List* to determine their meaning.

LIGHTHOUSES

A lighthouse is an important aid to navigation at night, but can also be used in the daytime. A raster/paper chart shows them as either a magenta teardrop symbol or a star with various technical data about their light and fog signals. A vector chart identifies them with a lighthouse icon. A *Coast Pilot* book tells you what they look like. With light structures surrounded by water, note the symbol for the riprap which often surrounds them, and don't go too close. The same often applies to other structures such as jetties.

Isolated Danger Mark

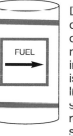

Special Purpose Mark

INFORMATION & REGULATORY MARKERS

These are used to alert you to dangers, exclusion and controlled areas, directions, and other regulatory matters and information. They have orange square, diamond or circle symbols with an orange band above and below the symbol displayed against a white background.

Information & Regulatory Markers

DANGER	BOAT EXCLUSION AREA	CONTROLLED AREA	INFORMATION

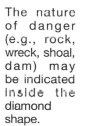
The nature of danger (e.g., rock, wreck, shoal, dam) may be indicated inside the diamond shape.

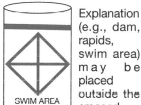
Explanation (e.g., dam, rapids, swim area) may be placed outside the crossed diamond shape.

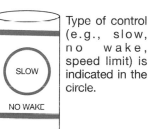
Type of control (e.g., slow, no wake, speed limit) is indicated in the circle.

Directions, distances and other non-regulatory information is displayed inside the square or rectangular symbol.

INTRACOASTAL WATERWAY SYSTEM (ICW)

This waterway on the East Coast and the Gulf of Mexico uses its own unique markings of a yellow triangle ▲ and a yellow square ■ . Since there is no obvious approach from seaward for the ICW, the Conventional Direction of clockwise rotation around the U.S. land mass is used. As a result, the marks toward the mainland side of the waterway are designated as marking the right side of the waterway by a yellow triangle ▲ , and the ones toward the sea mark the left side and have a yellow square ■ . When following the ICW from New Jersey to Texas, a mark with a yellow triangle should be left on the boat's starboard side and a mark with a yellow square on its port side, regardless of the color of the navigation aid on which they appear. The prudent navigator will follow charts closely and carry an up-to-date ICW cruising guide.

There are places along the Intracoastal Waterway where its waterway and a channel leading in from the sea coincide. If the directions of the two systems are the same, the yellow triangles will be on the red marks and the yellow squares on the green marks. But if the conventional direction of the ICW runs opposite to the returning from seaward direction of the channel, the U.S. Aids to Navigation System for the channel prevails and the yellow triangles will be on the channel's green marks and the yellow squares on the red marks. Extreme care should be taken when passing the junction of the ICW and a channel leading in from the sea. The mixture of marks can be very confusing, but if you follow the yellow ICW symbols, you should not get lost.

The Intracoastal Waterway is a network of protected inland water routes winding from New Jersey to Texas.

The yellow triangle on this red daymark indicates the starboard (mainland) side of the ICW channel.

The yellow square on this green daymark marks the port (seaward) side of the ICW channel.

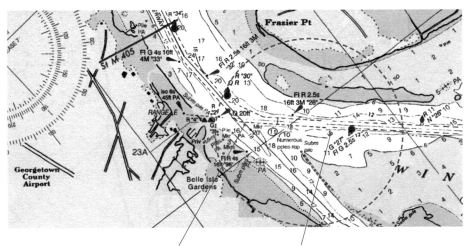

Junction of the Intracoastal Waterway and a channel leading in from the sea.

Channel leading in from the sea

WESTERN RIVER SYSTEM

This is used on the Mississippi River and its tributaries above Baton Rouge as well as certain other rivers emptying into the Gulf of Mexico. Its major differences from the U.S. Aids to Navigation System are:

- Aids to navigation are not numbered or lettered. *Numbers on marks represent mileages.*

- Safe water and isolated danger marks are not used.

- Lights on green aids show a single flashing green or white light; lights on red aids have a red or white group flashing light.

- Diamond-shaped crossing boards indicate where the channel crosses from one riverbank to the other.

REVIEW QUESTIONS

1. *One minute of latitude on a paper chart is equal to _____ nautical mile(s).*
2. *To find information on a buoy on a vector chart, use the _____ and click on the buoy.*
3. *_____ is the direction a boat is pointing.*
4. *The difference between Magnetic North on your compass and True North on a chart is called _____.*
   a. deviation   b. oscillation   c. variation
5. *When returning from seaward, red marks are kept to the _____ side of a boat.*

Answers:
1) one
2) cursor
3) Heading
4) c. variation
5) starboard

Chapter 15

BASIC NAVIGATION & PILOTING

KEY CONCEPTS

▶ Electronic-based navigation

▶ Depth sounders

▶ Autopilots

▶ Backup navigation

▶ Navigation using paper charts

▶ Planning a trip

▶ Piloting

The ease and efficiency with which we can accurately identify our position, especially on a powerboat moving at speed, is incredible and has revolutionized the way a recreational boater can navigate and pilot from point A to B. However, there is also the other side of the equation.

With this technology being perceived as simpler, the elements of complacency and overconfidence can and do creep in, and sound navigating fundamentals are forgotten or seen as not needed. Even when following a route on your chart plotter, you should always be looking for additional landmarks, buoys and depth to confirm what you are seeing on the screen. Operators who understand the advantages, but more importantly the limitations, of a GPS-based navigation system will be safer and more accomplished powerboaters. Many systems are similar in their use, but it is the responsibility of the operator to learn their specific system.

ELECTRONIC-BASED NAVIGATION

While chart plotter systems all have similar functionality, it is important to know that the keys operating those functions can vary from unit to unit. To be safe and efficient, the operator *has to know their system*. A combination of reading the manual, watching videos and experimenting with the system in an area known to the operator goes a long way to gaining familiarity with the unit.

SCALE

This is critical when using a plotter. Whether using raster or vector charts (see Chapter 14), finding the correct scale will provide the maximum amount of information. Zooming too far out, the detail is either too small to read or, in the case of vector charts, there could be essential information missing. One can also be too zoomed in which does not let you see upcoming dangers or can be pixelated and hard to read with raster charts.

TIP

When using a chart plotter, zoom in and out periodically while underway to ensure you see all potential dangers.

ORIENTATION

When using a chart plotter there are two ways you can have your screen image set up, depending on your skill or preference:

❶ North-Up Setting orientates the chart image in the same manner as a paper chart, with North at the top. Depending on their heading, some operators might not be comfortable with this setting, as it does not match what is seen "out the window."

❷ Head-Up Setting is the most common setting with recreational boaters where the boat points to the top of the screen. When using this setting, it resembles the head-up setting of the GPS navigation system in your car.

CURSOR USE

The cursor is essential to using your chart plotter effectively. Its primary role is to pan or look ahead, provide a latitude and longitude at its location and, with vector charts, provide additional information if the cursor is clicked over an object. The cursor may be manipulated by arrow keys, a rollerball or by a finger on touch screens. Beware that if you are panning ahead to check your route, once done you will need to use the "center vessel" feature to return the screen to your boat's actual position. If you don't, you could be monitoring an area that is miles from where you are and not the progress of your boat—a good way to run aground!

DETERMINING YOUR POSITION

The screen and its data box show your vessel's real-time position all the time. Normally this position is shown in latitude and longitude, which is useful if you ever need to relay your position to other boaters or authorities.

WAYPOINT

A waypoint is a specific location that is either an intermediate point within a route or a single destination point, and is identified by latitude and longitude coordinates. The operator can insert a waypoint using the cursor or touchscreen. Waypoints are also useful to mark an anchorage location or to help locate a Person in the Water (PIW) in a rescue situation. By activating the MOB (Man Overboard) button, a waypoint is generated for that location, giving a bearing and distance back to it.

KEY POINTS FOR NORTH-UP SETTING

- *Chart points to True North, the top of the screen.*

- *Boat will rotate, but the chart image will remain fixed.*

- *Not all systems will be able to accommodate this setting. It requires a heading input from a fluxgate or GPS compass to orientate correctly.*

- *Better for use with raster charts.*

- *More natural for route planning and using in coastal trips and passages.*

KEY POINTS FOR HEAD-UP SETTING

- *Boat always points to the top of the screen.*

- *When you alter your heading, the chart image will rotate while the boat icon points to the top of the screen.*

- *Works best with vector charts where the information such as depth will orientate to your heading.*

- *Good for channels and approaches, as it matches what you see ahead of you.*

Vessel's position

Cursor position data box

Vessel position data box

Destination waypoint (cursor position)

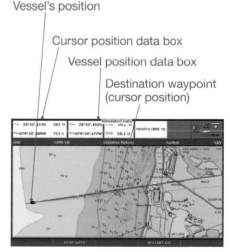

The vessel's real-time position is shown in the Ves Pos data box, and the destination waypoint's position is shown in the Csr Pos data box.

BUILDING A ROUTE

A route is a series of waypoints that has a start and works sequentially toward an end point or destination. A trip could involve numerous waypoints or just a few. To build a route, go to the route tab on the navigation menu, then use the cursor to select or create waypoints along your intended route. At the end, save and name the route.

STEERING TO A WAYPOINT ON A ROUTE

If you are navigating along a route, you will be steering to waypoints within the route. An active waypoint on your chart plotter will provide you with information as to how well you are progressing. Along with a boat icon showing your position on the screen, other real-time information is provided in the data box to help you stay on your intended course line.

Understanding the following points and terms will be important to use your chart plotter effectively and proceed safely along your route.

- BTW (Bearing to Waypoint) is a bearing (True or Magnetic) from your boat to the waypoint. When the BTW and COG are the same you should have little to no XTE. In other words, you are right on course!

- COG (Course Over Ground) is the track your boat is traveling along the seabed and is expressed in degrees (True or Magnetic). This might not be the same as your heading due to the impacts of wind and current.

- SOG (Speed Over Ground) is the speed your boat is actually achieving over the seabed and takes into account any impact of current.

- XTE (Cross-Track Error) is a distance measurement either to port or starboard off your intended course line. This can be caused by current, wind, inaccurate steering or any combination of these.

- DTW (Distance to Waypoint) provides a distance from your position to the waypoint. Using the distance and SOG, you can calculate your Estimated Time of Arrival (ETA) to a waypoint.

It is helpful to use the Heading and COG (vector) lines which extend from the boat icon. This will provide a visual representation of where you are pointed, how you are progressing along the seabed, and show the impact of current and/or wind explaining the cause of any cross-track error (XTE).

KEY POINTS FOR BUILDING A ROUTE

- *Have the scale zoomed in appropriately to place your waypoint so you do not miss any small detailed dangers.*

- *Allow for a margin of error by keeping the waypoints a safe distance from dangers without creating too much extra distance.*

- *Be cautious of setting waypoints close to a headland or a navigation aid where others may be putting theirs too. This could lead to a lot more traffic to deal with.*

- *Always do a "flyover" of your route once completed. Zooming both out for an overview and closer in to confirm the waypoints are where you set them.*

- *Saved routes can be reversed in the route menu, so you can return along the same path without having to create an additional return route.*

Cross-track error (XTE) is 158 feet to port of the waypoint bearing.

Waypoint

Steer to starboard to correct error.

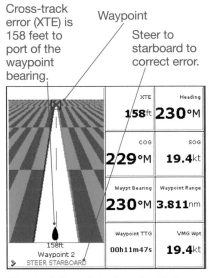

Chart plotter data box in Highway mode

Course over Ground (COG) line - green

Boat icon   Heading line - red

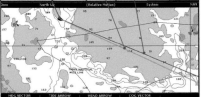

The boat's COG line is to starboard of its Heading line due to the impact of wind and current.

DEPTH SOUNDERS

This is a vital tool in helping to navigate in shallow waters and verify a boat's position as shown on the chart plotter or a paper chart. For example, recognizing that one should be in 12 feet of water according to the chart plotter and reading three feet on the depth sounder should alert the operator that there is a discrepancy. At this point, slow or stop the vessel and confirm your location. Depth sounders can also be used for coastal navigation by matching the depth readings with a position on a chart, or by following a certain depth contour while traveling along a shoreline.

A shallow water alarm can be programmed into the unit to alert you if you are nearing a specified minimum safe operating depth. This should be set at the maximum draft of your boat plus some additional safety margin added in. This depth alarm can also be used to detect if the boat is dragging an anchor at night.

AUTOPILOTS

Autopilots can be like having an extra set of hands, and are almost becoming standard equipment on modern sport, center console, express and trawler style powerboats. The autopilot, provided it has a heading feed, will steer the vessel on a set course decided by the operator. These units also provide a digital compass heading on the display and, in most cases, a rudder angle indicator. The heading can be adjusted by rotating a dial or pressing soft keys, depending on the manufacturer and model. Always read the owner's manual to understand the correct use and limitations of your specific unit.

There are three steering modes on an autopilot:

- **Standby mode** allows the operator the freedom to steer the vessel using the wheel. It will only go back to autopilot if engaged to do so.

- In **auto mode**, the vessel will steer a set heading with no allowance for current or wind effects on the vessel. This will require the operator to adjust

Water Depths Related to Transducer

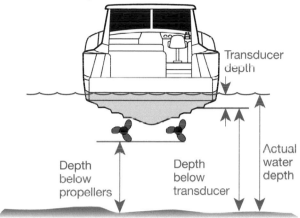

Depth sounders can be set to indicate the depth below the lowest part of the boat, below the transducer, or the actual depth of the water. Know which setting is used, and make sure the depth sounder displays the same units as your chart.

KEY POINTS FOR DEPTH SOUNDERS

- *It is very important to know how your sounder is configured. A reading that reflects water depth under the transducer is likely **not the lowest location on the boat**. Many powerboats have the props, pods or a keel lower than the transducer. If you know how deep your transducer is, or the distance between your transducer and the lowest part of your boat, your sounder can be programmed to display how much water is actually under the maximum draft of the boat. Alternatively, it could be programmed to display the actual depth from the surface, which would correspond to what is displayed on your charts.*

- *The depth sounder readings can be affected by water moving under the boat when docking or backing up to anchor. Allow the water to settle and it should read correctly again.*

- *Make sure the depth sounder is set to correspond to the measurement units on your charts, whether that is in feet, meters or fathoms.*

A multifunction display depicting water depth in feet.

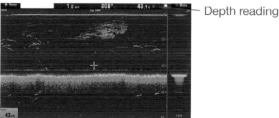

Depth reading

Some units have a Sonar feature displaying depth.

heading to stay on their intended course.

- In **track mode**, the vessel will steer directly to an active waypoint and make course alterations to adjust for tidal streams and wind influences. This mode will follow a route and prompt the operator at each new waypoint to accept the next turn. Not every model has this feature, which needs to be networked into your plotter.

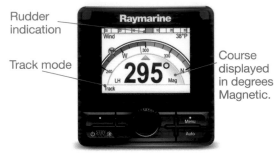

Rudder indication

Track mode

Course displayed in degrees Magnetic.

Photo Courtesy of Raymarine

BACKUP NAVIGATION

When making an electronic navigation system your primary means of navigation, there is always a risk of system failure from power supply, dropped signals, water damage, and hardware or software issues. ***Having an independent backup system is a must***, be it on a mobile device, laptop, or paper charts with plotting tools, a hand-bearing compass, and a hand-held GPS. Make sure you understand and use your backup system BEFORE you need it.

MOBILE DEVICES

With the amount of processing power now available on mobile devices, they can, in many cases, be quicker than slightly dated chart plotter units. Applications running raster chart, vector chart and compass applications can be downloaded to your tablet or smartphone and are far less expensive.

The essential principles of chart plotter use still remain but be aware not all navigation apps are created equal. Some testing is suggested prior to use in a known environment to check accuracy. As with all systems, it is important to spend time and become skilled with the controls, screens, menus and symbols of the application.

This option offers an affordable and accurate stand-alone navigation option for sport boats, where a console-mounted option might not be feasible. It also offers older vessels with more dated chart plotters a reliable secondary system.

KEY POINTS FOR AUTOPILOTS

- *One advantage of the autopilot is it allows you to keep your focus on navigating and collision avoidance by steering a straight course for you. This can also allow for operators to become complacent and not pay attention, so beware!*

- *If you are switching between standby, auto or track mode, confirm it is engaged in that mode. If not, you may end up somewhere you would rather not be.*

- *Glance down regularly to check that the unit is still engaged in auto or track mode. Some setups can disengage if the wheel is turned.*

- *When in confined waters such as a channel, you should be in standby mode and steer by hand so quick adjustments in course can be made.*

KEY POINTS FOR MOBILE DEVICES

- *GPS Enabled. Mobile devices that rely on triangulation from cell towers are subject to error based on cellular coverage for that area. Ensure your device has a built-in GPS (and it is ON) for superior accuracy.*

- *Night Use. The device/application might not have a setting to change the color palette for low-light use. This will leave the screen with more white light and impact the operator's night vision.*

- *Updates and Calibration. With all apps, regular updates are important to keep the system optimized while others, such as compass apps, might need calibrating prior to using for the first time.*

- *Screen Size. This can impact the ability to see dangers in detail, in particular when using a smartphone with a small screen. Correct scale is important for safe use.*

- *Power Supply. Your battery can drain rather quickly when running a navigation app with GPS positioning and the screen running constantly. Forethought should be given to how to power it for extended periods via battery packs or plug-in points.*

- *Protection. Be sure your device is in a waterproof case if exposed, and secure so it does not fall overboard or get damaged.*

- **Integration** Certain mobile chart apps can connect to the boat's chart plotter and transfer pre-planned routes into the plotter so planning can be done before a trip.

- **Easy to Use** The navigation apps are very user friendly and mobile users understand the platform. They do not carry a wide range of additional features but the simplicity allows for safer use for less experienced operators.

- **Chart Updates** These are done often, either automatically when opening the app, or by manually running the update feature. In many cases the mobile devices have more current charts than their fixed-unit counterparts, which require cards to be manually updated.

Paper Charts

It is easy to download a navigation app to your tablet and have an independent backup system, but paper charts are still around and make an outstanding backup.

NAVIGATION USING PAPER CHARTS

When you are using paper charts to determine your position and a course to steer to a destination, you'll need a compass to take bearings, plotting tools, and a flat surface large enough to lay out your paper chart.

Determining Your Position

Start by taking a *bearing*, which is an imaginary line joining a known charted point with your boat's position. In the illustration, bearing **Ⓐ** has been taken of a chimney stack with a hand-bearing compass. This compass reading is located on the inner magnetic ring of the compass rose and is then transferred as a line running from the stack on the chart using a parallel ruler or a chart protractor. Your position is somewhere on this line (line **Ⓐ** on the chart).

Take multiple bearings to fixed objects from your boat to determine your position. In the example shown, bearings **Ⓐ**, **Ⓑ** and **Ⓒ** have been taken from three objects and transferred to the chart and plotted. Since the boat is on all three lines, the boat should be at the point of intersection (called a *fix*), or was there when the last bearing was taken. In practice, all three lines rarely pass through the same precise point. Instead, they form a small triangle. If your fix was correctly performed with care, your position should be inside the triangle.

KEY POINTS FOR PAPER CHARTS

- *Paper charts are not reliant on a power source, so if power sources are limited to keep a mobile device charged, this might be a superior option.*

- *Paper charts do require some storage and need plotting tools such as dividers, pencils and parallel rulers or chart protractor. A flat work area is also required to plot positions and courses.*

- *Paper charts offer detail not always found on vector charts, which is helpful when planning out your trip beforehand.*

This hand-bearing compass is used to take bearings by sighting the object across the top of it and reading the projected compass numbers.

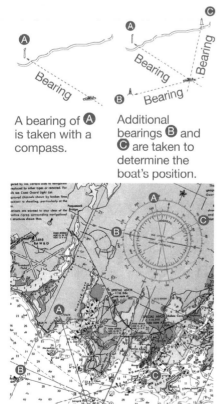

A bearing of **Ⓐ** is taken with a compass.

Additional bearings **Ⓑ** and **Ⓒ** are taken to determine the boat's position.

DETERMINING A COURSE TO STEER

With a compass and chart, once you know where you are, you can determine a *Course to Steer*. For instance, you are at point **A** on the chart and want to go to point **B**. Draw a line from **A** to **B**. Make sure there are no hazards such as rocks, reefs or shallow waters along the route. Now, transfer the line **A** – **B** to the compass rose (the line has been drawn for you on the chart.) Read the circled heading at the letter **B** on the inner magnetic ring of the compass rose. The heading is 272 degrees Magnetic (M), which is your compass course from **A** to **B**. To steer the course you have planned, steer to the compass heading you have plotted.

PLANNING A TRIP

Planning is an essential part of any time on the water. Whether it's a simple trip a mile away to a favorite afternoon anchorage or a trip up the coast, both require specific elements. Plugging in an unknown destination in your car is straightforward and involves little risk. Doing the same on your boat could be disastrous.

Use the following elements as a guideline to planning and executing a successful trip:

ASSESS

Before going anywhere you should always look at the viability of your trip. This will determine if you move any further than this first phase. Some key points to consider in your planning:

- **Distance** How far is the trip? Can it be done in one day? Is there enough fuel to make it without a fuel stop? It is better to know and plan for it than end up out of fuel in a potentially dangerous situation.

- **Identify Dangers** It is not wise to go on a trip to an unfamiliar place without knowing what potential navigational hazards there might be. These could be strong tidal streams or shallow water. Whatever the case may be, you need to be aware and know the limitations.

- **Weather** When coming into an inlet, is there a strong onshore wind which builds in the afternoon, or thunderstorms that develop late in the afternoon in the summer, or a sea breeze that causes a sea to develop in your local sound or bay? These are important considerations before committing to the next phase.

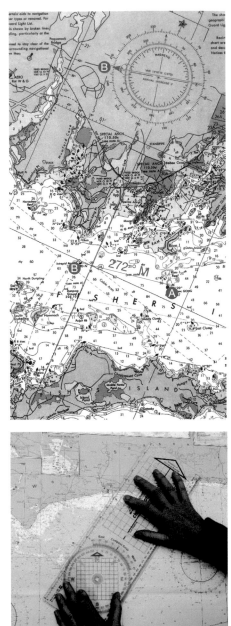

Plotting a course with parallel rulers requires walking the rulers across the chart to transfer information to and from the compass rose. A chart protractor does away with this inconvenience.

- **Crew/Guests** It might be a day with two- to three-foot seas which is fine in your mind, but some of the guests or crew might be susceptible to seasickness in these conditions. Also consider a tight dock scenario with a crosswind where line handlers with some experience might be needed.

- **The Boat** Knowing its limitations and seaworthiness are important to decide if it is safe to do the trip. Be aware of the load capacity of the boat, which includes people and gear, to avoid overloading it.

PLAN

Once you have decided the trip makes sense, you can begin planning the trip which involves factors other than navigating to your destination.

- **Route** Map out the route to your destination, taking into account: dangers; a safe haven if an issue develops or weather turns bad; and the limitations of the boat such as its height and draft. Determine at what speed you will run to arrive at your destination. Your planned departure time may be decided by tides, currents, or the check-in time at your destination slip.

- **Logistics** Where can you get fuel and what time does the fuel dock close? Does the dock space have the right shore power for you to plug in? Where can you get provisions? These are essential to a successful trip.

CHECK

With the plan in place, include these items in your pre-departure checklist:

- **Fuel Level** It is never wise to assume you have enough fuel. If you figure you will burn 2/3 of a tank, it is best to top off and give yourself a safety factor. As a powerboat operator, it is important to know how much fuel you use at a certain rpm and, if possible, the gallons per nautical mile.

- **Safety Equipment** Make sure you have at least one U.S. Coast Guard approved life jacket of appropriate size for each person on board. Confirm the locations and function of flares, throwable flotation device, first aid kit, bilge pumps, blowers, and any other safety equipment required by law.

- **Systems** Check your essential systems such as navigational equipment, VHF radio, night operation lights, engines and generator (if you have one), making sure startup is good.

- **Weather** A final check of the weather is never wasted time, as weather can change in a matter of a few hours.

- **Route** Last but not least, double check your route to make sure nothing has been missed and that the route is saved correctly.

GO

Once you have completed your assessment, planning and checks, you can get underway. But before you do, make sure you complete these few items:

- **Departure Plan** With any great journey there is a beginning, so departing your slip or mooring smoothly is always a great start. Assign your crew their responsibilities and ensure that everyone understands their role.

- **Crew/Guest Brief** Going over a safety plan is important, as not everyone knows your boat and not everyone is comfortable on the water. Point out the location of life jackets, fire extinguishers and other safety items. It's also a good idea to include the correct use of the head and VHF radio in your brief.

- **Send Out ETA** Once you have completed all of the above and just before casting off lines, provide an ETA along with your float plan to a shore contact (destination marina or a friend on shore). Use a window of 30 minutes either side of your anticipated time, as it can always be updated while underway.

It can be understood if you do not enter a route for a day trip to a local familiar spot, but it is another thing entirely if you do not check the weather, tides (if relevant), fuel levels, comfort and safety of your guests/crew, or do not share a float plan whether you are out for a few hours or heading out for the weekend.

PILOTING

Navigating close to the shoreline, entering or departing harbors can be the most challenging part of any trip. The operator needs to be focused and aware, as traffic is condensed and shallow areas are often in close proximity. Staying on your intended track while monitoring for collisions is critical to arriving safely.

KEY POINTS

- *Relying only on your chart plotter screen should not be considered safe. GPS systems can have errors that may show you in an incorrect position.*

- *Visual aids to navigation and other landmarks will confirm you are in your intended position.*

- *Observing the effects of current and wind on your boat will be more evident by sight than focusing on the screen.*

- *Having a pilotage plan identifying tides, currents, local dangers and buoys is considered prudent and seamanlike.*

- *Using a combination of ENCs and paper/raster charts will provide the most complete picture of your approach. Ensure you have the correct scale to provide the best amount of detail so you do not lose essential information.*

- *Your depth sounder will be a key tool when approaching shallow areas as added verification to help you stay in deeper water. Remember to factor in the height of the tide when reading off the soundings.*

- *Satellite photos, when available, also provide valuable information on depths, coastlines and hazards.*

TIP WHILE UNDERWAY

Once underway, continue to monitor the weather and evaluate your position and performance of the boat, including engine readings, throughout the trip.

- Printed or digital publications such as cruising guides offer useful information regarding how to best approach a harbor and local hazards. A quick call to your intended marina's dockmaster can also offer valuable local up-to-date knowledge.

RUNNING A RANGE

In medium- and longer-range piloting, a GPS or chart plotter will give you what you need to keep on your course track. In tighter situations, or in a strong crosscurrent where a navigator needs to use visual navigation rather than instruments, there is nothing more useful than a range. A range is formed by lining up two fixed objects on the same bearing, one closer to you than the other. The objects may be headlands, trees, buildings, towers, beacons, buoys or special range markers.

KEY POINTS RUNNING A RANGE

- *You can use a range to follow a channel, keep in safe water, or stay on course.*

- *If you are motoring across a current toward a destination, you need to adjust your course to compensate for the current's effect. You can determine how much to compensate by using a range.*

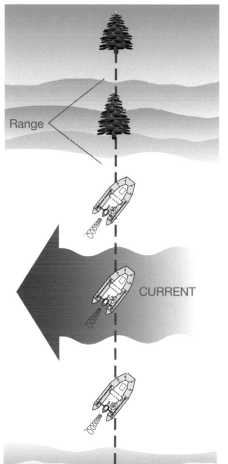

By lining up the two trees of this natural range, you will be able to reach your destination in a straight line.

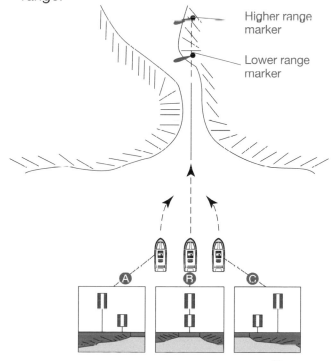

When the two range markers are lined up, boat **B** is in the center of the channel. If not, boat **A** should alter course to starboard and **C** to port with both alterations moving the boat toward the direction of lower (closer) marker and aligning the range markers.

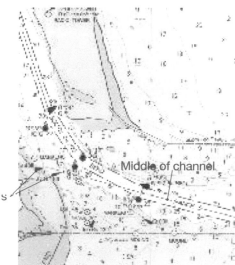

By lining up the two markers of this official range, you will be able to stay in the middle of the channel.

Phase 3 – Hypothermia

Full effect with loss of consciousness occurs in about 1 hour in very cold water. Hypothermia occurs when the temperature of the body core drops below normal. It can also occur during prolonged exposure to cool air and/or cool spray or precipitation. Signals include shivering in the early stages, lack of shivering in the later stages, impaired judgment, dizziness, numbness, and loss of consciousness. Action: if in water, minimize loss of heat by assuming the Heat Escape Lessening Posture (H.E.L.P.) position or Huddle group position; if on a boat, replace wet clothing with dry clothing and blanket, and warm gradually.

Phase 4 – Post-Rescue Collapse

After a person is rescued, blood pressure can drop suddenly, causing heart problems; and the lungs may be damaged from water. Get medical assistance as soon as possible. Until medical assistance arrives, follow the treatment steps listed in the hypothermia table below.

Hypothermia Prevention

Wear a life jacket and layered clothing suitable for the conditions. Best prevention in cold water includes wearing a dry suit or wetsuit. Capsizing and falling overboard are the causes for most in-water hypothermia situations. To reduce these risks: don't overload a boat or shift weight too much to a side; don't go out in conditions unsuitable for your boat; avoid use of alcohol; and don't reach too far over the side of a boat.

HYPOTHERMIA

SIGNALS

▶ Shivering

▶ Impaired judgment

▶ Dizziness

▶ Numbness

▶ Change in level of consciousness

▶ Weakness

▶ Glassy stare

(Physical symptoms may vary since age, body size and clothing will cause individual differences.)

TREATMENT

Medical assistance should be given to anyone with hypothermia. Until medical assistance arrives, these steps should be taken:

▶ Check breathing and pulse.

▶ Gently move the person to a warm place.

▶ Carefully remove all wet clothing. Gradually warm person by wrapping in blankets or putting on dry clothes. Do not warm person too quickly, such as immersing in warm water. Rapid rewarming may cause dangerous heart rhythms. Hot-water bottles and chemical heat packs may be used if wrapped in a towel or blanket before applying.

▶ Give warm, nonalcoholic and decaffeinated liquids to a conscious person only.

HEAT EMERGENCIES

Heat emergencies can also be life threatening. High temperature and humidity are the usual culprits. Be alert for signals whenever the temperature is around 90 degrees Fahrenheit and the relative humidity is more than 70 percent. Young children and elderly people are particularly vulnerable. The best preventive measure is to avoid dehydration by drinking plenty of water at regular intervals and staying in the shade.

HEAT EXHAUSTION

SIGNALS

► Cool, moist, pale skin

► Heavy sweating

► Headache

► Dizziness

► Nausea

► Weakness, exhaustion

TREATMENT

Without prompt care, heat exhaustion can advance to a more serious condition—heat stroke. First aid includes:

► Move person to cool environment.

► Remove clothing soaked with perspiration and loosen any tight clothing.

► Apply cool, wet towels or sheets.

► Fan the person.

► Give person a half glass (4 oz.) of cool water every 15 minutes.

HAZARDS

ELECTRICAL HAZARDS

When using electrical power tools near water or stringing extension cords along docks, make sure they are properly grounded and the power cords and connections do not make contact with the water. Overhead power lines can be a dangerous hazard. If they are touched by a long antenna, fishing rod, or some other tall metal object on your boat, the result could be shock or even electrocution. Look upward for power lines in boat launching sites or over water where they could be low lying. Another potential electrical hazard is snagging your anchor on underwater electrical cables. Check for cable markings on shore or cable location symbols on your chart before anchoring.

ACTION PLAN FOR ELECTRICAL INJURY

● *Never approach a victim of an electrical injury until you are sure the power is turned off.*

● *If a power line is down, wait for the fire department and/or power company.*

● *Contact a doctor or EMS personnel immediately.*

● *The victim may have breathing difficulties or be in cardiac arrest. Provide care for any life-threatening conditions.*

CARBON MONOXIDE HAZARDS

Carbon monoxide gas is very difficult to detect because it is odorless, tasteless and colorless. If you smell exhaust fumes from an engine, carbon monoxide (CO) is present. Exposure to CO gas can kill you at low concentrations over prolonged duration or high concentrations in a very short time. The best detection for this poisonous gas is a regularly inspected, marine-approved carbon monoxide detector in spaces where CO may collect. Symptoms of carbon monoxide poisoning include headache, nausea, dizziness, weakness and irritated eyes, and are often confused with seasickness or alcohol intoxication.

Carbon monoxide gas is generated from the combustion or burning of carbon-based fuels which include gasoline, oil, propane and charcoal. Sources include: exhaust leaks or outlets from engines and generators; space heaters; water heaters; grills; and propane stoves. Prevention includes: don't swim or sit near exhaust outlets while engines or generators are operating; avoid sitting in areas where wind can carry the gas; don't ride close behind a moving boat either by hanging onto the swim platform or on a short tow; avoid exhaust emissions when docked or rafted alongside another boat; ensure adequate fresh air circulation all through the boat; and perform regular inspection and maintenance of engines and generators and their exhaust systems.

PROPELLER STRIKES

Recent statistics indicate that 4 percent of fatalities are caused by strikes from propellers, but a propeller can also produce serious injuries. Bowriding and sitting on the gunwale of a moving boat increase the risk of falling overboard and getting hit by the propeller. To prevent runaway situations, the lanyard to the emergency engine cutoff switch (or remote wireless device) should be attached to the operator. When approaching a person in the water, the operator should keep the person in sight at all times and, when close, shut off the engine.

PROPELLER SAFETY TIPS

- *Keep propeller away from a person in the water.*

- *Turn off the engine when near a person in the water.*

Backflow from a low-head dam can hold a boat against the face of the dam and capsize it.

DAMS

These can present a very confusing and often misleading appearance to the boater. Many larger dams incorporate hydroelectric-generating plants, road crossings and, in some cases, bypass locks that allow boats to travel around the dam. These large dams are usually well marked and quite obvious. Other dams are not so obvious. Dams that allow the water to flow out of the bottom can trap an unsuspecting boat against the wall by the strong downward flow of the water. Low-head dams are designed to maintain a minimum water level upstream. To the unsuspecting boater upstream of the dam, it cannot be seen by the water flowing over it. Any boater who is downstream of the dam could get caught in the back-flow circulation and be pinned against the dam with the risk of a possible capsizing. Know the locations of these dams to avoid them.

Capsizing & Swamping

Most capsizes occur from overloading, improper weight distribution, or shifting weight of passengers or unsecured gear. Ensure that the maximum loading on the boat's Maximum Capacities label is not exceeded and the boat is loaded evenly fore and aft and from side to side. It is equally important not to overpower a boat with too large an engine. With a powerful outboard or stern drive, a boat can roll significantly if turned too sharply with a sudden burst of power at slow speed. On smaller boats, this could be enough to swamp or capsize them.

Should a capsize occur the cardinal rule is to, "Stay with the boat; don't swim for shore." An overturned boat is much more easily sighted than a swimmer. Everyone should be wearing a life jacket. Be aware that a person in the water under duress weakens very quickly. After a capsize, a head count and safety check should be taken to make sure everyone is alright and wearing a life jacket. If life jackets are not available, use improvised floating aids such as paddles, floorboards, ice coolers or buoyant containers. Use distress signals to attract attention for a rescue (e.g., sound signals, waving arms, flares).

Falling Overboard Prevention

Next to capsizing, falling overboard is the second leading cause of fatal boating accidents. It is also one of the most preventable. Many overboard situations occur before the boat even leaves the dock. Typically, these situations occur when passengers attempt to step aboard while carrying items and slip, or they step on the edge of the boat and lose their balance when the boat tips. Overboard incidents can also happen when people stand up or ride on the boat's bow, gunwales (outer edges) or seatbacks, or are thrown off balance by a careless driver making erratic or sudden changes in speed or direction. To help prevent falling overboard, use footwear with good traction and follow the maxim, "One hand for the boat and one hand for yourself."

PERSON-IN-WATER RESCUES

Rescuing a person in the water (PIW) is a four-stage procedure: return to PIW and make physical contact; attach PIW to boat; get PIW back aboard; and aftercare.

Return to PIW & Make Physical Contact

The procedure to return to the PIW will depend on the size of the boat and the conditions. Key elements are to: maintain sight of the PIW at all times, approach at minimum control speed with the PIW on the operator's side of the boat and close enough to make contact with a line or boat hook, and turn off the engine once contact is made.

Attach PIW to Boat

Pass a Lifesling (if available) or a looped line around the PIW and attach it to the boat. This will ensure that you don't lose the PIW if he or she weakens and cannot hold on

SAFETY TIP
There are communication and signaling devices that can be carried on a person to signal for help in case of a fall overboard or a capsize. These may include a personal locator beacon, laser flare, whistle, strobe light, rescue mirror, and orange smoke signals. In cold water conditions, carry a signal device that will continue to operate if overcome by the effects of cold water immersion.

SAFETY TIP
When getting aboard a boat or moving around, use three points of contact with the boat (both feet and one hand, or both hands and one foot) to prevent falling.

any longer. If the PIW is wearing a safety harness, attach the safety line to the harness and secure the line to the boat.

Get PIW Back Aboard

This can be the most difficult part of the process. Many boats may have a swim platform and ladder on the transom. If your boat does not, carry a portable ladder. With small low-sided boats, a PIW may be pulled in over the rail by lifting the PIW on a three-count bounce or rolling the PIW over the rail. Avoid using a stern drive or cavitation plate as a step because there is a risk of getting cut by the propeller. On larger powerboats with high sides, a strap or sling or rescue net can be rigged to lift a PIW. If there are any problems getting the PIW aboard or there is a grave and imminent threat to his or her life, activate the DSC Distress button, or make a Mayday distress call to the Coast Guard on your VHF radio, or call 911 on your mobile phone if coverage permits.

Aftercare

Take the greatest care of a rescued PIW who often will be suffering from varying degrees of hypothermia. Refer to the beginning of this chapter for suggested treatment.

Race Track Rescue Procedure

❶ If a person falls overboard, immediately swing stern and propeller away from PIW. Shout "Crew Overboard!" and throw buoyant objects such as cushions and life rings toward the PIW as soon as possible. Even if these objects do not come to the aid of the PIW, they will litter the water where he or she went overboard and help your spotter to keep the PIW in sight.

❷ Designate someone to spot and point to the PIW. The spotter should NEVER take his or her eyes off the PIW.

❸ Maneuver the boat to a position downwind of the PIW, staying close enough to the PIW to keep him or her in sight while allowing sufficient room to complete the maneuver.

❹ Approach slowly using minimum control speed, bow first, pointing into wind and waves with the PIW on the operator's side. This allows better visibility for the operator. Communicate with and reassure the PIW.

❺ Shift into NEUTRAL and coast to PIW, making physical contact with a paddle, boat hook or line. Turn off the engine once reliable contact has been made or if there is any risk of the PIW coming close to the propeller. Keep reassuring the PIW.

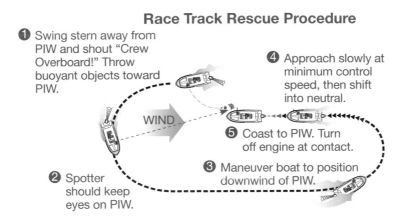

Race Track Rescue Procedure

❶ Swing stern away from PIW and shout "Crew Overboard!" Throw buoyant objects toward PIW.

❹ Approach slowly at minimum control speed, then shift into neutral.

WIND

❺ Coast to PIW. Turn off engine at contact.

❷ Spotter should keep eyes on PIW.

❸ Maneuver boat to position downwind of PIW.

LIFESLING RESCUE PROCEDURE

❶ If a person falls overboard, immediately swing stern and propeller away from the PIW. Shout "Crew Overboard!" and throw buoyant objects such as cushions and life rings toward the PIW as soon as possible. Assign a spotter to watch and point at PIW.

❷ Deploy the Lifesling by opening the bag and dropping the sling into the water. It will trail out behind and draw out the remaining line.

❸ Circle the boat around the PIW with the line and sling trailing astern (similar to circling a towline to a waterskier in the water). Take care not to run over the floating line.

❹ Contact is made with the PIW by the line and sling being drawn inward by the boat's circling motion. The PIW then places the sling over head and under arms, and fastens the snap.

❺ Upon contact, shift into NEUTRAL. Once the PIW is in the Lifesling, turn off the engine and pull the PIW close to the boat. Set up boarding equipment to bring the PIW aboard.

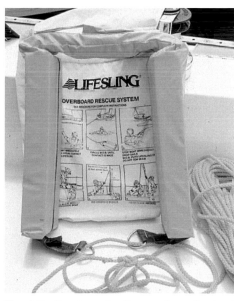

The Lifesling is a floating collar attached to the boat by a length of floating line that doubles as a hoisting sling to retrieve a PIW.

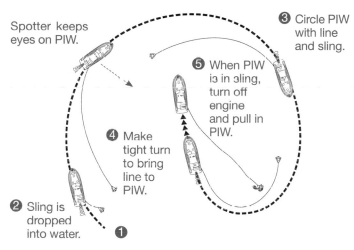

Spotter keeps eyes on PIW.

❸ Circle PIW with line and sling.

❺ When PIW is in sling, turn off engine and pull in PIW.

❹ Make tight turn to bring line to PIW.

❷ Sling is dropped into water.

❶

WILLIAMSON TURN RESCUE PROCEDURE

If a person falls overboard and the situation (e.g., at night or restricted visibility) makes it difficult to keep the person in sight, the Williamson Turn is the best method to use to return back along your track to the PIW's position. During the maneuver, maintain constant speed throughout the turns to keep the radius of turn constant. Try to use references other than the compass to avoid acceleration errors in the compass during the turn.

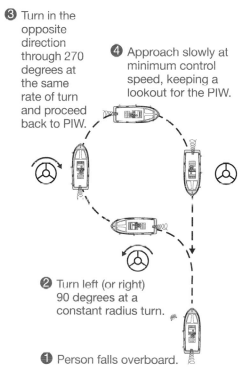

❸ Turn in the opposite direction through 270 degrees at the same rate of turn and proceed back to PIW.

❹ Approach slowly at minimum control speed, keeping a lookout for the PIW.

❷ Turn left (or right) 90 degrees at a constant radius turn.

❶ Person falls overboard.

DISABLED BOAT

RUNNING AGROUND

The severity of this situation depends on how fast the boat was moving and the hardness of the ground. The combination of high speed and a hard, rocky bottom can cause extensive damage to the hull, as well as serious injury to occupants. Slow and soft impact is most likely an uneventful self-rescue situation. After running aground, make a full damage assessment and check for leaks before freeing the boat. If the boat is holed you may not want to float free until you have stopped the flow of water.

Generally, when boats with outboards or stern drives hit bottom, the skeg and propeller will be the first to strike. If the neoprene hub (or shear pin) is still intact, you may be able to free the boat by quickly reducing the throttle to idle rpm and then shifting into NEUTRAL. Next, tilt the outboard motor into the shallow water position and try to carefully back off in the direction from which you came. Strong backing thrust from the propeller may pile sand up, blocking the hull from moving backward. Another alternative is to move everyone forward to raise the stern and push the boat off with a paddle. If the neoprene hub is damaged, you'll be able to run the outboard, but only at low power.

Skeg hits soft bottom

❶ Reduce throttle to idle rpm and shift into neutral.

❷ Tilt outboard to shallow water position and shift into reverse to back off.

If the boat is firmly stuck and the tide is rising, the best course may be to get an anchor out in the direction of deep water and keep a strain on it, and wait while the tide floats the boat off.

An anchor can also be used to help pull your boat free (*kedge off*). It can be placed in position by carrying it out in a small inflatable boat, or floating it with cushions or extra life jackets and swimming it out. Keep a strain on it the whole time you are attempting to free the boat. When the boat breaks free, take up on the line and keep it clear of the propeller.

PREVENTION FOR RUNNING AGROUND

- *Know the location of shallow water and underwater hazards.*
- *Know your position in relation to shallow water and underwater hazards.*
- *Maintain a lookout for indications of shallow water and underwater hazards.*

ACTION PLAN FOR RUNNING AGROUND

- *Check crew for possible injury.*
- *Determine damage to boat.*
- *Attempt to free boat without causing further damage.*

When kedging off, use a winch or bridle to increase the strain on the anchor line.

If you cannot get off, you will need the assistance of a professional towboat rescue service. If another boater offers to help, use great caution. Lines used to pull a grounded boat clear are put under tremendous strain as well as the chocks and cleats. Cleats on small pleasure boats frequently cannot withstand such loads. If a line should break or a cleat pulls away, injury can result.

FLOODING

If a boat is taking on water, it could be caused by damage to the hull from hitting an underwater object or crashing off waves at high speeds. Many outboard-driven powerboats have double hulls. If the operator suspects an impact was hard enough to damage the outer hull, every effort should be made to determine whether the space between the hulls is flooding. Another possibility is failure of a through-hull fitting, such as a seacock. An inboard engine offers additional possibilities, such as a broken hose line in its cooling system, a torn outdrive boot or a leaking seal at the stern tube on a fixed-propeller drive system.

ENGINE FAILURE

When a boat suddenly loses power and starts drifting, consider whether or not it is in danger. Quickly determine if it is drifting toward rocks, shallow waters or a heavy-traffic shipping channel.

- If there is no danger and you're drifting in safe waters, the best alternative may be to try to fix the problem or call the local towboat rescue service.

- If the water is shallow enough for anchoring, this could be the best alternative until help arrives. Being anchored in a fixed place will also make it easier for the towing service to find you.

- If land is nearby or the wind is favorable, another alternative may be to paddle the boat or even rig a sail from the boat's canopy. Remember, it is always safer to stay with the boat and not attempt to swim for help.

If you cannot fix the problem, you can call the local towing service on the VHF radio channel it monitors or via a mobile phone. You can also use the appropriate distress signals on board your boat to attract the attention of another boat (see Chapter 10). You should not activate the DSC Distress button or make a Mayday distress call to the U.S. Coast Guard unless there is a grave and imminent (actually happening) danger to the vessel or the life of a person(s) on board.

ACTION PLAN FOR FLOODING

If flooding occurs, make sure everyone is wearing a life jacket and follow these three steps:

- *Start pumping and bailing with large solid bucket.*

- *Locate leak.*

- *Stop the flow. You may be able to raise the damaged area above the waterline by shifting equipment and people. Pack a hole with some sort of plugging material, such as a shirt, extra life jackets, cushions or even a nerf ball. This temporary remedy may slow the water flow enough to slowly head for a near shore where the boat can be beached.*

If you cannot stem the flooding, this is the time to use your distress signals and push the DSC Distress button, or call the Coast Guard on Channel 16 of your VHF radio.

FIRE

Nothing can be more frightening than the sudden outbreak of a fire on board. The importance of strategically placed and fully charged fire extinguishers cannot be stressed enough (see Chapter 10 for fire extinguisher requirements). The most effective way of preventing a fire is ensuring that fuel and gear are stowed properly and that bilges are kept clean.

Most fires can be controlled, providing the boater acts immediately and properly. Know how to use your fire extinguisher and take the opportunity to practice its use. When using an extinguisher, sweep its discharge across the base of the flames and keep going until the extinguisher is empty. Watch the remnants for reignition. An easy way to remember proper procedure in an emergency situation is the acronym PASS: **P**ull pin, **A**im at fire base, **S**queeze handle, **S**weep side to side using short bursts.

Types of Fires	Extinguishing Methods
Class A: wood, paper, cloth, rubber, some plastics	1 Water, poured or hosed, on flames 2 Dry chemical extinguisher 3 Fire blanket for contained galley fires 4 FE-241, FM-200 automatic extinguishers (Halon replacements)
Class B: flammable liquids including diesel, oil, gasoline, alcohol	1 Dry chemical extinguisher 2 Carbon dioxide (CO_2) extinguisher 3 FE-241, FM-200 automatic extinguishers
Class C: live electrical fires	1 Carbon dioxide (CO_2) extinguisher 2 Dry chemical extinguisher 3 FE-241, FM-200 automatic extinguishers

The Fire Triangle

Some form of fuel, heat and air are the three elements necessary for fire to occur.

ACTION PLAN FOR FIRE

- *The first person to see a fire should shout "Fire!" and everyone should move on deck wearing a life jacket.*

- *Steer the boat so as to lessen any wind and to keep the smoke clear of people on board.*

- *If danger seems imminent and life threatening, use your distress signals and activate the DSC Distress button, or make a Mayday distress call to the Coast Guard on Channel 16 of your VHF radio, or a 911 call on your mobile phone if coverage permits.*

- *Prepare to abandon the boat.*

TOWING & BEING TOWED

There are professional towboat rescue services in many areas that will respond to your request for a tow. They can be reached by VHF radio or mobile phone. Keep their telephone numbers on board your boat in case you need to call them. If you ever need a tow or have to help another boat in trouble, consider the following:

- A towline of 100 feet of ½-inch or ⅝ inch double braided nylon is recommended. If an anchor line is used, make sure it is in good condition. If the nylon line breaks under load, it has a dangerous whipping action.

- If there is no mooring eye on the stem of the bow to be towed, rig a bridle (see detail) to split the load. If the reliability of the cleats or eyes is questionable, it may be necessary to wrap the towline completely around the boat.

- Do not stand near or in line with the towline and bridle, in case it breaks or the cleats pull out.

- Everyone should wear a life jacket.

TOWING TIPS

- *Operator of towboat briefs boat to be towed and a means of communication (i.e., hand signals or VHF radio) is established.*

- *Start the tow slowly, maintaining a steady strain on the towline, and tow at a moderate, safe speed.*

- *Adjust the length of the towline so that both boats climb up and slide down waves at the same time.*

- *Make wide turns.*

- *Avoid bow-down trim to maintain steering control.*

- *On the boat being towed, raise the outboard motor to the UP position and lock it. If the boat weaves out of control, you may have to lower the motor to help it track, which will require a much slower towing speed.*

- *Steer towed boat with rudder (if applicable) to follow behind towboat.*

- *Allow plenty of time for the tow to slow down before attempting to release the tow.*

- *Be prepared to shorten up on the towline when entering an anchorage.*

- *Tow to the nearest safe anchorage, harbor or marina.*

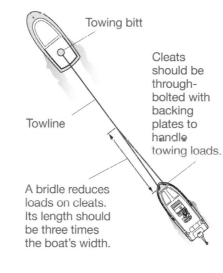

Towing bitt

Cleats should be through-bolted with backing plates to handle towing loads.

Towline

A bridle reduces loads on cleats. Its length should be three times the boat's width.

REVIEW QUESTIONS

1. *If your boat capsizes, you should _____ the boat.*
   a. leave   b. recover   c. anchor   d. stay with

2. *To recover a person from the water it is best to approach from _____ of the person.*

3. *If your boat experiences engine failure and you are not in grave and imminent danger, you should _____.*
   a. swim to shore   b. tie onto a channel buoy   c. stay with the boat   d. make a Mayday call

4. *When using a fire extinguisher, sweep the discharge across the _____ of the flames.*

5. *To extinguish a diesel or gasoline fire, you should use _____.*
   a. water   b. a fire blanket   c. a wet chemical extinguisher   d. a dry chemical extinguisher

Answers: 1) d. stay with   2) downwind   3) c. stay with the boat   4) base   5) d. a dry chemical extinguisher

Chapter 17

LAUNCHING & TRAILERING

KEY CONCEPTS

▶ Trailering

▶ Ramp launching & hauling out

▶ Hoist operation

A boat on a trailer expands the range of boating opportunities, and your ability to easily use a ramp or hoist will add to the enjoyment of your on-the-water experience. Preparation and a little maneuvering practice with your vehicle and trailer are the keys to success.

TRAILERING

The combined weight of boat and trailer affects the vehicle in several ways:

1 its ability to pull and stop;

2 weight on the hitch may depress the vehicle's rear suspension where the front wheels become light on the road, making it difficult to steer and blinding oncoming drivers with high headlights;

3 additional wear on brakes, transmission, suspension and tires as well as possible engine overheating.

Check the owner's manual (or contact a dealer) for manufacturer's limits, towing weight limitations, warranty requirements and suggested packages for towing.

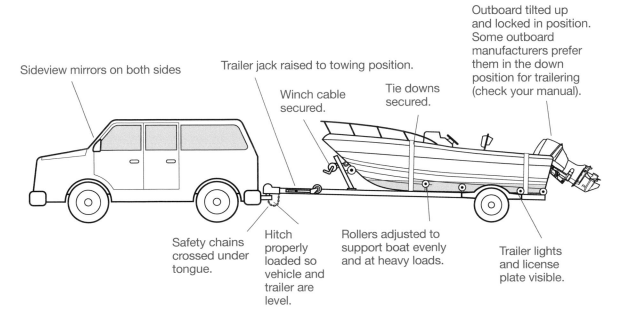

Sideview mirrors on both sides

Trailer jack raised to towing position.

Winch cable secured.

Tie downs secured.

Outboard tilted up and locked in position. Some outboard manufacturers prefer them in the down position for trailering (check your manual).

Safety chains crossed under tongue.

Hitch properly loaded so vehicle and trailer are level.

Rollers adjusted to support boat evenly and at heavy loads.

Trailer lights and license plate visible.

TRAILER INSPECTION

Trailer Hitches

Conventional hitches come in five classifications (I, II, III, IV, V) that are rated for different gross trailer weights and tongue weights. Avoid hitches attached to bumpers. The weight on a hitch ball (tongue weight) typically ranges from 5 percent to 10 percent of the combined weight of the trailer and boat with fuel and gear. If the tongue weight is too light, the trailer can swerve back and forth (fishtail) on the road. If it's too heavy, the vehicle will be difficult to steer.

Safety Chains

Safety chains should be used and crossed under the tongue and attached to the vehicle's frame. They should not drag on the ground or come under tension when making a tight turn.

Tires & Brakes

Tires (including the spare) should be inflated to recommended pressure and trailer brakes checked to ensure they are working properly. Brakes are activated either electrically or with a surge hydraulic system. Each type has its pros and cons. Check your state law and talk with experienced boaters in your area to determine what type best meets your needs. Many states require trailer brakes when the combined weight of the trailer and boat exceeds 3,000 pounds, but the limit can go as low as 1,500 pounds.

Wheel Bearings

Check wheel bearings for signs of wear (each side of the hub has a bearing). Signs of worn bearings are: noise as wheel rotates; wheel wobble; smoke or excessive heat at the hub; or grease residue sprayed on wheel or boat. Bearings should be removed and checked every 1,000 miles or at the beginning of each season. Waterproof bearings and/or spring-loaded bearing protector caps are recommended. Lubricate the bearings with marine-grade waterproof grease, being careful not to use too much.

DRIVING TIPS WHILE TRAILERING

- *Allow extra time and space to accelerate and stop.*

- *When slowing down or stopping, gradually increase pressure on trailer and car brakes. Avoid hitting the brakes hard. This is especially dangerous on wet roads and could jackknife the trailer. Sudden stops while turning may also jackknife the trailer.*

- *If the trailer starts to fishtail, minimize steering and slowly reduce speed until the fishtailing stops.*

- *When driving downhill, shift into lower gear to avoid excessive brake wear.*

- *When turning, make a wider turning radius to prevent the trailer from hitting an obstacle on the inside of your turn. Use the rearview and sideview mirrors to check trailer clearance to the obstacle.*

- *In windy or truck-passing conditions, trailers may have a tendency to fishtail. Tow at a slower speed in these conditions.*

- *Reduce speed for bumps or depressions in the road.*

- *When backing a trailer, avoid oversteering. Turn the bottom of the steering wheel in the direction you want the back of the trailer to turn.*

- *Some states have lower speed limits for trailering.*

- *Check the trailer, boat and tie downs periodically.*

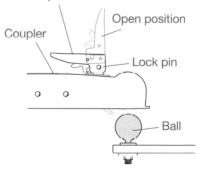

Ball should match coupler size and should be lightly greased. There are three ball sizes: 1⅞ inches (typically rated for 2,000 pounds); 2 inches (rated anywhere from 3,500 pounds to 6,000 pounds); and 2⁵⁄₁₆ inches (6,000 to 10,000 pounds). The coupler usually has the ball size marked on it along with the maximum gross weight and maximum tongue weight (combined weight of the trailer and boat on the ball).

BOAT SUPPORT

Be sure roller supports or bunks (pads) support the boat evenly along centerline, near chine and at transom, and at locations where weight is concentrated. Secure gear to prevent movement and lock outboard or stern drive in towing position. Make sure tie downs are snug and secured. Drain plugs should be removed and stowed.

LAUNCHING

1 Get the boat ready to launch in an area that does not block the ramp. Insert and secure drain plugs, remove tie downs (except for winch cable), unplug wiring connector, add boat gear, attach bow and stern lines, connect fuel line attachments, and complete starting checks. Allow the trailer's wheel bearings and lights to cool before launching to avoid damaging them by sudden cooling.

2 Back trailer slowly down ramp until boat is in water. Use rearview and sideview mirrors to keep both sides of ramp in view when backing. Know where the end of the ramp stops to avoid running the trailer's wheels off it. Many ramps have a mark to indicate its end. Avoid immersing the vehicle's exhaust pipes in the water. A tongue extension may be required to launch deeper draft boats or for shallow slope ramps.

3 Park in first gear or PARK and place a chock behind the vehicle's rear wheel.

4 Have someone take the bow line so the boat won't float away.

5 Detach the winch cable from the boat.

6 Start the boat and back away.

7 Remove the vehicle and trailer from the ramp as soon as possible.

SPARE PARTS LIST

☐ Trailer bearings, seals and grease
☐ Trailer tire
☐ Bulbs for trailer lights
☐ Trailer jack and lug wrench
☐ Tie downs and lines

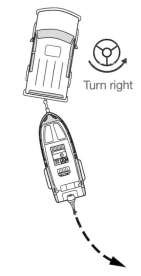

Turn right

When backing a trailer, turn the bottom of the steering wheel in the direction you want the trailer to turn.

CAUTION
Be aware of slippery ramps. They can cause injury or make it difficult for vehicles with or without four-wheel drive to pull a boat up the ramp. Before launching, open a window in case the vehicle accidentally slips off the ramp and becomes submerged.

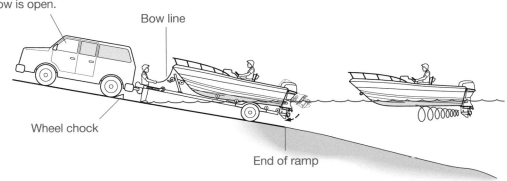

Window is open.

Bow line

Wheel chock

End of ramp

HAULING OUT

1 Back trailer down ramp until about two-thirds of the rollers/bunks are in the water. Park in first gear or PARK and place a chock behind the rear wheel.

2 Approach trailer slowly, lining up the centerline of the boat with the centerline of the trailer, shift into NEUTRAL to let boat float on the trailer. Some people prefer to use the engine to get on the trailer, called power loading, but be aware that some ramp facilities may prohibit this method.

3 Attach winch cable to the mooring eye on bow stem and take up cable until bow is snug against stop. Lock cable. Be sure to operate the winch while standing to one side to avoid getting hit if the cable breaks.

4 Check that the center of the transom is over centerline of trailer if there are no trailer side posts or guide rails. If the transom is off centerline, try shifting into FORWARD gear at the throttle's IDLE setting and turn outboard to swing transom over centerline. Do not advance throttle.

5 Raise outboard or stern drive and lock.

6 Pull trailer up ramp at slow, steady speed.

7 Clear the ramp area.

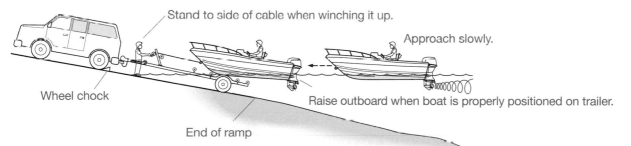

Stand to side of cable when winching it up.

Approach slowly.

Wheel chock

Raise outboard when boat is properly positioned on trailer.

End of ramp

WASHING BOAT & TRAILER

There is an increasing problem with boats and trailers picking up aquatic nuisance species (e.g., zebra mussels) from one body of water and introducing them to other waters or lakes. Away from the ramp and run-off areas, remove the drain plugs and wash down the trailer, boat and boat's gear with high water pressure. Flush the outboard's cooling system with a flusher attachment to the water hose. Remove contents of live wells and bait buckets on land.

HOIST OPERATION

If a hoist is not operated properly, it can result in serious damage and injury. Some facilities require specific personnel to operate the hoist. If you are not at such a facility and haven't operated the hoist before, ask an experienced person to demonstrate or help. Operate the hoist carefully and don't rush. Oftentimes, safety rules will be posted. Be sure to review them carefully beforehand.

HOIST PREPARATION

- ☐ Drain any water from the boat and close the drain plugs securely before launching.
- ☐ Check the condition of the lifting slings, their fittings, and the attachment points on the boat. Their breaking strength should be at least twice the weight of the boat fully loaded, including fuel and gear.
- ☐ Slings are fitted so the boat is level when on the hoist.
- ☐ Slings are securely fastened.
- ☐ Bow and stern lines are attached to boat.
- ☐ Outboard or stern drive is locked in the UP position.

REVIEW QUESTIONS

1. The weight on a hitch ball is known as _____.

2. If the tongue weight is too light, a trailer may swerve back and forth, or _____. If this occurs, _____ speed.

3. When backing a trailer, move the _____ of the wheel in the direction you want the back of the trailer to turn.

4. When launching, once the trailer is backed down the ramp, park in first gear or PARK and place a _____ behind the vehicle's rear wheel.

5. To avoid introducing nuisance species from one body of water to another, it is important to _____ the trailer, boat and boat's gear after hauling out.

Answers:
1) tongue weight
2) fishtail; reduce
3) bottom
4) chock
5) wash down/wash

Chapter 18

OTHER BOATING ACTIVITIES

KEY CONCEPTS

▶ Personal watercraft

▶ Waterskiing & towed devices

▶ Diving activities

▶ Hunting & fishing

▶ Paddlesports

PERSONAL WATERCRAFT (PWC)

How Does a Water Jet Work?

Personal watercraft are propelled by a water jet drive, which is powered by a gasoline engine located inside an engine compartment. A water jet illustration in Chapter 1 shows how water flows into the jet intake and accelerates through the water pump and squirts out the exit nozzle. It is the jet of water exiting the nozzle that propels the PWC forward. If there is no water coming out of the nozzle, the PWC won't move. When you increase the throttle, water is pumped through the nozzle at a higher speed, resulting in greater thrust that moves the PWC faster. While some models may have a deflector mounted behind the nozzle to deflect or reverse the exiting water, many may not have this feature to stop or reverse the PWC. In this case, you will have to turn off the engine to stop. Make sure you allow enough distance for your watercraft to come to a stop.

Steering

The exit nozzle is movable and is used to steer the PWC. The direction of the nozzle is typically controlled by a handlebar. If you turn the handlebar to the right, it will turn the nozzle to the right causing the thrust from the water jet to turn the PWC to the right. Your steering control improves with the speed of the water exiting the nozzle. Higher engine speeds increase flow and produce greater steering response. If you reduce the throttle to idle or the engine stops, you lose steering control and the amount varies depending on whether your PWC has a device to reduce this loss. In the worst case, the PWC won't change direction even if you turn the handlebar. This occurs because the steering thrust of the jet drive becomes ineffective if the PWC is moving faster than the thrust. A common mistake is to turn while reducing the throttle and then discover you can't change direction.

Rear view of a PWC steering nozzle.

Capacity & Stability

PWCs are designed to carry a maximum number of people and/or weight. The recommended capacity can be found in the owner's manual or on the manufacturer's decal. If you exceed these limits, the performance of the PWC could be dangerously affected and could result in capsizing. When operated under the maximum capacities limit with the weight of the occupants centered in the middle, PWCs are stable. When getting on board, keep your weight centered. If a PWC happens to turn upside down, it should be rolled back upright in the direction recommended by the manufacturer. Failure to do so could result in damage. Check the owner's manual for the direction of rotation and look for a rotation decal on the stern of the PWC.

Maximum Capacities label indicating the PWC is limited to 3 persons or 530 pounds (240 kilograms).

Fueling

Two key points to remember when fueling:

- Fill the tank away from the water, if possible, to avoid polluting the water with fuel spills. Do not overfill your tank.

- Gasoline vapor is heavier than air and will sink. After fueling and/or before starting the engine, open the engine compartment and let it ventilate for at least four minutes. If you smell gasoline, check for fuel leaks.

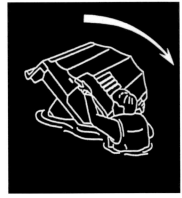

The arrow on this rotation decal indicates the PWC should be rotated clockwise to bring it upright after capsizing.

Starting a PWC

The basic steps are:

1. Complete the pre-start list (includes fuel, oil, required equipment, manufacturer's checks).

2. Position the PWC in an adequate depth of water (as per owner's manual) to avoid ingesting sediment or vegetation into the water jet drive.

3. Get on the PWC.

4. Attach the lanyard of the emergency engine cutoff switch to your wrist or life jacket.

5. Start the engine as per manufacturer's manual.

Falling Off & Reboarding a PWC

If you fall off, PWCs typically have an emergency engine cutoff switch that will turn off the engine as soon as you fall off. However, this cutoff switch will only work if its lanyard is attached to the switch and to you. As soon as the lanyard is pulled off the switch, the cutoff switch is activated. Some older models may not have this feature and will circle at idle speed until you can swim over and grab them. Be aware that if the idle speed is set too high, it may be difficult to catch the circling PWC. If you need to reboard the PWC, it should be done from the rear, pulling yourself over the back end and keeping your weight centered.

EQUIPMENT & OPERATING REGULATIONS

PWCs are subject to the same laws, Navigation Rules and equipment requirements that govern boats of the same size. There are additional regulations and requirements specific for PWCs that vary with each state.

- Each person on a PWC must wear a U.S. Coast Guard approved life jacket; a high-impact vest type is recommended and often required.

- Wearing a wetsuit or dry suit is recommended in cool air or water conditions.

- Drivers must attach the lanyard of the emergency engine cutoff switch to their wrist, life jacket or clothing (if applicable). If a PWC is equipped with a self-circling device, it must not be disabled.

- Drivers must meet the state's minimum age limit and education requirements.

- PWCs cannot be operated from sunset to sunrise (some states specify a half hour after sunset to a half hour before sunrise, or other variations—check with your state).

- The Navigation Rules apply to PWCs—know them and obey them.

- Obey Slow No Wake restrictions.

- Avoid high-speed operation in shallow water, which can cause damage to the water jet pump and environmental erosion.

WATERSKIING & TOWED DEVICES

In addition to high-speed boat-handling skills, waterskiing and towing wakeboards or tubes require additional considerations and skills. States and local jurisdictions may have additional requirements and limitations.

EQUIPMENT & OPERATING REGULATIONS

- Appropriate USCG approved high-impact life jacket (inflatable type is not suitable) must be worn by a skier.

- Towline: typically 75 feet, but maximum length limitation may vary depending on use and state and local regulations.

- Federal regulations prohibit skiing or towing after sunset and before sunrise; some states have different time limitations—check with your state.

Wearing a life jacket is always required when operating or riding on a PWC.

Photo Courtesy of U.S. Coast Guard

KEY POINTS FOR PWC

- *Accident statistics indicate the most common accidents for PWCs are collisions with other vessels or hazards. To help reduce these accidents: keep a proper lookout at all times; stay a proper distance from vessels and objects; and always operate your PWC in a safe manner.*

- *Read the operating instructions in the manufacturer's manual and familiarize yourself with stop/start and throttle controls.*

- *Take into account that steering control is drastically reduced or lost when rapidly reducing speed from high to low.*

- *Keep a constant lookout for other boats and objects.*

- *Always look around and behind before turning.*

- *Do not make sudden changes in direction when near other boats.*

- *Do not jump wake close behind another boat (many states prohibit this within 100 feet).*

- *Do not weave through congested traffic.*

- *Be considerate of other boaters and people onshore; avoid operating in the same area for any length of time and avoid making excessive noise (altered mufflers or cutout devices are prohibited in many states).*

- Have an observer in the boat to watch the skier or towed device, and relay signals to the driver; many states require an observer even if a boat has a rearview mirror.

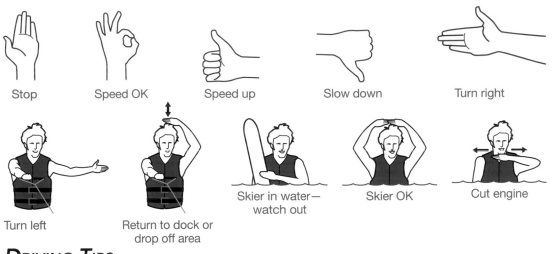

Stop   Speed OK   Speed up   Slow down   Turn right

Turn left   Return to dock or   Skier in water—   Skier OK   Cut engine
              drop off area   watch out

Driving Tips

- *Use hand signals to communicate.*

- *Wait for a start signal from a skier before accelerating and steer straight.*

- *Use a lower speed for inexperienced skiers.*

- *Make wide turns.*

- *Return immediately once a skier falls or drops off.*

- *Make a slow approach when operating near a person in the water—be especially careful with a propeller-driven boat.*

- *Turn off the engine when picking up or dropping off a skier in the water.*

- *Allow a 200-foot wide corridor (or twice the towline length) for the skier to avoid contact with objects.*

DIVING ACTIVITIES

Under Inland and International Navigation Rules, a vessel engaged in diving operations during the day may display a rigid replica of International Code Flag ALPHA not less than 3.3 feet (1 meter) in height. The ALPHA flag is exhibited only by a vessel engaged in diving operations and signifies its inability to maneuver in accordance with the Rules. It has no special separation or maneuvering requirements for other boats other than to keep out of the way of the diving vessel.

International Code Flag ALPHA represents the letter A.

The Diver Down flag has no official status in federal regulations. It is recognized by the Coast Guard as a flag indicating diving operations and, unlike the ALPHA flag, it is used to mark locations of divers in the water. Many states have enacted regulations requiring the display of the Diver Down flag and specifying standoff distances. A minimum of 100 feet is recommended but divers frequently stray

Diver Down Flag

considerable distances from their marker and separations of up to 300 feet in open waters are recommended. Like the ALPHA flag, the Diver Down flag should be of rigid construction and conspicuously displayed. A vessel conducting diving operations should only display the flag to mark the site of diving operations, not when running to or from the site.

HUNTING & FISHING

If you use your boat to hunt or fish, you should be aware that capsizing and falling overboard account for the greatest number of fatalities (almost 70%) and occur most frequently in boats under 20 feet in length. Eight out of ten fatalities were NOT wearing life jackets. People often hunt or fish in remote areas or during periods of the year (fall, winter or spring) when conditions are cold, weather can change rapidly, and other boaters or marine patrols may not be around if help is needed. You should be aware of the risks of cold water shock and hypothermia (see Chapter 16). Immersion in cold water is the #1 killer for people who hunt with a boat.

When you fish or hunt, wear a life jacket. It could save your life.

Photo Courtesy of U.S. Coast Guard

Water Temp. (°F)	Exhaustion or Unconsciousness	Expected Time of Survival
60 to 70	2 to 7 hours	2 to 40 hours
50 to 60	1 to 2 hours	1 to 6 hours
32.5 to 40	15 to 30 minutes	30 to 90 minutes

This table depicts examples of time periods that a person may be able to survive in various water temperatures. (Adapted from U.S. Coast Guard Table)

The best prevention for hypothermia is to dress appropriately in layers, wear a life jacket and a wool or fleece hat, and for cold water wearing a dry suit or wetsuit is recommended. Alcohol does not mix with boats and cold weather. Not only will alcohol impair your judgment and balance, it will have an adverse effect on the body's ability to avoid hypothermia.

Federal regulations require life jackets be carried for each person on board the boat, but if you hunt or fish you should wear your life jacket. If you fall overboard, many boats do not have a good and easy method of getting the person back on the boat and it may take some period of time, especially if you are bulked up with warm clothing that becomes very heavy as soon as you try to emerge from the water. Trying to put a life jacket on in the water is difficult and tiring, and can increase heat loss.

SAFETY TIPS

- *Observe all boating safety rules and regulations. When you hunt or fish, you are a boater and must comply with safe boating practices and regulations.*

- *Wear your life jacket.*

- *Don't overload your boat beyond the limits of the Maximum Capacities label.*

- *Keep the boat evenly balanced.*

- *Keep weights low.*

- *Carry a VHF/DSC radio or mobile phone.*

BOAT DESIGN

Boat design affects the risk of capsizing and swamping. Many of the smaller boats used for hunting and fishing may have low freeboard and/or a flat bottom for shallow water operation. Both of these features can increase the risk of swamping or capsizing if you overload the boat with people and gear, put too much weight on one side, get caught in rough weather, or anchor from the stern. Boats that have elevated pedestal seats for fishing will have their center of gravity adversely affected when people are sitting in them, which increases the risk of capsizing at smaller angles of heel (tipping).

PADDLESPORTS

Canoeing, kayaking, rafting, rowing, and stand up paddleboarding (SUP) are popular water sports, and all use watercraft that are propelled by paddles or oars. The easily driven performance of these types of watercraft comes from their light weight and hull shape, but these performance-enhancing features also make them more susceptible to capsizing. With their narrow beam and small amount of draft, they can roll over if the weight of the people and equipment is not kept low and near the centerline. Standing up and shifting your weight to the side can cause capsizing. Avoid reaching too far over the side. If picking up an item in the water, get next to it so your shoulders don't lean over the side. With their low freeboard, powerboat wake and rough water conditions could cause these watercraft to capsize or swamp, or paddleboarders to fall. All boat operators should be particularly careful when operating near these watercraft. Knowing how to swim and wearing a life jacket are smart safety fundamentals. Accident statistics indicate that 50 percent of canoe and kayak fatalities were while fishing, 25 percent had consumed alcohol, and a large majority were not wearing life jackets. If you are new to these sports, take a hands-on course. For more information about these courses, contact the American Canoe Association or your state boating department.

If you capsize, stay with your craft and try to hold onto your paddle. Hold onto the upstream or upwind end to avoid getting pinned between the hull and a hazard, and float on your back keeping your feet downstream and on the surface to avoid getting them caught in the bottom. Use your free arm to swim to shore.

Federal regulations require life jackets for paddleboarding and they should always be worn. In cold conditions, wear a wetsuit or dry suit to protect against hypothermia.

Wear a life jacket whenever you canoe or kayak.

Photo Courtesy of U.S. Coast Guard

SAFETY TIPS

- *Wear a properly fitted U.S. Coast Guard approved life jacket.*
- *Know how to swim and paddle.*
- *Know how to self-rescue your craft if it capsizes.*
- *Paddle with a buddy.*
- *Don't paddle or row while under the influence of alcohol.*
- *Be aware of weather and water conditions and forecasts.*
- *Avoid conditions that exceed your skills and experience.*
- *Leave a float plan with a friend or relative.*
- *Wear appropriate clothes, headwear and footwear for air and water temperatures. Wearing bright colors and using brightly colored paddles increases your visibility to other boaters who may not see you low in the water. If in doubt, raise your paddle vertically.*
- *Attach a waterproof bag to carry your personal items (e.g., sunscreen, water, VHF/DSC radio or mobile phone).*
- *Check for leaks and carry a bailer.*
- *Don't overload your craft.*
- *Distribute weight evenly, centered side to side and front to back, and keep it low.*
- *Position your weight over the centerline when getting in or out.*
- *Avoid standing up and moving to the side. If you have to move around, keep a secure footing and grip on the watercraft by using the three-points contact method (two hands and one foot in contact or one hand and two feet in contact).*
- *Paddle or row into or away from waves that might capsize or swamp your craft.*
- *Beware of rapids, low-head dams and other hazards along the route.*
- *Paddle near a shore in open waters and avoid channels used by other boats or vessels.*

REVIEW QUESTIONS

1. A jet of water exiting from a movable _____ is used to steer a PWC.

2. If the throttle is suddenly cut from high speed to idle speed on a PWC, loss of _____ control may occur.

3. When fueling a PWC, you should ventilate the engine compartment for at least _____ minutes before starting the engine.

4. A waterskier is required to wear a U.S. Coast Guard approved high-impact _____ .

5. If you see a red flag with a white diagonal stripe, it marks the location of _____ and you should keep at least _____ feet from the flag.

Answers:
1) nozzle
2) steering
3) four
4) life jacket
5) divers; 100

SOUND SIGNALS & NAVIGATION LIGHTS

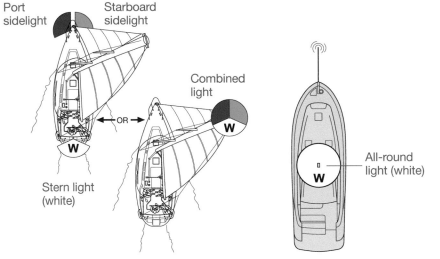

Port sidelight   Starboard sidelight

All-round light (white) can be seen from all directions.

Light requirement for a powerboat underway whose length is less than 39.4 feet (12 meters).

Port sidelight   Starboard sidelight

Masthead light (white)

Sternlight (white)

Light requirement for a powerboat (or sailboat using an engine) underway whose length is less than 164 feet (50 meters).

Port sidelight   Starboard sidelight

Combined light

— OR —

Stern light (white)

All-round light (white)

Light requirement for sailboats underway. In addition to sidelights and a sternlight, a sailboat under sail may display a red all-round light over a green all-round at or near the top of the mast, but these lights shall not be exhibited in conjunction with the combined light (as shown in the illustration). A sailing boat less than 23 feet (7 meters) long may use a flashlight instead of navigation lights, provided it is turned on in sufficient time to prevent a collision.

Light requirement for an anchored boat less than 164 feet (50 meters).

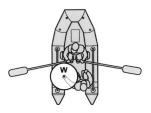

Light requirement for a boat being rowed or paddled: a flashlight is turned on in sufficient time to prevent a collision.

Sound Signals

● A short blast is about one second's duration.
— A prolonged blast is from four to six seconds' duration.

For vessels in sight of each other:

● **One short blast** indicates *altering* course to starboard (International), or *intending* to alter course to starboard (Inland) when meeting or crossing.

●● **Two short blasts** indicate *altering* course to port (International), or *intending* to alter course to port (Inland) when meeting or crossing.

●●● **Three short blasts** indicate engine is in reverse (although vessel may still be moving forward).

●●●●● **Five short blasts** = danger.

For vessels in restricted visibility:

— One prolonged blast every two minutes indicates a vessel under power.

—●● One prolonged blast followed by two short blasts every two minutes indicates a vessel under sail. Be aware that other vessels will also sound this signal (e.g., vessels engaged in towing, fishing, pushing, and vessels restricted in their ability to maneuver).

Other sound signals:

— One prolonged blast is sounded by a vessel nearing a blind bend of a channel or fairway, or when departing a berth.

For other sound signals consult the *Navigation Rules: International-Inland*.

AIDS TO NAVIGATION SUMMARY

LATERAL AIDS TO NAVIGATION

Lateral marks (below) indicate channels, safe water (mid-channel), and preferred channels (junction buoys) as well as the side on which to leave them when returning from seaward.

PORT SIDE OF CHANNEL

GREEN CAN

▶ odd numbered

▶ leave to port

GREEN DAYMARK

▶ odd numbered

▶ leave to port

GREEN BUOY/GREEN LIGHT

▶ odd numbered

▶ leave to port

PREFERRED CHANNEL BUOY: GREEN TOPMOST BAND

▶ preferred channel to starboard

▶ may have green light (Fl 2+1)

▶ may be lettered

STARBOARD SIDE OF CHANNEL

RED NUN

▶ even numbered

▶ leave to starboard

RED DAYMARK

▶ even numbered

▶ leave to starboard

RED BUOY/RED LIGHT

▶ even numbered

▶ leave to starboard

PREFERRED CHANNEL BUOY: RED TOPMOST BAND

▶ preferred channel to port

▶ may have red light (Fl 2+1)

▶ may be lettered

MIDDLE OF CHANNEL

SPHERE/RED & WHITE VERTICAL STRIPES

▶ safe water either side

RED & WHITE VERTICAL DAYMARK

▶ safe water either side

RED & WHITE VERTICAL BUOY

▶ sound/light signal flashes a short and long white light (Morse A)

▶ safe water either side

ISOLATED DANGER & SPECIAL PURPOSE MARKS

BLACK & RED BANDS WITH TOPMARK BUOY

▶ has a topmark of two black spheres

▶ may have white light group flashes of two every 5 seconds

▶ marks an isolated danger with navigable water all around

YELLOW BUOY

▶ yellow mark with black letter(s)

▶ may have a yellow fixed or flashing light

▶ marks a special feature or area (e.g., pipelines, traffic separation schemes, spoil areas, jetties)

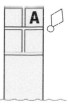

LIGHTHOUSES

Lighthouses fall into the category of lighted beacons and are fixed to the sea bottom or on land. Raster and paper charts indicate a lighthouse with either a magenta teardrop symbol or a star and identify the characteristic flashing sequence of its light (e.g., flashing, occulting, group flashing or isophase). Examples: Fl 15s indicates light flashes once every 15 seconds; Fl(2) 5s indicates a Group Flash 2 every 5 seconds.

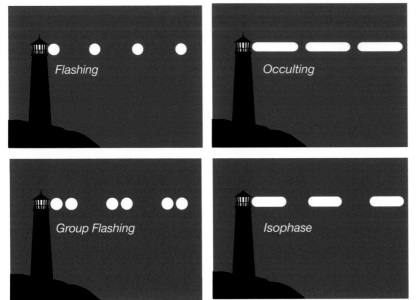

A **flashing** light is on in short bursts interspersed with longer periods of darkness.

A **group flashing** light repeats multiple light signals.

A **composite flashing** light repeats irregular multiples of signals, or example "2+1". This means that within its time cycle the light will flash a group of 2 flashes followed by a short pause, then a third flash.

An **occulting** light is on most of the time and "winks" off according to its charted sequence. Sometimes called a "black flash," these lights are easy to take bearings on.

An **isophase** light has equal periods of light and darkness.

INFORMATION & REGULATORY MARKERS

These markers with their orange symbols and bands are used for dangers, warnings, directions, and other regulatory matters and information.

Danger	**Boat Exclusion Area**	**Controlled Area**	**Information**
		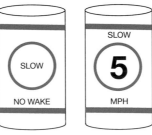	
The nature of danger (e.g., rock, wreck, shoal, dam) may be indicated inside the diamond shape.	Explanation (e.g., dam, rapids, swim area) may be placed outside the crossed diamond shape.	Type of control (e.g., slow, no wake, speed limit) is indicated in the circle.	Directions, distances and other non-regulatory information is displayed inside the square or rectangular symbol.

GLOSSARY OF BOATING TERMS

Including radio phonetic alphabet (in parentheses)

A (ALPHA)

Abaft - toward the stern relative to a position (e.g., abaft the beam).

Abeam - off the side of (at right angle to) a boat.

Aboard - on a boat.

Adrift - a boat drifting without control.

Aft - at or toward the stern or behind a boat.

Aground - a boat whose bottom, keel or skeg is touching the sea bottom.

Aids to navigation (ATONS) - include beacons and buoys used to determine a boat's position or safe course, or to warn of dangers or obstructions.

Alternator - a device which generates electricity from an engine.

Amidships - at, or toward the center of a boat.

Astern - behind the stern of a boat.

Athwartships - a direction across a boat from side to side.

B (BRAVO)

Back - a counterclockwise change of wind direction.

Bail - to empty a boat of water.

Balance - the relationship of a boat's athwartship (sideways) orientation to the surface of the water.

Barometer - a weather forecasting instrument that measures air pressure.

Battery switch - the main electrical cutoff switch.

Beam - the width of a boat at its widest point.

Bear away - to fall off, turn away from the wind.

Bearing - the direction from one object to another, usually expressed in degrees.

Below - the area of a boat beneath the deck.

Berth - 1. the space in which you park your boat. 2. a bed on a boat.

Bight - a loop in a line.

Bilge - the lowest part of a boat's interior, where water collects.

Bimini - a sun awning used to cover the cockpit or flying bridge.

Bitter end - the end of a line.

Block - a pulley on a boat.

Boat hook - a pole with a hook on the end used for grabbing hold of a mooring or an object in the water.

Boat speed - the speed of a boat through the water.

Bottom - 1. the underside of a boat. 2. the land under the water.

Bow - the forward part of a boat.

Bow line (BOW - line) - a line attached to the bow.

Bowline (BOE-lin) - a knot designed to make a loop that will not slip and can be easily untied.

Breast line - a short dockline running perpendicular from the beam (at mid-length) of a boat to the dock.

Broach - a sudden, uncontrolled and powerful turn when running down a large wave. The boat will also roll onto its side and could capsize in extreme situations.

Bulkhead - a wall-like structure that runs athwartships on a boat, usually providing structural support to the hull.

Bunk (*see* Berth, definition #2)

Buoy - a floating navigation mark or mooring ball.

Buoyancy - the ability of an object to float.

C (CHARLIE)

Cabin - the interior of a boat.

Can - an odd-numbered, green buoy marking the left side of a channel as you return from seaward.

Capsize - to roll a boat onto its side or upside down and it does not return to its upright position.

Cast off - to release a line from a boat and not bring it aboard.

Cavitation - vaporized bubbles disrupt water flow on the propeller blades causing loss of thrust and erosion of the blades' surface.

Centerline - the midline of a boat running from bow to stern.

Chafe - wear on a line caused by rubbing.

Channel - a waterway where the water is deeper than the surrounding area and is often marked by navigation marks.

Chart - a nautical map.

Chart datum (*see* Datum)

Chart plotter - an electronic device used to display charts and determine positions, bearings, distances and courses.

Chine - the sharp edge formed at the intersection of the topsides and bottom of a boat.

Chock - a fitting mounted on the deck through which dock lines and anchor lines are led.

Choke - a device for controlling the mixture of air and fuel for an engine.

Cleat - a fitting used to secure a line.

Coaming - the low protective wall surrounding the cockpit.

Coastal waters - include the U.S. waters of the Great Lakes, U.S. territorial seas and those waters directly connected to the Great Lakes and territorial seas where any entrance exceeds 2 nautical miles between opposite shorelines to the first point where the largest distance between shorelines narrows to 2 miles.

Cockpit - the open area that is recessed below the deck or gunwale.

Coil - to loop a line neatly so it can be stored.

Companionway - the steps leading from the cockpit or deck to the cabin below.

Compass (fluxgate) - an electromagnetic instrument that indicates a boat's heading digitally in degrees True or Magnetic.

Compass (magnetic) - a magnetic instrument that indicates the direction in which a boat is headed in degrees Magnetic.

Compass (satellite) - an instrument that determines True North using GPS positioning and is unaffected by the Earth's magnetic field. It indicates a boat's heading in degrees True.

Compass protractor - a plotting instrument oriented to latitude/longitude lines on a chart.

Compass rose - the twin circles on a raster or paper chart which indicate the direction of True North and Magnetic North.

Console - a structure in a cockpit or inside a boat on which the boat controls and instruments are located.

Contour line - a line of constant water depth on a chart.

Converter - a device that may be used to convert voltage from AC (alternating current) to DC (direct current).

Course - the direction in which a boat is steered or to be steered.

Course Over Ground (COG) - the direction in which a boat is traveling across the sea bottom.

Crew - anyone on a boat who helps the operator.

Crosscurrent - the direction that is perpendicular (at 90 degrees) to the direction of the current (horizontal movement of water).

Cross-Track Error (XTE) - the distance and direction that a boat is off its intended course to an activated waypoint.

Crosswind - when the wind direction is perpendicular (at 90 degrees) to a boat's course or its centerline.

Current - the horizontal movement of water caused by tidal action, wind and other forces.

D (DELTA)

Datum - 1. a standard vertical reference from which depths are indicated on a chart, and tide depths are calculated. 2. a standard geographic coordinate system (latitude and longitude) of the earth's surface from which the position of a boat or object can be determined.

Dead Reckoning (DR) - used to determine a boat's position calculated from course steered and speed (distance) through the water.

Deck - the mostly flat surface area on top of a boat.

Deck plate - a plate in a deck covering a fill line to a fuel or water tank, or a pump-out line to a holding tank.

Deviation - is the magnetic compass error caused by metal objects with magnetic properties (e.g., iron and steel).

Diameter (propeller) - the dimension of the circle made by the rotation of the tip ends of the propeller blades.

Dinghy - a small boat that can be rowed, sailed, or propelled by a small motor.

Directional stability - the ability to hold a straight course.

Displacement - the weight of a boat; therefore the amount of water it displaces.

Dividers - an instrument used for measuring distances or coordinates on a paper chart.

Dock - 1. a structure to which a boat can be tied. 2. the act of bringing a boat to rest alongside the structure.

Dock line - a line used to secure a boat to a dock.

Dodger - a canvas shield in front of the cockpit of some boats that is designed to protect people from spray.

Downcurrent (*see* **Downstream**)

Downstream - the direction that the current (horizontal movement of water) is flowing toward.

Downwind - away from the direction of the wind (where the wind is blowing toward).

Draft - the vertical distance from the water's surface to the deepest point on a boat.

E (ECHO)

Ease - to let out a line until tension is eased, but the line does not hang slack.

Ebb - an outgoing current.

Electronic Navigation Chart (ENC) - a standardized electronic chart with multiple layers of digital navigation information, commonly known as a vector chart.

Emergency engine cutoff switch - a switch that shuts off the engine when activated.

EPIRB - Emergency Position Indicating Radio Beacon

F (FOXTROT)

Fairway - the center of a channel.

Fall off (*see* **Head down**)

Fathom - a measurement of the depth of water. One fathom equals six feet.

Fender - a flexible cylindrical or spherical object used to protect the sides of a boat when coming in contact with a dock or another boat.

Fitting - a piece of nautical hardware.

Fix - a boat's position determined by bearings.

Flake - to lay out a line on deck using large loops to keep it from becoming tangled.

Float plan - an itinerary of your intended trip, left with a responsible party onshore.

Float switch - a switch for an electric bilge pump that is activated when water raises a floatable lever to a certain level.

Flood - an incoming current.

Fluxgate compass (*see* **Compass, fluxgate**)

Following sea - waves coming from behind a boat.

Fore - forward.

Forepeak - a storage area in the bow (below the deck).

Forward - toward the bow.

Fouled - tangled.

Freeboard - the height of a hull above the water's surface.

G (GOLF)

Gear - generic term for boating equipment.

Gearshift - the control that changes the direction of an engine and its propulsion system (propeller or jet drive) from neutral to forward or reverse.

Give-way vessel - the vessel required to give way to another vessel when they may be on a collision course.

GPS compass (*see* **Compass, satellite**)

Great Lakes - means the Great Lakes and their connecting and tributary waters including the Calumet River as far as the Thomas J. O'Brien Lock and Controlling Works (between mile 326 and 327), the Chicago River as far as the east side of the Ashland Avenue Bridge (between mile 321 and 322), and the Saint Lawrence River as far east as the lower exit of Saint Lambert Lock.

Ground tackle - the anchor and rode (chain and line).

Gunwale (GUNN-nle) - the top edge of the topsides or where the topsides and deck meet.

Gust - an increase in wind speed for a short duration.

H (HOTEL)

Hard over - to turn the tiller or wheel as far as possible in one direction.

Hatch - a large covered opening in a deck or the top of a cabin.

Haul in - to take in a line.

Head - the bathroom or marine toilet on a boat.

Heading - the direction that a boat is pointed at, usually expressed in degrees.

Head down - to change course away from the wind.

Head off (*see* **Head down**)

Head up - to change course toward the wind.

Headway - progress made in the forward direction.

Heave - to throw.

Heavy weather - strong winds and large waves.

Heel - the sideways lean of a boat.

Helm - the tiller or wheel.

Helmsman - the person who drives a boat.

Hold - a line handling term to not let any line out, but be ready to act when directed.

Holding ground - the sea bottom used to hold a anchor.

Holding tank - a tank that stores sewage from a marine toilet.

Hull - the body of a boat formed by the bottom, topsides, and deck.

Hull speed - the theoretical maximum speed of a boat determined by the length of its waterline.

I (INDIA)

Inboard - 1. inside the rail or gunwale of a boat. 2. when referring to an engine that is located inside the hull.

Inlet - a narrow opening or passage in the shore from open water (e.g., ocean, gulf, lake, sound).

Inverter – a device that converts DC (direct current) to AC (alternating current).

Isobar – a line of equal atmospheric pressure depicted on a weather map.

J (JULIET)

Jury rig - an improvised, temporary repair.

K (KILO)

Kedge off - to use an anchor to pull a boat into deeper water after it has run aground.

Keel - a vertical fin running along the centerline of a powerboat's bottom to improve its tracking ability by reducing its sideways slip in the water.

Kill switch (see **Emergency engine cutoff switch**)

King spoke - a marker on the steering wheel which indicates when the rudder is centered.

Knot - one nautical mile per hour.

L (LIMA)

Land breeze - a wind that blows from land toward the sea.

Lash - to tie down.

Latitude - a measurement measured north or south from the equator in units of degrees, minutes, decimals of minutes or seconds.

Lazarette - a storage compartment accessed through the deck, usually located in the stern.

Lee shore - the shore to which the wind is blowing.

Leeward (LEW-erd) - the direction away from the wind (where the wind is blowing to).

Leeward side - the side of a boat that is away from the wind.

Leeway - sideways slippage of a boat in a direction away from the wind or current.

Left-hand (propeller) - a propeller that rotates counterclockwise in forward gear when viewed from astern (behind).

Lifeline - plastic coated wire, supported by stanchions, around the outside of a deck to help prevent people from falling overboard.

Lifesling - a floating sling that is attached to the boat by a length of floating line and is used to rescue a person in the water.

Lift (propeller) - is produced by a pressure difference from each side of a propeller blade when the propeller is rotating.

Line - a nautical term used for rope.

List - the sideways lean of a boat.

Longitude - a measurement measured east or west of a line running from the North Pole through the Greenwich Observatory in England to the South Pole in units of degrees, minutes, decimals of minutes or seconds.

Lubber's line - a small post in a compass used to help determine a course or a bearing.

Lull - a decrease in wind speed for a short duration.

M (MIKE)

Magnetic - in reference to Magnetic North rather than True North.

Make fast - to secure a line.

Marine Sanitation Device (MSD) - a system that includes toilet, holding tank and connecting lines and valves.

Marlinspike - a pointed tool used to loosen knots.

Master switch (see **Battery switch**)

Mayday call - the internationally recognized distress signal for a life-threatening emergency.

Mooring - a permanently anchored buoy to which a boat can be tied.

N (NOVEMBER)

Nautical mile - a distance of 6,076 feet or 1.15 statute miles, which equals one minute of the earth's latitude.

Navigation aids (see **Aids to navigation**)

Navigation lights - lights on a boat (i.e., sidelights, sternlight, masthead light, etc.) that are used to identify watercraft and help avoid collisions when operating from sunset to sunrise and during restricted visibility.

Navigation plan - includes compass headings, distances and estimated times to help determine a boat's position or route during a trip.

Navigation Rules - laws established to prevent collisions on the water.

No-Discharge Zone (NDZ) - an area where the discharge of any treated and untreated sewage is prohibited.

Nun - a red, even-numbered buoy, marking the right side of a channel as you return from seaward.

O (OSCAR)

Offshore - away from or out of sight of land.

Offshore wind - a wind blowing from the land toward the sea.

On board - on a boat.

On the beam (see **Abeam**)

Onshore wind - a wind blowing from the sea toward the land.

Outboard - 1. outside or toward the rail or gunwale of a boat. 2. when referring to an engine that is located outside the hull (outboard motor).

Overtaking - a boat that is catching up to another boat and about to pass it.

P (PAPA)

Painter - a line attached to the bow of a small boat.

Pan-Pan call - the internationally recognized distress signal for an urgent situation.

Parallel rulers - an instrument with two rulers linked parallel by hinges used to plot a course on a paper chart.

Pay out - to ease a line.

Pendant - a length of line or wire used to attach a boat to a mooring.

Pennant - a small flag used for signaling.

Personal Flotation Device (PFD) - a life jacket or life vest.

Piling - vertical timber or log driven into the sea bottom to support docks and/or secure dock lines.

Piloting - near-shore navigation used to determine a boat's position by visual references (e.g., aids to navigation, landmarks, and water depths).

Pitch (propeller) - the theoretical distance that a propeller would advance in one revolution in a solid material (no slippage).

Planing - when a boat reaches a speed where it is running on top of the water and no longer restricted by its bow and stern waves.

Plot - applying calculations to a chart to determine course or position.

Port - 1. the left side of a boat when facing forward. 2. a harbor. 3. a window in a cabin on a boat.

Power trim - hydraulic adjustment of the angle of outboard motors or stern drives while underway.

Power-driven vessel - any vessel propelled by machinery.

Prevailing wind - typical or consistent wind conditions.

Prop walk - the side force generated from the rotation of a propeller, which results in a boat's tendency to turn slightly instead of tracking straight.

Propeller - a hub with radiating blades used for propulsion.

Pulpit - a stainless steel guardrail at the bow and stern of some boats.

Pumpout station - a location where boats can empty their holding tanks.

Q (QUEBEC)

Quarter - the sides of a boat near the stern.

R (ROMEO)

Radar reflector - a metal object designed to be detected by other vessels' radar.

Rail - the outer edges of a deck.

Range - 1. the alignment of two objects that indicates the middle of a channel, safe water, or is used to stay on course. 2. a distance that is used to define the position of a boat or object from a known point. 3. the visual distance that a light may be seen. 4. the vertical distance between high and low water (tide).

Raster Navigational Chart (RNC) - a digitized image of a paper chart.

Raw water - water from outside a boat brought in through hoses for engine cooling or toilet flushing.

Restricted visibility - any condition in which visibility is restricted by fog, mist, falling snow, heavy rainstorms, sandstorms, or any other similar causes.

Rhumb line - a straight course between two points.

Right-hand (propeller) - a propeller that rotates clockwise in forward gear when viewed from astern (behind).

Rode - line and/or chain attached to an anchor.

Route - a series of pre-planned waypoints on either a GPS or chart plotter that define a trip.

Rudder - the underwater fin used to steer a boat.

Rules of the road (*see* **Navigation Rules**)

Running lights (*see* **Navigation lights**)

S (SIERRA)

Safety harness - a body-type harness worn by a person and attached to the boat by a tether to prevent the person from falling overboard or being separated from the boat.

Sailing vessel - any vessel under sail provided that propelling machinery, if fitted, is not being used.

Scope - the ratio of the amount of anchor rode deployed to the distance from the bow to the bottom.

Scupper - a cockpit or deck drain.

Sea breeze - a thermal generated wind that blows from the sea toward the land.

Seacock - a through-hull fitting with a valve.

Seaplane - any aircraft designed to maneuver on the water.

Secure - to make safe or tie a line to a cleat.

Sécurité call - an internationally recognized signal to warn others of a dangerous situation.

Set - 1. the direction of a current. 2. to dig an anchor into the sea bottom to prevent it from dragging.

Shackle - a metal fitting to connect lines, wire, chain and other fittings.

Shoal - shallow water that may be dangerous.

Skeg - 1. a triangular fin on the centerline at the aft end of a powerboat's bottom to improve its steering and tracking ability. 2. a triangular fin at the bottom of the lower unit of an outboard motor.

Skipper - an informal term for a person in charge of a boat.

Slack - 1. to release all tension on a line and let it hang slack. 2. when the velocity of water current is at minimum or zero speed.

Slip - 1. the space in which you park your boat. 2. to cast off from a mooring.

Snub - to hold a line under tension by wrapping it on a winch or cleat.

Sole - the floor in a cockpit or cabin.

Solenoid switch - an electrical switch that shuts off the flow of propane.

Soundings - water depths depicted on a chart and measured from the sea bottom to the chart datum.

Speed Over Ground (SOG) - a boat's speed across the sea bottom.

Spring line - a line running forward or aft from a boat to a dock or another boat to keep the boat from moving forward or aft, or to rotate a boat when powering against it.

Squall - a short intense storm with little warning.

Stanchion - a stainless steel support at the edge of a deck that holds the lifelines.

Stand-on vessel - the vessel required to maintain its course and speed when it may be on a collision course with another vessel (unless the give-way vessel does not take action to avoid a collision).

Starboard - the right side of a boat when facing forward.

Steerage - ability to control the direction of a boat when steering with a wheel or tiller.

Steerageway - minimum amount of boat speed needed to control its direction.

Stem - the centerline of the forward part of a hull running along the profile from the deck to approximately the waterline.

Stern - the after end of a boat.

Stow - to store an item in a locker or a secure place.

Sump - 1. a cavity in the bilge to collect water. 2. a tank where drain water from showers and iceboxes collect.

Swamped - a boat filled with water.

T (TANGO)

Tackle - an arrangement of blocks and line that provides a mechanical advantage.

Take in - to bring a line aboard a boat.

Tether - a length of line connecting a safety harness to the boat.

Throttle - a device for controlling the engine's revolutions per minute (rpm).

Tide - the vertical rise and fall of water level due to the gravitational effect of the moon and sun.

Tiller - a lever or handle used to steer a boat instead of a steering wheel.

Toe rail - a low rail around the outer edges of a deck.

Topsides - the sides of a boat between the waterline and the deck.

Track - the direction a boat has run or will follow if it stays on its heading.

Transom - the vertical surface of the stern or back end of a boat.

Trim - 1. the relationship of a boat's forward and aft orientation to the water's surface. 2. to adjust the angle of an outboard motor or stern drive to the boat and the surface of the water.

Trim tab - a pivoting plate attached to the transom which can be adjusted to effect the trim of a boat.

U (UNIFORM)

Underway - when a vessel is not at anchor, tied up, or aground.

Upstream - the direction that is opposite to the direction of the horizontal movement of a current.

Upwind - toward the direction of the wind (where the wind is blowing from).

V (VICTOR)

Variation - the angular difference between Magnetic North and geographic (True) North in units of degrees and minutes.

V-berth - a bunk in the bow of a boat that narrows as it goes forward.

Veer - a clockwise change of wind direction.

Velocity Made Good (VMG) - the speed a boat has made toward its destination.

Ventilation (propeller) - air from above is drawn onto the propeller blades disrupting water flow over the blades that causes a sudden loss of thrust and increase in engine rpm.

Vessel - any watercraft, including powerboats, sailboats, person watercraft (PWC), and ships.

Vessel engaged in fishing - any vessel fishing with nets, lines, trawls, or other fishing apparatus which restricts maneuverability, but does not include a vessel fishing with trolling lines or other fishing apparatus which do not restrict maneuverability.

VHF - abbreviation for Very High Frequency, a two-way radio commonly used for boating.

Visibility - Vessels shall be deemed to be in sight of one another - only when one can be observed visually from the other.

W (WHISKEY)

Wake - waves caused by a boat moving through the water.

Waterline - the horizontal line on the hull where the water surface should be.

Waypoint - a geographic point or location used in navigation and usually expressed in latitude and longitude.

Western Rivers - means the Mississippi River, its tributaries, South Pass, and Southwest Pass, to the navigational demarcation lines dividing the high seas from harbors, rivers, and other inland waters of the United States, and the Port Allen-Morgan City Alternate Route, and that part of the Atchafalaya River above its junction with the Port Allen-Morgan City Alternate Route including the Old River and the Red River.

White caps - waves with foam tops.

Windage - the amount of surface area of a boat that is presented to the wind.

Windlass - a type of winch used for handling anchor rodes (line and/or chain).

Windward - the direction toward the wind (where the wind is blowing from).

Windward side - the side of a boat closest to the wind.

X (XRAY)
Y (YANKEE)
Z (ZULU)

INDEX

Appendix

ABOUT US POWERBOATING

WHO WE ARE

US Powerboating offers the nation's best and most comprehensive on-the-water training and education courses for recreational boaters. Our hands-on courses are taught by Certified Powerboat Instructors who empower students with the skills and confidence they need to get more out of their boating experience and become safer powerboat operators. US Powerboating's courses are offered through approved schools, community programs, clubs and marinas.

US Powerboating is an affiliate of US Sailing, a non-profit 501(c)(3) organization and the National Governing Body for the sport of sailing in the United States. US Sailing works to achieve this mission through a wide range of programs and events, geared towards providing an equal level playing field for all sailors. US Sailing sets the course enabling sailors to enjoy the sport for a lifetime.

OUR MISSION

Our mission aligns closely with the strategic objectives of the U.S. Coast Guard's Boating Safety Division. We aim to support them in their mission to make America's water ways safer for all and to minimize property damage, personal injury and loss of life by creating a new generation of educated and experienced recreational boaters.

OUR COURSES

US Powerboating's philosophy is that there is no substitute for practical, hands-on experience. After all, you wouldn't drive a car without taking driver's education so consider us your source for Driver's Education for Boaters.

Our courses are offered by Course Providers and at Powerboat Schools around the country. They are taught by knowledgeable, professional instructors who are dedicated to ensuring you get the most out of your educational experience. With offerings ranging from beginner to advanced, we are sure we have something for everyone.

We strive to emphasize the fun side of boating while ensuring that you feel safe, comfortable and confident!

ACKNOWLEDGMENTS

A number of US Powerboating/US Sailing powerboat instructors, trainers and other experts were involved in reviewing and editing revised editions of Start Powerboating Right! which was originally written by Dick Allsopp and Timothea Larr. Important contributions by volunteers to the content of previous editions include Dick Allsopp, Steve Colgate, Rob Crafa, David Forbes, Lynn Lynch and Karen Prioleau.

Led by Timothea Larr, this fourth edition would not have been possible without the diligent efforts of several individuals including Gordon Colby, Kevin Horan, Eddie Persichetti, Karen Prioleau, Paul Prioleau, Scott Souders and Juan Watson. Gordon Colby wrote major and important revisions to life jacket designations and approval labels in Chapter 10 (*Equipment & Requirements*). Scott Souders, Eddie Persichetti, Paul Prioleau and Juan Watson served as primary contributors to Chapter 11 (*Onboard Systems*). With keen input from Karen Prioleau, Paul Prioleau and Kevin Horan, Juan Watson spearheaded the rewrite of Chapters 14 and 15 (*Basic Navigation & Piloting Concepts* and *Basic Navigation & Piloting*). Additionally, Juan Watson, Karen Prioleau and Paul Prioleau contributed to the addition of pod drives and the Automatic Identification System in other chapters.

ADDITIONAL THANKS

Scott M. Carson, Graphic Designer, provided the layout and several illustrations for this publication.

US Sailing staff contributors: Betsy Alison, Adult Director; Stu Gilfillen, Director of Education; Pat Crawford, Copy Editor; Bradley Schoch, Instructional Designer; Jessica Servis, Education and Outreach Manager; and Karen Davidson, Adult Programs Operations Manager.

Cover photos courtesy of Grady White Boats

LOOKING FOR A RECREATIONAL BOATING SAFETY SKILLS COURSE?

The new National On-Water Standards (NOWS) are American National Standards that identify best practices course providers should follow when delivering skills-based instruction in recreational boat operation for beginners. They were developed through one of the largest collaboration projects ever conducted in recreational boating, funded in part by the Sport Fish Restoration and Boating Trust Fund, administered by the U.S. Coast Guard.

Consider the following when shopping for a recreational boating safety course for operating powerboats, sailboats, and human-propelled craft (such as kayaks, stand-up paddleboards, canoes, and rowboats).

Use this QR Code to see a short video about the development of the NOWS.

Visit https://www.usnows.org/review-standards for a complete list of the boating safety skills that a course provider should include in their beginner-level courses and the quality standards for the instruction they should provide.

- ■ Display this National On Water Standards (NOWS) logo on their website or course materials indicating they have self-assessed and declared their beginner-level courses align with NOWS.

- ■ Make available a declaration of conformity statement that identifies the course's level of conformity with NOWS.

- ■ Make available information about how the course is delivered according to NOWS including instructor credentials, student/instructor ratio, approach to student feedback, quality of the boats and safety equipment, and safety protocols they follow.

- ■ Teach boating safety skills identified in the NOWS indicating they are following best practice standards for what skills they should be teaching in their entry-level courses.

- ■ Deliver instruction primarily on the water with students learning through direct and personal experience operating the boat.

- ■ Have instructors work directly with students while on the water as students learn to operate the boat/craft.

- ■ Include what boat operators need to DO (skills) with what they need KNOW (for example, navigation rules) to safely operate a recreational boat.